DACHAU TO THE DOLOMITES

Tom Wall is a retired official of the Irish Congress of Trade Unions and is a master's graduate of UCD. He is a regular contributor of essays and reviews on historical themes for *Dublin Review of Books*.

DACHAU TO THE DOLOMITES

The Untold Story of the Irishmen,
Himmler's Special Prisoners and
the End of WWII

TOM WALL

MERRION
PRESS

First published in 2019 by
Merrion Press
An imprint of Irish Academic Press
10 George's Street
Newbridge
Co. Kildare
Ireland
www.merrionpress.ie

9781785372254 (Paper)
9781785372261 (Kindle)
9781785372278 (Epub)
9781785372285 (PDF)

British Library Cataloguing in Publication Data
An entry can be found on request

Library of Congress Cataloging in Publication Data
An entry can be found on request

Cover front (above): Dachau Main Gate, 1945 (PhotoQuest/Getty Images).
Cover front (below): Group of *Prominenten* outside Pragser Wildsee Hotel, May 1945.

Printed in Ireland by SPRINT-print Ltd.

CONTENTS

For Berni

PREFACE AND ACKNOWLEDGEMENTS

At the entrance to the exhibition in the Dachau Concentration Camp Memorial Site, there is a large wall map listing the numbers of prisoners from each country held in that notorious place. A figure '1' is superimposed on a map of Ireland. On a visit, intrigued by who this fellow Irishman might be, I began a journey of discovery. I soon learned that he was John McGrath, from Elphin in County Roscommon, who, prior to the war, had managed cinemas in Dublin and Cork before becoming the manager of the Theatre Royal in Dublin. It was a rare stroke of good fortune on my part, to establish contact with Tom Callan, who had met John McGrath. I am forever indebted to him and to his good friend John Kelly, for their assistance and for the research they undertook on my behalf. With their help, and with the assistance of the Historical Disclosures Unit of the British Army Personnel Centre in Glasgow, I discovered a great deal about this enigmatic man's military career. He left few accounts of his adventures; he has no surviving close relatives and any personal letters or documents seem to have been lost. However, I learned that aspects of his time as a German prisoner have been recounted by others, including a number of fellow British officers detained with him as special prisoners. They all came to be integrated into a VIP group, known as the *Prominenten*, assembled for hostage purposes by the SS during the final months of the war.

The origins and odyssey of this extraordinary group – containing leading statesmen, clergy, aristocracy, aristocrats and generals – then became the focus of my research. A number of books containing reminisces of some survivors were published after the war. These include works in English by Sigismund Payne Best, Peter Churchill, Bertram James, Kurt Schuschnigg, Fey von Hassell, and a biography of Harry Day. I have drawn extensively from these accounts. Other important *Prominenten* reminisces include Léon Blum's *Le Dernier Mois* and Isa Vermehren's *Reise durch den letzen Akt*. Payne Best's book, *The Venlo*

Incident, contains the most extensive description of the events dealt with here, but it is not always an accurate account, as will become evident. Harry Day, along with others in my tale, played a prominent part in what has become known as 'The Great Escape': however, as this story has been extensively told, I make only a brief reference to it here. I have, though, drawn from Tim Carroll's excellent work on the subject in respect of some biographical detail.

The British National Archives contain a number of relevant files and I benefited greatly from the helpfulness and efficiency of the staff in Kew and likewise at the Imperial War Museum in London. Some relevant US and German archive materials were sourced online. Newspaper reports and rare books were accessed at the National Library in Dublin and I am most grateful for the assistance of the staff at that institution. Cuttings from Roscommon newspapers relating to John McGrath were kindly provided by Caitlin Brown of Roscommon County Library. The library service was most helpful in securing the most relevant books from their archives. I am also grateful to Dr Caraline M. Heiss and Jens Kappel of the Pragser Wildsee Hotel in Italy for granting me access to their archive on the *Prominenten*. Georg Grote of University College Dublin generously shared his knowledge of the history of the South Tyrol.

A number of friends provided assistance and encouragement. My good friend and neighbour Tom McCaughren shared his expertise as a writer. My dear friend Stephen McCarty, who accompanied me to Dachau and the South Tyrol, was a constant source of knowledge about the Second World War and much else besides. Martin McGarry kindly assisted with some German translations. Maurice Earls was a constant source of help, as was his co-editor of *Dublin Review of Books*, Enda Doherty. Both allowed me to develop my writing skills through contributions to their excellent journal. Margaret Geaney helped with early proofreading. My hill-walking colleagues, whom I regaled with aspects of my story, remained constant in their encouragement, despite, no doubt, going beyond their boredom threshold at times. Particular thanks is due to Conor Graham of Merrion Press for his belief in the manuscript and for his commendable professionalism in guiding the final product towards publication, greatly aided by Fiona Dunne. Last, but far from least, I am eternally grateful to my wife Berni, who provided sound advice and encouragement, and to Ciara and Ronan for their support.

On a technical point, in the text I have used British equivalent ranks instead of burdening the general reader with German military and SS titles. Endnotes provide information on sources. The abbreviations used in respect of the principal archival institutions are listed below:

INA – Irish National Archives
IWM – Imperial War Museum
UKNA – British National Archives, Kew

INTRODUCTION

On 6 May 1945, a posse of international reporters and photographers were transported by American troops deep into the Dolomites in Northern Italy. They were told that they were about to meet a large number of important prisoners of the SS, among them prominent politicians, statesmen, nobility, clergy and military leaders from a number of countries. The destination was a hotel located on the shores of a lake overhung by high cliffs. On arrival, as the occupants of the hotel emerged, the newsmen would have recognised Léon Blum, the former premier of France; Kurt Schuschnigg, former Austrian Chancellor; and Miklós Kállay, the former Prime Minister of Hungary. Another familiar face would have been that of Martin Neimöller, the Lutheran pastor who had been imprisoned on Hitler's orders. They interviewed a spokesman for the group – an Englishman wearing a monocle – who introduced himself as Captain Sigismund Payne Best, a British Secret Service officer who had been kidnapped by the Germans during the early weeks of the war. Accompanying him was Colonel John McGrath, an Irish-born officer. Other British officers present included survivors of the mass escape from Stalag Luft III in 1943. With them were four Irish NCOs and soldiers. It must have surprised assembled members of the press to find among the group a number of German aristocrats and former Wehrmacht generals.

The group was known as the *Prominenten*, although not all were famous or well-known. Most had disappeared into concentration camps years earlier, before being assembled as Nazi hostages during the final weeks of the war. There were, in all, eighteen nationalities represented. The German contingent included a large group of civilians – men, women and children, all relatives of those executed for their part in the plot to kill Hitler. News of the sudden discovery of these former SS hostages became a minor sensation internationally, to be as quickly forgotten when Nazi Germany officially surrendered three days later.

The context for their assembly as hostages was the machinations of high-ranking leaders of the SS. As the 'Thousand Year Reich' collapsed into rubble and all hopes faded, some of its leading lights competed with each other in their attempts to interest the Western Allies in dialogue. They included Heinrich Himmler, Ernst Kaltenbrunner and Walter Schellenburg, who each attempted to use hostages in order to save the regime or, as a final resort, themselves. Hostage-taking has a long history in conflict, but seldom before had the practice been applied with such implausible intent. Feelers had been put out by intermediaries signalling the prospect of the release of prominent prisoners as a prelude to peace talks. After being assembled in Dachau Concentration Camp, the *Prominenten* had been transported to the Alps. Their removal to an Alpine redoubt was designed to prevent their liberation by the advancing Allies, and to allow more time for their use as barter.

This book is in four parts, the first of which relates to the confinement, as special prisoners of war, of the principal characters in our story. Sachsenhausen was where most were initially held, although the Irishmen in the group had previously been billeted in a special camp where the *Abwehr* (German Army Intelligence) hoped to persuade Irish-born British servicemen to switch sides. The special prisoners were mostly kept in demarcated compounds within their concentration camps, separated from the main prisoner population. They were held as *Nacht und Nebel* ('Night and Fog') prisoners, that is, prisoners whose existence was to be kept secret. Although for most of the time they were treated more favourably than regular concentration camp prisoners, they were always in danger of execution, a fate some did not escape.

The chapters in Part II are set in Dachau, where different groups of special prisoners were assembled in separate compounds. They were a diverse group in terms of nationality, background and political orientation; notable hostages are introduced in these chapters. Among them were a number of high-ranking German officials who had been suspected of plotting against Hitler. Part III tells the story of their journey into the Alps, eventually arriving in the South Tyrol. The final chapter of this section deals with the attempts of the hostages to free themselves from their SS guards, who were believed to have been under orders to murder some or all of them. Part IV details the travails of the group after they found themselves stranded in a frozen hotel high in the Dolomites.

It is a true story involving some exceptional men and women, many of whom displayed great courage and perseverance. It was not always, however, a harmonious collective, for there were conflicts within the group and among them were a few mavericks and villains. These include a number of fascinating individuals whose background story are told in five addenda. Some are revealed to have led extraordinary double lives involving deception and treachery. Addendum III recounts the love story of Count Alexander von Stauffenberg and Fey von Hassell, two prisoners of kin who joined the hostages on their journey into the Alps.

THE CAST

The following is a summary profile of the members of the hostage group and associated characters who will feature in a number of chapters.

Austrian

Kurt von Schuschnigg was Chancellor of Austria until the Anschluss. He was voluntarily accompanied in captivity by his wife Vera. Their child, Maria (known as 'Sissi'), was born in captivity. He was arrested for his opposition to union with Germany.

British Military Contingent

Captain Peter Churchill was an intelligence officer with the Special Operations Executive (SOE) who was captured in France while assisting the French Resistance. He had fallen in love with his courtier, Odette Sansom, who was arrested alongside him. In the hope of saving both of their lives he pretended to be a relative of Winston Churchill, and that he and Odette were married.

Lieutenant Colonel Jack Churchill was known as 'Fighting Jack' or 'Mad Jack'. He was a commando renowned for going into battle with a Scottish broad sword, a longbow and a set of bagpipes. He was captured in Yugoslavia in 1944 while leading a group of partisans and fellow British commandos in battle against the Germans who believed, wrongly, that he was related to the British Prime Minister.

Sergeant Thomas Cushing liked to be known as 'Red' – due to the colour of his hair, not his politics. As with all members of the Irish group, he was captured after Dunkirk in 1940. He was among a small group detained in a special Irish camp who volunteered for training by the Germans for sabotage missions. He had previously been in the US army.

Wing-Commander Harry Day was generally known as 'Wings'. Day was captured while leading an RAF squadron on a mission in 1939. As a senior British officer he led numerous escape attempts, including what became known as The Great Escape, following which fifty of his comrades were executed.

Major Johnnie Dodge was an American-born officer of the British army who was related, through his mother's second marriage, to Winston Churchill.

Flight Lieutenant Sydney Dowse was captured after being shot down in 1941. Alongside Harry Day, he was a serial escaper and a survivor of The Great Escape.

Squadron Leader Hugh Falconer was an SOE agent captured in Tunis during a covert operation. He joined some of the British group during their journey to Dachau.

Flight Lieutenant Bertram James was known as 'Jimmy'. James was another survivor of The Great Escape who was reunited with some of his colleagues in Sachsenhausen.

Lieutenant Colonel John McGrath was an Irish First World War Veteran, recalled to the colours in 1939. Up until then he had been manager of the Theatre Royal in Dublin. After a period in an officers' POW camp, he acted as senior officer in a camp established by the *Abwehr* in the hope of winning Irish recruits for anti-British espionage and sabotage. McGrath secretly set about sabotaging the project.

Private Patrick O'Brien volunteered or pretended to work for the Germans while in the Irish camp.

Captain Sigismund Payne Best was a Secret Service officer kidnapped by the Germans in the Netherlands, in what became known as the Venlo Incident.

Gunner John Spence worked for a German propaganda radio station beamed at Ireland. He joined the other Irish in Sachsenhausen, where he came under suspicion of being an informer.

Lieutenant Colonel Richard Stevens worked for MI6 and was captured, along with Payne Best, in Venlo on the Dutch–German frontier. The two were probably the earliest British spies captured by the Germans during the war.

Corporal Andrew Walsh was trained by the Germans, like Cushing and O'Brien, to undertake sabotage missions until it became clear that he planned to double-cross them.

French

Léon Blum was a former French Premier and leader of the Socialist part. He was accompanied by his wife Jeanne who voluntarily joined him in detention. He had been put on trial by the collaborationist Vichy government before being taken into captivity in Germany.

Monsignor Gabriel Piguet was arrested by the Gestapo for sheltering a wanted priest. The Bishop of Clermont-Ferrand, he had also arranged for Jewish children to be hidden in a school in his diocese.

Flight Lieutenant Ray Van Wymeersch was a member of the Free French Air Force under the command of the RAF. He joined the other RAF continent in the Sachsenhausen after being recaptured following The Great Escape.

Prince Xavier de Bourbon lived in France most of his life and fought with the Belgium and French armies. A Spanish aristocrat, he was the Carlist pretender to the Spanish throne.

Italian

Mario Badoglio was the son of Marshal Pietro Badoglio. His father was the head of the Italian Armed Forces and Prime Minister for a period after the overthrow of Mussolini.

Colonel Davide Ferrero was the founder of an Italian partisan group. Ferrero was arrested by the Germans and detained in Dachau.

General Sante Garibaldi was a grandson of Giuseppe Garibaldi, the renowned Italian liberator. Sante took up residence in France where he linked up with the French Resistance, resulting in his arrest by the Gestapo in 1943.

Tullio Tamburini was Chief of Police in Mussolini's Italian Social Republic prior to his arrest and detention in Dachau.

Greek

General Alexandros Papagos was Commander in Chief of the Green Army. He was accompanied in detention by members of his former high command and two orderlies.

German Military Prisoners

Colonel Bogislaw von Bonin had been chief of the operations section of the German army's general staff. He was arrested for making a tactical retreat near Warsaw, thereby contravening Hitler's orders. Despite this, he maintained his military rank and honours while in captivity.

General Alexander von Falkenhausen was a former Governor of Belgium during its occupation. He was arrested on suspicion of being associated with a plot to kill Hitler.

General Georg Thomas bore some responsibility for the Nazis' brutal treatment of the inhabitants of occupied Russian territory, even while involved in some anti-Nazi plots.

General Franz Halder was involved in plots to overthrow Hitler during the early years of the Nazi administration. The former Chief of the Army General Staff, he was accompanied by his wife Gertrud in captivity.

Colonel Fabian von Schlabrendorff was a cousin and adjutant to Major General von Henning von Tresckow, and directly involved in plots to kill Hitler.

German Civilian Prisoners

Dietrich Bonhoeffer was a Lutheran pastor and theologian who opposed the Nazis.

Georg Elser was a would-be assassin of Hitler. He planted a bomb in the Bürgerbräukeller in Munich, which exploded soon after Hitler had left.

Friedrich Engelke claimed to be a civil servant but was almost certainly an SS colonel stationed in France during the occupation.

Wilhelm von Flügge was an executive of I.G. Farben with links to the German opposition.

Dr Erich Heberlein was a former German ambassador to Spain who was detained along with his wife Margot.

Fey von Hassell was a daughter of the former German ambassador to Italy and opposition leader, she was arrested soon after the execution of her father.

Heidel Nowakowski was purported to be a lover of an SS officer before being interned in Dachau for reasons unknown.

Prince Friedrich Leopold of Prussia was a cousin of the Keizer and was arrested in 1944 along with his secretary and partner, Baron Fritz Cerrini, because of their homosexuality.

Josef Müller was a Bavarian lawyer and leading Catholic politician. He was a link man with the Vatican in a conspiracy to overthrow Hitler.

Martin Niemöller was an evangelical pastor and renowned opponent of the Nazi regime who was arrested on Hitler's orders.

Prince Phillip of Hesse was an active Nazi who considered himself to be an intimate of Hitler until he was arrested in 1943. He was closely related to German and British royalty and his wife was a sister of the King of Italy.

Sigmund Rascher was a doctor in Dachau who conducted appalling, cruel experiments on prisoners.

Hjalmar Schacht was president of the Reichsbank and economics minister in the Nazi administration before he fell out of favour.

Alexander von Stauffenberg was a brother of Clause and Berthold von Stauffenberg, both of whom were executed for their roles in the attempt to kill Hitler on 20 July 1944. Alexander was arrested under the *Sippenhaft* ('kin liability') laws.

Fritz Thyssen was a leading German industrialist and financier of the Nazi regime. He was arrested after announcing his opposition to the invasion of Poland.

Isa Vermehren was a popular cabaret artist who was arrested after her brother, who was a German intelligence officer, defected to the British.

Wilhelm Visintainer was a former circus clown who became a prisoner trustee assigned to service the needs of the special prisoners.

Paul Wauer was a Jehovah's Witness who, like most of his fellow co-religionists, was imprisoned and later assigned as a trustee to service the special prisoners.

SS Guards

Ernst Bader was an SS lieutenant in charge of one element of the SS guards that were believed to have earlier been part of an *Einzsatzgruppen* unit involved in the murder of civilians behind the lines in Poland and Russia.

Edgar Stiller was the Lieutenant in charge of the special prisoners in Dachau, and assigned the duty of escorting the *Prominenten* to the Alps.

Hungarians

Miklós Horthy was the son of Admiral Horthy, the Regent of Hungary.

Miklós Kállay was formerly the Prime Minister of Hungary.

The Soviets

General Ivan Bessonov was a senior NKVD officer, who, after his capture in 1941, agreed to work for the Germans. Before falling into disfavour, the Germans intended that he would command a group of turned Russian POWs to act as anti-Soviet partisans.

Lieutenant Yakov Dzhugashvili was Stalin's son from his first marriage. He was captured and used by the Nazis for propaganda purposes. He was imprisoned at Sachsenhausen with some of the Irish captives.

Lieutenant Vassily Kokorin was a nephew of the Soviet Foreign Minister. An officer in the Soviet Air Force, he was a close friend of Stalin's son, with whom he shared a cell at Sachsenhausen.

Major General Pyotr Privalov was a former university lecturer and decorated solider. The highest-ranking among the Soviet contingent, he was captured near Stalingrad.

Yugoslav

Colonel Hinko Dragic was an officer in the Yugoslavian Army. He was arrested after the German invasion and imprisoned in Flossenburg Concentration Camp, where he managed to become part of the *Prominenten*.

PART I

SPECIAL PRISONERS

Each concentration camp had an elite of privileged prisoners, no more than ten percent of the population, and admission to this exclusive club depended on an inmate's position in the internal hierarchy, which was determined by myriad factors such as ethnicity, nationality, profession, political beliefs, language, age, and the time of arrival in the camp.

—Nikolaus Wachsmann, KL

Following the defeat of France, about 40,000 British troops joined an estimated 1.8 million French, Belgium and Dutch prisoners of war in Germany. The provisions of the Geneva Convention were largely observed, although, in breach of its terns, a small proportion of prisoners were transferred to concentration camps. Some were selected for punishment due to repeated escape attempts or for political or security reasons. While some had to endure the deprivations of ordinary concentration camp inmates, others were given special status, housed in isolated compounds and allowed more favourable treatment. These included a number of the British Army and Air

Force prisoners, who were held with Russians and natives of other combatant countries. They were placed in Sachsenhausen and later Dachau, where they were joined by prominent Germans suspected of traitorous intentions against the Nazi regime. Two British Intelligence officers were included in the group.

CHAPTER ONE

KIDNAPPED AT VENLO

Captain Sigismund Payne Best seems to have relished being a spy for he did not go out of his way to hide it. In his mid-fifties, tall and gaunt, his grey hair combed back, he sported a monocle and was fond of wearing tweed suits and spats. Comparisons with P.G. Wodehouse's Bertie Wooster come to mind and a contemporary colleague regarded him as 'an ostentatious ass, blown up with self-importance'.[1]

While there seems little doubt that Payne Best had an inflated opinion of himself, his upper-class twit appearance could mislead. Although quite the English country gentleman, with all the mannerisms and prejudices of his time and class, he was well travelled and spoke Dutch, French and German fluently, having been a student in Munich for a number of years. He worked for British Intelligence during the First World War before settling in Holland, where he married and established an import–export business which provided him with cover when he resumed his intelligence work before the outbreak of the Second World War.

The Hague, 9 November 1939

Payne Best was not in the best of form as he entered his office in The Hague on that fateful morning. It was still quite early and he had only had a few hours' sleep. He wasn't looking forward to the long drive to Venlo, which was close to the German frontier. He picked up the morning newspaper and glanced at the headline. It appeared that there had been an attempt to kill Hitler the previous day. A bomb had exploded in a beer hall where Hitler had been speaking and a number of people were killed, but not the Führer, who had left the venue beforehand. This perplexed Payne Best, who wondered if this had anything to do with the German officers he was due to meet in Venlo.[2] They claimed to represent an anti-Hitler faction within the *Wehrmacht* and the meeting was to discuss a possible coup. However, before proceeding, they needed assurances that the British would treat with them after their accession to power. Such an assurance was required, they informed the British, before the coup could be attempted. Payne Best must have wondered, reading the newspaper, if the coup had already begun. The news added to his anxiety about the planned rendezvous.

A number of clandestine meetings had already taken place in The Hague. These involved a Major Schaemmel and another German officer, both claiming to be emissaries of senior *Wehrmacht* generals. Also in attendance was Major Richard Stevens, a fellow British Intelligence officer based in the Passport Control Office (PCO) of the British embassy. Less exotic in appearance than his colleague, he was, at forty-six years old, the younger man. Although his hairline was receding, his hair was suspiciously dark for a man of his age and he sported a toothbrush moustache. Before the war he had been based in India and had mastered a number of languages. The Secret Intelligence Service traditionally ran their agents from embassy PCOs. It provided them with diplomatic immunity, but made for poor cover when the practice became common knowledge. It was for this reason that Claude Dansey, the deputy chief of MI6, established a parallel foreign intelligence network, known as the 'Z' organisation. Payne Best was Dansey's man in the neutral Netherlands.[3]

The covert contacts with the Germans convinced a doubtful Payne Best that the emissaries were genuine and Stevens shared his optimism. Following approval from London, the two Englishmen were in a position to respond positively, if cautiously, on behalf of His Majesty's Government. They had been authorised to promise aid and support to the plotters. As evidence of this, their German contacts had been supplied with a radio transmitter with which to maintain contact with a British Secret Service station in The Hague. Schaemmel had promised that while a post-Hitler administration would restore independence to Poland, Czechoslovakia and Austria, it would seek the return of former German colonies in Africa.[4]

The meeting in Venlo was to finalise matters and it was anticipated that one of the leading German generals involved in the conspiracy would attend. So that he would be fresh for the planned meeting, Payne Best arranged for his trusted Dutch chauffeur to drive himself, Stevens and a Dutch Intelligence officer named Lieutenant Dirk Klop to Venlo. All four set off in Payne Best's distinctive Lincoln Zephyr for the three-hour journey. It was only two months since the declaration of war and so far only minor skirmishes had occurred. Their discussions with the Germans raised the alluring prospect of the war ending while still in its early stages. As they journeyed towards their rendezvous the two Englishmen must have believed they were about to make history. The glittering prospect of being instrumental in ending the war seemed almost within their grasp. The Foreign Secretary, Lord Halifax, ever keen for a negotiated settlement, was excited about the prospect, as was Prime Minister Neville Chamberlain. Payne Best was initially suspicious about the contact who had initiated the process, even writing to his superiors in London, stating that the man was most likely an *agent provocateur*. The report was ignored. Instead, Steward Menzies, then acting head of MI6, told Chamberlain and Halifax what they both wanted to hear: that there was a real prospect of Hitler being overthrown, of peace being restored.[5] Payne Best put aside his earlier suspicion after meeting the German contacts. There were, at that time, a number of German generals plotting against Hitler, the most prominent of which was General Franz Halder, the chief of the *Wehrmacht* General Staff, but the people they were about to encounter were not part of this conspiracy. The British had fallen for a well-executed German intelligence sting.

When they reached the meeting place – a café close to the German frontier – they were confronted by SS troops armed with submachine guns. Their leader, 'Schaemmel', was in reality Walter Schellenberg, an SS protégée of Reinhard Heydrich. Klop tried to resist and was shot and fatally wounded. At gunpoint, Stevens and Payne Best were handcuffed and hustled into a car which sped across the nearby border into Germany.[6] Schellenberg won plaudits for his leading role in the kidnapping and was personally congratulated by Hitler. He later became head of foreign intelligence within the SS; it was in this role that he tried to arrange for Stevens and Payne Best to be exchanged for German POWs, but this action was vetoed by Himmler.[7] When we encounter him again in our story, he will be acting as Himmler's emissary in a number of attempts to use hostages as bargaining chips near the end of the war.

The capture of the two intelligence officers was more than just an embarrassment for the British. Unaccountably, Payne Best had in his possession a list of the names and addresses of British agents and Stevens was carrying secret codes.[8] Both are believed to have supplemented this material by telling the Germans all they knew about MI6 operations in continental Europe.[9] As a result, a number of British agents and informers are likely to have been shot. The Venlo Incident, as it was to become known, was a disaster for British Intelligence and made the British wary of all future contacts with Germans purported to be anti-Hitlerite.

***

The bomb intended to kill Hitler was planted by an obscure young man acting alone : Georg Elser, a skilled carpenter and clock-maker from a small Swabian town. Of the many attempts to assassinate Hitler, none was as carefully planned and as skilfully executed as the time bomb he planted at the *Bürgerbräkeller* in Munich the day before Payne Best and Stevens were captured. Only unforeseen circumstances prevented him from altering world history.

Every year since 1933, the Nazis have commemorated the 'Beer Hall Putsch', a failed coup attempt in 1923 that centred on the *Bürgerbräkeller*, a beer hall in Munich. The finale of the commemorative event would always involve a lengthy address by Hitler to a gathering of Nazi dignitaries and Brown Shirt veterans. His speech would invariably begin at 8:30 p.m. and last for two hours. Elser had worked for months before the 1939 event to create a double-clock time bomb, which he managed to install inside a pillar where Hitler was due to make his address. The bomb was primed to explode at 9:20 p.m. when, as on all previous occasions, Hitler should be about half-way through his speech. However, on this occasion fog threatened to close Munich airport and Hitler, anxious to return to Berlin that night, started speaking earlier than planned and left at 9:07 p,m., having cut his speech short. The bomb exploded, as planned, thirteen minutes later. It killed seven people positioned near the lectern Hitler had used. Elser was arrested that night while trying to cross into Switzerland.

The Germans planned to kidnap Payne Best and Stevens months before Elser's attempted assassination of Hitler, so any connection made between these events could only have been an afterthought. Nevertheless, it was not unreasonable for the Germans to suspect a link. It seemed inconceivable that Elser could have acted alone. The Nazis were convinced that he had had assistance and was acting under the direction of others. Now they had proof that British Intelligence were intent on supporting an anti-Hitler plot. All three suspects were handed over to the Gestapo and interrogated separately. Elser alone was tortured, and savagely so. He was beaten to a pulp and, on Hitler's orders, was heavily injected with Pervertin, a stimulant then believed to be a truth serum. The top leadership of the SS and Gestapo were involved. Dr Albrecht Böhme, then in charge of Munich Kripo, the Criminal Police, described a scene he witnessed:

> I happened to became witness to a brutal scene that was played out, in the presence of Nebe [Arthur Nebe, Chief of Kripo, and later also an anti-Hitler conspirator] and me, between SS Reichsführer and Chief of German Police Heinrich Himmler and the prisoner Georg Elser. Elser was bound up, and Himmler was kicking him hard with his boots and cursing wildly. Then he had a Gestapo operative unknown to me drag him into the adjoining washroom of the Munich Gestapo chief and beat him there with a whip or (I couldn't see) some similar instrument, so that he cried out in pain. Then he was bundled, quick time, before Himmler and kicked again. But Elser, who was groaning and bleeding profusely from his mouth and nose, made no confession; he would not have been physically able to, even if he wanted to.[10]

From an early stage Elser confessed to the bombing, but insisted that he acted alone. He was tortured to make him identify his supposed accomplices, and to connect him to Stevens and Payne Best. Another suspected accomplice, the mastermind in Hitler's mind, was the hated Otto Strasser, a former Nazi who had formed a leftist fascist break-away, the 'Black Front'. Strasser was based in Switzerland at that time and it was assumed that Elser was attempting to join him there when he was arrested. Strasser, like Payne Best and Stevens, had no prior knowledge of the assassination attempt. Hitler, though, continued to believe Strasser was involved and later tasked Schellenberg with poisoning him in Lisbon, but the SS man failed to locate him. Strasser survived the war.

Elser was quite prepared to relate all the details of his workings, but he was not going to invent collaborators. Apart from truthfulness, he was proud of his work. He didn't hide his motives; he hated Hitler, whom he deemed a warmonger and responsible for his brother's imprisonment. The Gestapo decided to test his ability. They demanded that he replicate the time bomb after providing him with the necessary materials. He readily assembled the clock mechanism wiring, detonators and housing cabinet. This astonished his interrogators, who came to accept that he acted alone. [11] But matters had gone too far for this to be admitted. German newspapers had headlined the capture of the British agents and declared them complicit in the plot to kill Hitler. The event became world news. It was a propaganda triumph for the Nazis. There was no possibility that Stevens and Payne Best, now notoriously linked to Elser, could be exonerated. Payne Best and Stevens faced the prospect of a show trial with a predetermined outcome; their extinction. But Hitler was in no hurry; it was best left until the end of the war, when victory was secured. Then it could be demonstrated to the people of a conquered Britain that their own government was to blame for their misfortune. The event, though, had a more immediate benefit for Hitler: he later used the involvement of the unfortunate Klop as a pretext for the invasion of the Netherlands.

Sachsenhausen Prison Section, 1940–3

After weeks of interrogation in Berlin, Stevens and Payne Best were taken to the prison section of Sachsenhausen concentration camp, known as the *Zellenbau* ('bunker'). The prison section was used to house prisoners under interrogation for political 'crimes', with execution frequently being the final stage of the process. Elser was later brought there also. They were each held in isolation cells with no natural light, permanently handcuffed, manacled to the wall at night, with SS guards continually in attendance. These discomforts were mild, though, when compared to what others suffered. Prisoners in punishment cells were regularly tortured. From the compound outside, they often heard the cries of prisoners who had been suspended on a pole, their wrists tied behind their backs and connected to a high hook so that their toes were just off the ground. Left in this position, their shoulder ligaments would tear and their joint would dislocate, causing excruciating pain.[12] It soon became evident that Payne Best and Stevens were receiving comparatively favourable treatment as, over time, their conditions improved. Their shackles were removed, their food rations were adequate and they were allowed to take daily exercise. Facilitated by his fluent German, Payne Best managed to establish cordial relations with most of his guards, and from some he managed to secure cigarettes. Stevens fared less well in this regard and, according to Payne Best, he became depressed.[13]

Elser, recovering from his earlier torture, also began to enjoy improved conditions. He was allocated a large cell, was supplied with adequate amounts of food (although he ate little), and was provided with materials and tools to make items of furniture and musical instruments. This favourable treatment astonished the SS guards and irritated the more Hitler-adoring of them. It didn't make sense to them that the Führer's would-be assassin should enjoy such privileges. Then, a rumour circulated that Elser was merely a stooge of the SS; the bomb had been a Nazi plot to gain sympathy and support for Hitler and Elser was just a bit player and fall guy. Although Elser was strictly isolated, and it was forbidden for other prisoners to have any contact with him, this rumour spread among guards and prisoners in the bunker. Payne Best certainly believed it.

In his book, *The Venlo Incident*, Payne Best, although admitting that he never met him, claimed that Elser managed to smuggle a series of notes to him in which he gave an account of his life and his involvement in the *Bürgerbräkeller* plot. He says Elser told him that he had been detained in Dachau as an 'anti-social' before the war and, while there, he was induced by the SS to undertake a mission. The supposed scheme was to plant a bomb that would only be detonated after Hitler left and which was designed to kill some anti-Hitler plotters. According to the story Payne Best related, Elser was promised that he would be allowed to escape to Switzerland after the bomb went off, a promise that was reneged on. His comfortable billet in Sachsenhausen was less than adequate compensation. This story, and Payne Best's description of how he learned about it from Elser, is implausible. There is no factual evidence for the assertion that Elser was detained in Dachau as an 'anti-social'. And why would Elser lie about being complicit in a Nazi conspiracy? And if he was working for the SS, why would they torture him? How or why would he scribe his life story to a man he had never met and, given the ever-present SS guard, manage to smuggle out succeeding missives? Payne Best claims the writing was in indelible ink; how would Elser have obtained the necessary chemicals? It is likely Payne Best heard the story from the guards, with whom he was on friendly terms. The part about Elser smuggling material to him had to be invented, possibly to enhance his book's narrative and to obscure his actual source. It is now widely accepted that Elser acted entirely alone, but at the time Payne Best was writing his book there were a number of speculative stories portraying Elser as a stooge – Payne Best may have been influenced by these accounts. Payne Best's The Venlo Incident is the source for much of what has been written about the Prominenten. The lesson is to treat his accounts with caution.

Payne Best was detained for five years, the latter years in relative comfort. He recounts that he was visited by Himmler on one occasion during a tour of the camp in June 1942. It is plausible that Himmler would want to meet the Englishman, especially as he had been intimately involved in his case and Elser's. Less plausible is Payne Best's claim that he infuriated Himmler by refuting his suggestion that that British stories of German atrocities were false; Payne Best alleges that he told the Reichführer that their actions were even worse than stated.[14] If he was so audacious, he didn't suffer any consequences. He was soon put on double rations, permitted to purchase alcohol from the SS canteen, had his own electric cooker, was supplied with a typewriter and even had a small library in his cell. Following their occupation of the Netherlands, the Germans went to the trouble of retrieving his wardrobe – which included a number of tailored suits – from the Hague. In addition, he obtained a wireless set which allowed him to listen to the BBC. He could exercise outside for an hour or two daily and he grew vegetables and flowers on a patch of ground.

It began to seem that the SS were attending to his needs, more in the manner of dutiful servants than as guards. Adjacent to scenes of mass murder and barbarity, where prisoners suffered from hunger, torture, sickness and exhaustion, Payne Best was allowed to live the life of a cosseted tenant. He was not alone among the characters we will encounter that were relatively well cared for, although no other British captive – with the possible exception of his colleague Stevens – was treated with such consideration. Why was he so privileged? He himself, unconvincingly puts it down to guile on his part and to the decency of some of his SS guards. He was on quite friendly terms with the camp commandant, Anton Kaindl – 'a good friend to me' – and the head of the prison block, Kurt Eccarius – 'a very decent fellow'.[15] Both were regarded by most as odious and were later convicted of war crimes. Other factors were at play. It is likely there was an order to treat him well to ensure that he would be a presentable defendant, or witness, at the envisaged trial. He and Stevens are believed to have provided valuable information during interrogation.[16] Could it be that he was rewarded for his good behaviour? His conditions began to improve in late 1942. By then it was becoming clear to the Germans that the war was not going as planned. The thoughts of some in the Nazi leadership turned to ways by which the British might consider a ceasefire. Perhaps an intelligence officer, one who was obviously a Germanophile, might be able to assist. The idea of using select prisoners for this purpose probably germinated about this time.

Stevens spent just over a year in Sachsenhausen. To ensure his isolation from Payne Best, he was transferred to Dachau where, as we will later discover, he also enjoyed rare privileges. Before then, another British officer had entered the bunker. John McGrath was an Irishman who had earlier been held in a special camp for Irish POWs. Although he did not meet with Payne Best or Stevens in Sachsenhausen, they were later to become acquainted in Dachau under very different circumstances.

CHAPTER TWO

THE IRISH CAMP

Friesack Camp, June 1941

Major John McGrath, a tall, well-built, middle-aged man, was apprehensive about the task he was about to undertake. He was being driven to a POW camp north of Berlin, where he was about to take on the role of Senior British Officer (SBO) in a camp designed to turn British servicemen with Irish backgrounds into traitors. There had been disciplinary problems at the camp and the Germans felt that a senior officer, preferably one sympathetic to their designs, would improve matters. They had sought an Irish-born officer from a Catholic nationalist background and McGrath seemed to fit the bill. The son of a Roscommon farmer, both his mother and father's families were active in Irish nationalist politics; even more encouraging from a German perspective, was the fact that he had indicated a willingness to co-operate with them.

The Germans were mistaken about McGrath. He had only agreed to go to Friesack at the urging of a senior officer, in his previous camp in Laufen. Like many Irish servicemen, McGrath had mixed allegiances, but he was never going to dishonour his uniform. His relative's involvement in the Irish War of Independence happened after he moved to England in 1911. Although, like the majority of his class and religion, he was brought up in a nationalist environment, this was of the early twentieth-century constitutional and parliamentary variety that was, for the most part, 'culturally and politically comfortable with the trappings of empire'.[1] Before the Easter Rising in 1916, careers in the police or British Army were seen as legitimate options for young Irish Catholics and McGrath was no longer resident in Ireland when the post-1916 transformational change occurred within Irish nationalism.

The mission he was about to undertake was, as he was later to describe it, to 'investigate and endeavour to smash' the Germans' project.[2] It was a difficult and dangerous task. He had to convince the Germans he was prepared to fight for Ireland against Britain while, at the same time, win the confidence of the men and conspire with them to frustrate the Germans' plans.[3] For this role, McGrath would have had to draw upon whatever acting skills he had gleaned during his previous work in cinemas and theatre management in Ireland. He seems to have proved a capable actor, for he 'played the collaborator so convincingly that, for a time, even the British thought he had gone over to the other side'.[4]

However, it seems not all the Germans were convinced. He had been wined and dined in Berlin in the company of a number of German officers before being taken to the camp. Jupp Hoven, a member of the *Abwehr*, was the host and he was joined at the restaurant table by his friend and colleague Helmut Clissmann. Both had lived in Ireland before the war when they were involved in an Irish–German Academic Exchange service, most likely a cover for intelligence work. While there, they cultivated relationships with a number of senior IRA activists. Clissmann married a Sligo woman, Elizabeth Mulcahy, whose family were immersed in the Republican movement. Over dinner in Berlin, he confided to McGrath that his wife wished to return to Ireland and, knowing he had good business connections, sought his advice about finding her suitable employment. Whether this was a genuine request on his part, or a stratagem to gain McGrath's confidence is unclear, but in the course of the discussion, he began to doubt the Irish officer's collaborative potential. Clissmann is likely to have conveyed his doubts to Hoven, but the latter doesn't seem to have shared his friend's suspicions, at least not at that time. Even if Hoven had some concerns about McGrath's commitment, there wasn't a ready alternative. The previous SBO had been removed when a camp informer disclosed that the officer was leading an escape party. Other candidates for the position were likely to be Anglo-Irish, or have had a family tradition of service to the British Empire, making them probable British Intelligence plants.

On entry into the camp, McGrath's forebodings appeared justified. 'From the hour I entered the place I knew it meant trouble,' he later recalled.[5] The inmates were unhappy, suspicious and resentful. German promises of better food and recreation had not been kept and the majority of the prisoners were without proper footwear or clothing.[6] They were not allowed to write home, no Red-Cross parcels were being delivered and they were left without soap or cigarettes. Other grievances related to inadequate food and the absence of canteen facilities.[7] Adding to the discontent, many of the inmates felt they had been tricked or forced into the camp and were fearful that their very presence there could be viewed as disloyal. McGrath sensed that he was suspect in the eyes of these men. Seeing him arrive in the company of *Abwehr* officers, the inmates could be excused for assuming him to be a renegade officer, an aspiring Casement.[8]

McGrath was a veteran of the First World War, having seen action in the Dardanelles and France, where he was promoted to the rank of Captain. Wounded twice, he spent the final year of that war in a military hospital in Blackpool (see John McGrath: Truth and Invention, Addendum I). He remained a reserve officer in the inter-war years, even after he returned to Ireland. He could have readily avoided returning to duty in 1939. He was then forty-five years old and living in a neutral country. He had a good job – he was manager of The Royal, Dublin's premier theatre – but he immediately answered the recall. His return to service may not have been entirely a matter of contractual obligation. Through his employer and good friend, Louis Elliman, he had friendly contacts with the Jewish Community in Dublin and the anti-Semitism of the Nazis is likely to have appalled him. Perhaps, to quote the Irish poet Francis Ledwidge, a casualty of the First World War, he decided to join England's fight 'because she stood between Ireland and an enemy common to our civilisation'.[9] McGrath was assigned to the Royal Engineers and embarked with the British Expeditionary Force to France. Like thousands of others, he was left behind after the Dunkirk evacuations. He fought on and was wounded before being forced to surrender. We can safely assume that McGrath proved to be a brave and resourceful officer during the retreat for he was awarded a field promotion to major.

The evacuation of British troops from Dunkirk in 1940 is lauded, not without cause, as a heroic event; a deliverance snatched from the jaws of defeat. Less well known is the plight of the forty thousand service personnel who didn't board the boats. Those left behind fought on before surrendering, in many instances only when their ammunition and supplies were exhausted.[10] They were force marched from France to Germany during which time they were given little food and had to forage from fields. Notwithstanding occasional rain showers, it was a hot summer and in some French towns the inhabitants left out buckets of water for the prisoners which the German guards regularly kicked away. They were forced to drink ditch water and most suffered from dysentery as a result. They slept in open fields, often in their wet clothes. Whips, truncheons and rifle butts were employed on stragglers. McGrath later claimed that he escaped with a number of others and he was at liberty for three days, but a face wound led to his being identified and he was recaptured.[11] Through France, Belgium and Luxembourg the POWs trundled, until after two weeks, hungry, dirty and exhausted, they reached the German frontier town of Trier. There they were paraded through the streets as war trophies to be mocked and spat at, before being dispatched to various prisoner-of-war camps. About two hundred didn't make it; those who couldn't keep up or tried to escape were shot, including one of those who attempted to escape along with McGrath. This was an ominous start to what was to be five long years of captivity for thousands of British POWs. It was an experience unlikely to endear even nationalist Irishmen to their captors.

McGrath was first placed in an officers' camp in Laufen, a town on the Bavarian side of the Austrian border near Salzburg. Conditions were difficult at first, but later improved. Officers were treated much more favourably than regular POWs. Under the Geneva Convention they could not be forced to work and were relatively free to mingle and organise their own activities. McGrath seems to have had a relatively benign existence for most of the eight months he spent there. He had access to a library, attended lectures and, with Red Cross parcels supplementing camp fare, he was reasonably well nourished.[12] He couldn't have viewed the prospect of a move to a special Irish camp with much enthusiasm. During interrogation he refused, on a number of occasions, to be persuaded to go there. Whatever the content of the information provided by the Germans, it would have been clear to him what they had in mind. When his superior officer in Laufen, Brigadier Nicholson, suggested that he volunteer to go there in order to find out what was going on, he was obliged to give the matter serious consideration. It is possible that a coded message was sent to Nicholson suggesting Irish-born officers consider volunteering for this mission, for there is evidence that other British officers with Irish backgrounds were asked by MI9 to pretend to the Germans that they were anti-British and to double-cross them.[13] In any event, he sought the guidance of the most senior officer in captivity, the somewhat optimistically named General Victor Fortune, who had surrendered the remnants of his 51st Highland Division to Rommel after Dunkirk. Fortune is believed to have encouraged McGrath to take up the offer. The Irishman was also required to train some trusted men in the use of codes developed by the War Office that had been designed for intelligence purposes in letters posted home.[14]

McGrath agreed to take on the task and decided to self-promote himself from major to lieutenant colonel in the process.[15] He told himself that this would increase his credibility within the ranks in Friesack, although it's doubtful that this would greatly impress anyone, especially as he was still going to arrive in a major's uniform. It should, however, have led to his pay being increased as, under the Geneva Convention, the imprisoning power was obliged to pay officers according to rank. In any event, he may have felt he deserved a promotion for his gallantry in France, and for the dangerous task he was about to undertake.

The Germans, following their victory in France, had begun a process of identifying and segregating some POWs along ethnic and national minority lines. Breton, Flemish and Irish were among those chosen for special attention. The Irish section of the Friesack Camp was initially intended to facilitate the recruitment of Irish POWs into an Irish Brigade as per Roger Casement's efforts in the First World War. Sean Russell, the IRA Chief of Staff, proposed the idea to the Germans, but he died aboard a German U-boat before the scheme could be put into effect. The intention had been to land him in Ireland to coordinate German–IRA actions directed against Britain. The Germans had contingency plans to land an expeditionary force in Ireland, either in the event of a British re-entry into the Irish Free State, or as a prelude to a German invasion of Britain. In either case, they hoped an Irish Brigade, formed from Irish POWs, would fight alongside the Germans against the auld enemy. Following the failure of the Battle of Britain, the invasion plans were shelved and the task of the Irish camp in Friesack was downgraded to one of selecting and training a number of men deemed suitable for sabotage and espionage work.

The project came under the remit of Dr Edmund Veesenmayer, later to be directly complicit in Holocaust crimes, but at that time responsible for Irish matters, in particular liaison with the IRA. Hoven had been assigned by him to manage the Irish camp and he held the view that most Irishmen serving in the British forces had only joined because of economic necessity.[16] His contacts with the IRA during his time in Ireland may well have coloured his view about the extent and depth of Irish Anglophobia. It is estimated that there were more than 100,000 Irish in British uniforms throughout the war and motives for enlisting varied greatly. For many, especially those who joined before the war, an inability to find gainful employment at home would have been a factor, but there was no necessary correlation between this and anti-British sentiment. The attitude of Irish recruits towards Britain was likely varied and nuanced, and, like many involuntary emigrants, resentment was as likely to be directed homeward.

The selection of ordinary POWs for Friesack had begun in late 1940. Some merchant seamen and civilians were also included in the selection process. Prisoners were promised improved conditions and offered the prospect of release from captivity should they cooperate. The process involved POWs being questioned about their reaction to a theoretical British invasion of the Irish Free State and how they felt about a united Ireland. The purpose was to gauge Irish nationalist and anti-British sentiment. Frank Ryan, a legendary Irish Republican, participated, albeit briefly and reluctantly, in the selection process at the request of the *Abwehr*. A charismatic figure, he had left the mainstream IRA for the left-leaning Republican Congress and later fought with the International Brigade in Spain. He had become friendly with both Clissmann and Hoven during their time in Ireland and they were instrumental in having him removed from a Spanish prison, where he faced execution. Clissmann, with whom he shared accommodation for a time,[17] asked him to help verify claims of past IRA involvement by certain prisoners. Ryan, who was not introduced under his own name, withdrew from the process when one of the Irish servicemen recognised him.[18] Presumably, he feared reports portraying him as collaborating with the Nazis. Francis Stuart, the Irish writer who had taken up an academic post in Berlin University just before the war – an arrangement facilitated by Clissmann – also participated in the vetting process.[19] Unlike Ryan, Stuart had no qualms about being associated with Nazi propaganda, at least not at that time, for he later went on to make weekly broadcasts on a German propaganda radio station directed at Ireland.[20]

For some reason the selection process was slipshod and even chaotic. The Germans found the initial responses disappointing, so an adjudged absence of hostility to the possibility of German support for Ireland in the event of British occupation was deemed sufficient reason for selection. One decidedly hostile group was dispatched to Friesack in error following a mix-up of lists, and because the camp was a secret project they were kept there.[21] At its peak, about 180 Irish prisoners were housed in Friesack. When one considers that there were likely to be close to 1,000 Irish-born servicemen in POW camps in 1940, this represented only a small percentage of the total. Of those sent to Friesack, only about a dozen volunteered for sabotage or radio training and, it seems for most of these, it was just a ruse to get home and, or, to enjoy the privileges on offer. Volunteers for training were provided with rented accommodation in Berlin, paid an allowance and permitted relative freedom of movement, an alluring prospect at a time when there were few air raids or food shortages in the German capital.

After McGrath settled in the camp he consulted with the senior NCOs present. One of them was a fellow 'sapper', Sergeant-Major Whelan from Cork, who was actively warning prisoners against having any dealings with the Germans.[22] But McGrath decided on a different approach. He had learned that a number of prisoners had already volunteered to undergo training in radio communications and sabotage. This presented him with a dilemma; if he attempted to stop them, it would have exposed him and undermined his plans. His approach was to sanction their 'collaboration' provided they agreed that on landing in Ireland or Britain they would immediately report to the authorities and make no contact with the IRA. In clandestine briefings, he promised those he felt he could trust that 'he would stand by all' if 'they were not influenced by the Germans to undertake anything behind my back'.[23] Although most assured him of their support, McGrath wasn't confident that all would comply with his instructions to double-cross the Germans. There were, in addition, three or four active collaborators and informers outside of his influence. These were hated by the vast majority of inmates and when McGrath publicly set his face against them it enhanced his credibility as SBO with the rest.

Among the prisoners spoken to by McGrath were 'Sergeant' Thomas Cushing; Lance Corporal Andrew Walsh and Private Patrick O'Brien all from Tipperary. All three had joined the British Army before the war and, after being placed in Friesack, volunteered for training by the Germans. All were considered at the time to have strong nationalist and anti-British sentiments. Cushing was the dominant personality among the three. A chaplain who spent some time in the camp considered him 'too active a man to stand prison life' and someone who would 'do and say anything to get out of prison'. The priest, though, didn't believe that he would, in the end, do anything to help the Germans.[24] One of the *Abwehr* officers in the camp painted a more disparaging picture of Cushing during post-war interrogation, when he described him as a stool pigeon who had informed the Germans of McGrath's predecessor's escape plan.[25] Although it's not clear if McGrath knew of this, he had his suspicions about Cushing from an early stage. While it remains a matter for conjecture, it is unlikely that Cushing seriously contemplated working for the Germans. He felt little commitment to any cause, least of all that of his jailers, though he may have intended to make a final call depending on which side he perceived as offering the best opportunities for freedom and survival.

Cushing made the most of the freedom afforded him during his training in Berlin. He was less interested in sabotage techniques than the opportunity to indulge in his passion for drink. When captured in Normandy, he and a few colleagues were found to be inebriated, having earlier taken shelter in a well-stocked wine cellar. He was, as he later defined himself, a 'soldier of fortune'[26] and a feckless one at that. He claims to have been involved with the IRA during the Irish War of Independence and Civil War, but this is highly unlikely as he would have been only about ten years old in 1921.[27] He was sent to live with a relative in America at the age of fifteen where he subsequently enlisted in the US Army. There, he was regularly in trouble for being drunk and brawling. Soon after his return to civilian life, he claims he enlisted in the Lincoln Brigade to fight on the Republican side during the Spanish Civil War.[28] He liked to be known as 'Red' Cushing, but this was in reference to his hair colour, not his politics. In fact, he often boasted about his anti-Communism, something that would have placed him at some risk within the International Brigade. The problem with Cushing as a source is that he is entirely unreliable. Barry McLaughlin, who has researched Irish participation in the International Brigade during the Spanish Civil War, is doubtful that he was ever in Spain, or at least not on the Republican side.[29] Although he spent his time in captivity known as 'Sergeant Cushing' he wasn't a sergeant.[30] In the chaos that was Friesack, he had convinced the Germans and his fellow prisoners that he held that rank, most likely to avoid manual work, as under the Geneva Convention NCOs were only required to do supervisory work. Although some in the *Abwehr* had confidence in him, at least one considered him to be 'a rank opportunist, without backbone or moral fibre, a loud mouthed braggart with little courage or intelligence, whose reliability was highly doubtful'.[31] He may well have been a braggart, but he was also clever, if irresponsible. The assignment for which Cushing was being trained would have had him transported to Central America on a mission to blow up a lock on the Panama Canal where he had been stationed during his service with the US Army. That the *Abwehr* could believe that Cushing would carry out such a dangerous and difficult mission for them, in a place where he could easily abscond, illustrates the irrationality that permeated the whole Friesack venture.

Cushing was, by all accounts, loquacious. To use an Irish expression, he had the gift of the gab, and he seems to have used this talent to charm women he met during his stay in Berlin. According to a fellow trainee 'he led a wild sort of life in Berlin and seldom slept in his own room'.[32] One of his alternative sleeping quarters was the lodgings of a former model. He sought permission from the Germans to marry her, but his request was refused.[33] Whether he was lovestruck or just hoping to use her as a ticket to gain more freedom, it's impossible to say, although, as he makes no mention of her subsequently, it's safe to assume he was not inconsolable. It was likely through her that he became friendly with some German black-marketeers, an association that attracted the attention of the Gestapo. He also got into trouble for 'getting drunk and singing Irish songs in a café' where he offered 'to fight all and sundry'.[34] It's not difficult to conceive how this might have occurred: the sight of a drunk, obstreperous, tall, red-haired 'Britisher' having a good time in the company of a German woman, was bound to provoke some *Wehrmacht* soldier on leave. These skirmishes may have troubled the *Abwehr*, but of greater concern was the fact that the Irishmen might be defying strict orders not to fraternise together, for the Germans didn't want them disclosing their respective assignments to each other. In fact, Cushing was meeting regularly with Andy Walsh.

Lance Corporal Andy Walsh, a RAF aircraft fitter, had been considered by the *Abwehr* to have the most potential. He was described as tall and dark with 'large, rather tragic brown eyes'.[35] The *Abwehr* judged him to be intelligent and 'a mature, determined and quiet person, who seemed to have genuine Irish nationalist feelings', although, like Cushing, he had a fondness for drink. In fact, he was probably only semi-literate at best.[36] Walsh was being trained by the Germans to blow-up a power station within the large aluminium works in Kinlochleven in Scotland where he had worked before the war. He was at an airport in Oslo, about to board a plane from which he was to be parachuted out over Scotland, when he was arrested. It was the day after he had met with Cushing in Berlin. Already under suspicion, Cushing was being followed and he and Walsh had been seen to be 'behaving very furtively' and exchanging notes.[37] A report was filed the following day leading to a decision to arrest them both, by which time Walsh had left for Oslo. Walsh seemed to be the type of person everyone felt drawn to. The Germans, prior to his arrest, felt confident that he was on their side, while McGrath felt certain he could trust him to comply with his instructions to report his presence to the British authorities. In fact, Walsh was as unreliable as Cushing and, like his companion, he had been making up for lost drinking time in the bars of Berlin, befriending Germans involved in the black market and smuggling.

After their arrest, Cushing and Walsh were faced with a classic 'prisoner's dilemma': whether to deny everything in the hope that the other would do the same, or accuse the other before being betrayed by him. Both chose the latter course, fiercely accusing each other of planning to double-cross the Germans, and implicating John McGrath into the bargain. Another Irish 'trainee' Private William Murphy was also arrested at this time.[38] Their confessions were likely to have been extracted after fairly rough treatment by the Gestapo. Walsh later described being kept 'in total darkness' with very little food and being 'beaten up and kicked'.[39]

The other Tipperary man, Patrick O'Brien, was also undergoing training in Berlin at that time. He was considered by the *Abwehr* to be of sub-normal intelligence although their judgement may have been influenced by his insolence towards them. Within Friesack he had played the role of an 'irrepressible comedian' according to one account. When Jupp Hoven would appear, O'Brien would usually greet him with: 'Hello Joe, how's the scheme going?'[40] (Hoven was known to the inmates as Gestapo Joe.) If he was of below-average intelligence it might explain, but not excuse, a disturbing aspect of

O'Brien's persona. He was arrested by the criminal police for molesting a child living in his lodgings in Berlin.[41] The *Abwehr* convinced the enraged parents to withdraw the charges, presumably to avoid any disclosures about the nature of his assignment.

Despite McGrath being fingered by Walsh and Cushing, no immediate action was taken against him and he remained at Friesack for another few months. Perhaps, the authorities felt they couldn't believe anything Cushing and Walsh told them, but later they discovered more compelling evidence of McGrath's attempts to undermine their project. This may have been the result of the inadvertent action of a good friend.

About a month after McGrath arrived in Friesack, he was joined by a young Irish priest. Hoven, dressed as a civilian, had earlier visited Rome seeking to have an Irish Catholic chaplain assigned to Friesack. He alleged that this was the wish of the camp inmates. In fact, no such request had come from the men and it seems the Germans hoped that a priest, ideally one with strong Irish nationalist or pro-German sentiments, might assist with their plans. A number of religious orders were contacted before Hoven had success with the Society of African Missions in Rome. The Superior agreed to one of his young priests, Thomas O'Shaughnessy, being seconded to Friesack for a six-month period with salary and costs being paid by the German government. O'Shaughnessy seems to have been selected because he was studying German at that time.[42] Hoven may have assumed from this that the priest had pro-German sympathies, but, if so, he was again mistaken. O'Shaughnessy was not at all pleased with the arrangement. He suspected the motives of the Germans and feared he might end up as their captive rather than their employee. Although assured by Hoven that there was no military or political scheme afoot, he was not convinced. Before departing, he told his Superior that he would use a code in his letters to Rome. In the event of there being no problem, he would state that he was 'studying German', but if he found the camp was a 'political racket', he would write that he was 'studying Italian'. In the latter event, he expected that he would be immediately ordered to return to Rome. While in Friesack, he wrote a number of times, repeatedly emphasising that he was 'studying Italian', but his Superior, who had apparently forgotten the conversation about the codes, was merely impressed with his young charge's commitment to expanding his capability with languages.[43]

O'Shaughnessy, like McGrath earlier, was appalled at what he saw when he entered the camp. It seemed to him that the men were in rags: presumably their only clothing was the uniforms they had been wearing when captured. The men also viewed him with suspicion at first, some believing that he was an IRA agent disguised as a priest.[44] McGrath was also cautious initially, although the two men were soon to become good friends and allies. Most of the prisoners worked outside the camp during the day, so the two of them spent a great deal of time in each other's company. Together they successfully lobbied for the delivery of Red Cross parcels and achieved other improvements, which endeared them to the prisoners. It helped also that news spread about angry words being exchanged between the priest and a despised academic whose role was to propagate the virtues of National Socialism in lectures delivered to camp inmates.

McGrath took O'Shaughnessy into his confidence and they became allies in their secret endeavours to frustrate the Germans' intentions. Both men tried to counter the ceaseless propaganda inflicted on the inmates. Apart from lectures, a loudspeaker system broadcast news of repeated German success on the battlefield. The invasion of the Soviet Union had begun shortly before O'Shaughnessy arrived, and each victory announcement was preceded by a trumpet fanfare.[45] Tracts, believed to have been written by Lord Haw-Haw, were distributed. Although all this was a source of annoyance to the men, the seeming invincibility of the enemy was affecting morale. McGrath tried to convince the men that they would win in the end and to ignore their propaganda although, for a time, even he had his doubts.[46] There were a number of escape attempts from Friesack which both McGrath and O'Shaughnessy were likely to have been privy to or have aided.[47] These only led to short periods of freedom, but even this was seen as a victory of sorts over the 'Boche'.

When the time came for O'Shaughnessy to return to Rome, McGrath prepared a five-page briefing document for British intelligence which the priest agreed to hide on his person. The document contained information about the camp and the names of persons being trained by the Germans. It seems McGrath was making certain that none of them would succeed in any sabotage operations. The document had an added importance for the Irish officer in that it would provide proof of his continued loyalty. O'Shaughnessy, at some risk to himself, smuggled the report to Rome. McGrath had asked that it be delivered to the British envoy to The Holy See, D'Arcy Osborne, but instead he met with the Irish Ambassador, Thomas Kiernan, and showed him, or perhaps just told him about, McGrath's document. O'Shaughnessy soon travelled to Lisbon via Spain and managed to get on a flight to London where he briefed a British Intelligence agent about Friesack. He told him about the document in his possession which he intended to deliver to Irish officials when he reached Dublin. There he met with Joseph Walsh, the Secretary of the Department of External Affairs, and senior Irish Intelligence officers. He also met with the Taoiseach, Éamon de Valera, who seemed more interested about conditions in Lisbon than in hearing about Friesack.[48]

In Rome, information about the existence of the document had somehow become known to the Germans. The Irish Ambassador sent a coded message to Dublin containing information about O'Shaughnessy's visit and McGrath's report and it seems the Germans had broken the code.[49] As a consequence, McGrath was arrested by order of the head of *Abwehr II*, Erwin von Lahousen.[50] A search of his room seemed to provide evidence that he was gathering information on those being trained by the *Abwehr*, although McGrath insisted that all they found was a list of recipients of Red Cross parcels.[51] He was handed over to the Gestapo in November 1942 for in-depth interrogation.[52] He was stripped and his uniform, even his shoes, were ripped apart, presumably in the hope of finding documents or other incriminating items. When nothing was found, he was taken to Sachsenhausen and deposited in a cell in the camp's prison. His future prospects were dim. His action in smuggling out details about Friesack would have been viewed by the Germans as espionage, for which the death penalty applied.

By this stage, any hopes the *Abwehr* had for the Irish camp were rapidly fading. Apart from the escape attempts, a riot had occurred in which loudspeakers were disabled and propaganda posters torn down and burnt.[53] The *Abwehr* decided to abandon the project and the inmates were dispersed to other camps. Walsh, Cushing, Murphy and O'Brien were deemed to know too much and, after a period of Gestapo detention, they too were sent to Sachsenhausen, although to a different section than McGrath. His position was more serious. He was being accused of having espionage contacts outside Friesack[54] and was threatened with execution unless he named them.[55] He was, as he later said, 'locked up in an ordinary prison cell, with not even the privileges of a convict. I was now under the S.S. for whom I have not a good word to say.'[56]

Beyond this terse statement, McGrath never recounted his experiences in the Sachsenhausen bunker. Judging by the experience of others, he would have been kept in solitary confinement and manacled to the wall or floor during the night. He would have been subjected to a process of 'intensified interrogation', kept in isolation and deprived of sleep.[57] McGrath, although physically diminished, survived the ordeal. He may have been spared execution due to news of his presence in Friesack being made known to the British and Irish authorities thanks to Father O'Shaughnessy. The Germans were anxious to keep secret their executions of prisoners, not least a citizen of a country the Germans wished to remain neutral.

McGrath would have suffered most from being isolated. A naturally gregarious person, his only human contact was with his ever-present guards, but as he didn't speak German he, unlike Payne Best, wouldn't have been able to establish any meaningful communications with them. Payne Best and Stevens were in the same bunker at that time, although they were kept apart and he never met them there, although McGrath caught a glimpse of the former on one occasion. The Irishman continued to be deprived of all home contacts. His father had died in 1936, but he didn't know if his mother was alive or dead. In fact she was alive, and writing to the war office expressing her concern about not hearing from her son for over a year. She died in October 1944 without ever knowing if her son was alive or dead.

John McGrath spent ten months in solitary confinement in the Sachsenhausen bunker before being taken to Dachau. The reputation of his new abode would have been known to him and he would have journeyed there with some trepidation. He was not to know it then, but his relocation was to result in some improvement in his conditions.

We will encounter McGrath again. In the meantime, we will focus on the misadventures of other military figures who were later to become his colleagues in the *Prominenten*. Among them, his former charges in Friesack – Cushing, Walsh, Murphy and O'Brien – who were located in a special section of Sachsenhausen, sharing accommodation with two notable Soviet prisoners.

CHAPTER THREE

THE DEATH OF STALIN'S SON

Near Moscow, March 1945

Meeting with Stalin at his *dacha*, Marshal Zhukov asked the General Secretary if anything had been heard of his son Yakov. Yakov Dzhugashvili, Stalin's son from his first marriage, had been captured by the Germans while serving as a lieutenant in charge of an anti-tank battery in 1941. Stalin remained silent. Zhukov must have regretted asking. Three years previously, when given command of the defence of Leningrad, he had ordered that 'all the families of those who surrender to the enemy will be shot'. Although echoing a similar order by Stalin, he would not have known that this could, technically at least, imply that Stalin be shot. However, Stalin eventually replied, saying 'Yakov is never going to get out of prison alive. The murderers will shoot him.'[1]

Sonderlager 'A', Sachsenhausen Concentration Camp, 14 April 1943

Almost two years prior to this conversation, Yakov Dzhugashvili stood alone outside his prison hut in despair, hurting physically and mentally. A short time earlier he had been in a brawl with some Irish prisoners who were billeted with him. He asked to see the Camp Commander, probably to request a transfer, but the request was denied. His mental anguish may have hurt more than any blows he received. He had earlier been taunted by the allegation that his father was responsible for the murder of thousands of Polish officers and intellectuals, whose remains had been discovered in a mass grave in Katyn Forrest. The news had been broadcast on German radio the previous day. He may not have believed it, but it was another reminder of his awful predicament. His relationship with his father was never good. Despite his best efforts to win his approval, Stalin seemed to dislike him.[2] Now he had irredeemably shamed him by allowing himself to be captured by the Germans.

It was dusk and past curfew and he was being ordered to go into his hut. He remained standing. A rifle was trained on him from the watchtower. With increasing urgency he was being warned that he would be shot if he didn't obey. Some of his fellow prisoners, including Thomas Cushing, watched from a hut window. He still wouldn't move. Perhaps he reasoned that this was a way out of his dilemma. A sacrificial death might reconcile him with his father, a last act of tortured fidelity. It would at least end his torment.

Dzhugashvili suffered bouts of depression,[3] which is not surprising given his background. He was the only child of Stalin's first marriage to Kato Svanidze. She died when he was an infant and he was left in the care of his maternal grandmother and aunt in Georgia while Stalin pursued his revolutionary career. His father had little or no contact with him until he was taken to Moscow by his mother's relatives at fourteen years of age in 1921. Stalin was at that time a close ally of Lenin within the Communist Party and he was in a position to provide his son with a good education. To the disappointment of his father, Yakov didn't do well in school; which must have been, at least partly, attributable to the fact that he spoke only Georgian when he arrived. Although installed into the Stalin household, which now included two uncles and an aunt who had travelled with him from Georgia, he seems to have been despised by his father, who considered him soft and worthless.[4] Stalin regularly humiliated Yakov in front of others, referring to him as 'my fool'.[5] He was, however, protected somewhat by his stepmother, Stalin's second wife, Nadezhda Alliluyev, known in the household as Nadya.[6] When he was only sixteen years old, Yakov announced that he wanted to marry a fellow high school student, but Stalin objected – not so much because of their youth, but because he didn't approve of the girl's 'social behaviour' and the fact that she was the daughter of a priest.[7] Yakov married his sweetheart notwithstanding, but the union didn't prosper; a child died in infancy before the couple separated, in part at least due to Stalin's interference. The separation didn't improve the father-and-son relationship. In his early twenties, following another disagreement, an upset Yakov attempted suicide. He put a gun to his chest, but the bullet narrowly missed his heart and he was only wounded. This further alienated him from Stalin who told Nadya that Yakov was 'a hooligan and a blackmailer, with whom I have nothing in common and with whom I can have nothing further to do. Let him live wherever he wants with whomever he wants.'[8] Stalin, rather than seeing Yakov's action as a cry of despair at his father's relentless disapproval, viewed it as an attempt to exert pressure on him.[9] For eight years they were completely estranged.

He remarried – again Stalin didn't approve – and his new wife Yulia bore him a daughter, Gulia, in 1938. By then he was a Red Army officer cadet and this contributed to a reconciliation of sorts that allowed him return to the Stalin household. Relations, though, were still not easy. Nadya, was no longer there to protect him – she committed suicide in 1932 – and Yakov had a tempestuous relationship with his half-brother, Vasily. More tragedy followed. His maternal aunt and uncle along with his uncle's wife, all of whom had accompanied him from Georgia, were arrested in 1937 during the 'Terror'.[10]

When the Germans invaded on 22 June 1941, Dzhugashvili was ordered to the front in charge of an artillery unit. Before leaving, he telephoned his father who urged him to 'Go and fight!'[11] His unit entered combat on 27 June, but they were soon encircled by the Germans and he was captured when attempting to make his way back to Red Army lines. Although not wounded, he claimed to have been stunned by heavy bombing 'otherwise I would have shot myself', he told his German interrogators.[12]

Although he had fought bravely before being captured, he was suspected by his Soviet commander of willingly surrendering to the Germans.[13] Irrespective of the circumstances of his capture, Yakov knew Stalin would have been angered by it and he would have feared for his wife and 3-year-old daughter. Yulia was arrested, although her husband probably didn't know of this during his captivity. Stalin would have been particularly angered when the Germans used his son's capture for propaganda purposes. A leaflet containing a photograph of him looking somewhat dazed and dishevelled in the presence of two German officers was dropped over the Russian front. The accompanying text read:

Stalin's son, Yakov Dzhugashvili, full Lieutenant, battery commander, has surrendered. That such an important Soviet officer has surrendered proves beyond doubt that all resistance to the German army is pointless. So stop fighting and come over to us.[14]

This was the only propaganda the Germans extracted from him. He steadfastly refused to collaborate with the Nazis who wanted him to make propaganda broadcasts. His treatment in captivity alternated from being cosseted in a fashionable hotel to being ill-treated and half-starved in prison camps. The Nazis continued to pressurise him to work for them. They wanted him to act as nominal head of Vlassov's renegade Russian army, but he steadfastly refused to be linked to the turncoat general. He even refused to address SS guards by their military title, using only their surname; an unnecessary act of defiance that led to retaliatory punishments.

After Stalingrad, it is believed that Hitler offered to exchange Dzhugashvili for Field Marshal von Paulus. Stalin is said to have responded, 'I will not exchange a soldier for a marshal',[15] a comparison that owes as little to Communist egalitarianism as it does to notions of parental care. Before being sent to Sachsenhausen, he was interned in a special *oflag* near the Baltic port of Lübeck where he was billeted with Polish officers[16] who might have been expected to be hostile to Russians and Communists. However, contrary to expectations, Dzhugashvili became friendly with some of the Polish officers and joined them in a futile attempt to escape.[17] Robert Blum, the son of Léon Blum, the French statesman, whom we will encounter later, shared a cell with Dzhugashvili in Lübeck.[18]

Stalin's son was, potentially at least, the most valuable prisoner held by the Nazis. His friend and cell mate, Vassily Kokorin, was another prize captive, being a nephew of the Soviet Foreign Minister, Vyacheslav Molotov. Molotov was second only to Stalin within the Soviet leadership and would have been assumed to have influence over the Soviet leader. In fact, Molotov, described by Lenin as 'the best filing clerk in Russia',[19] was, like others in the Kremlin hierarchy, in abject fear of Stalin. Kokorin, Molotov's sister's son, was a Soviet Air Force officer who had been wounded before being captured, by which time his feet had been severely frostbitten with the result that most of his toes had to be amputated.[20]

The Irishmen with whom Dzhugashvili had brawled was none other than the Friesack 'collaborators' who had been arrested by the Germans when they realised they were likely to be double-crossed. Thomas Cushing, while charming and entertaining at times, could be short-tempered and quick to use his fists. O'Brien was even more disreputable; as we have learned, he was suspected of child molestation and had himself boasted of picking fights with co-workers on work details, especially foreigners.[21] Walsh was the only one others regarded as normal: a fourth Irishman present, Private William Murphy, was mentally unstable.

The four Irishmen and the two Soviet prisoners were billeted in the same hut. This was within a newly built compound, known as *Sonderlager* 'A', located on the north-eastern perimeter of Sachsenhausen Concentration Camp. It was built to house special prisoners whom the SS wished to keep segregated from the general camp population. Why the Irish group were housed there is unclear; it may have been because they were still considered to warrant equivalent POW status, but, because they knew so much about secret missions they could not be sent back to normal POW camps. Walsh and Cushing shared accommodation and appear to have overcome their differences arising from their mutual accusations in Berlin, although, perhaps not entirely, for the sound of raised voices was regularly heard from their quarters.

Originally housing political prisoners, Sachsenhausen and its satellite camps contained over 30,000 prisoners by early 1943, including Communist, Social Democrats, Jehovah's Witnesses, homosexuals, criminals and 'anti-socials'. It also housed thousands of Soviet captives along with political and military prisoners from other occupied countries. Although gas chambers had only just been installed, its reputation as a death camp had already been well established. Thousands of prisoners had already been executed. Jewish prisoners had been transported to Auschwitz for extermination in 1942. However, its primary function by 1943 was to supply slave labour to local industries. Thousands worked in factories in nearby Oranienburg where they laboured for up to twelve hours a day, nourished by only small amounts of bread and watery soup.

Cushing and the other Irish inmates did not have to endure these conditions. During daylight hours, they could roam freely within their small compound. The civilian clothes they had been wearing during training were taken from them and they were re-supplied with military attire. They weren't assigned work and occasional Red Cross parcels provided them with much needed extra food and cigarettes. It had been some months after their arrival in Sachsenhausen when they were joined by Dzhugashvili and Kokorin who shared with them a washroom and toilet. They, as special prisoners, enjoyed better conditions than their Soviet compatriots in the main camp, who were treated appallingly. However, their treatment was harsher than that of the Irish. Despite being officers, the two were required to work and, like all Russian prisoners, they had no access to Red Cross parcels.

At first, relations between the Russians and the Irishmen appear to have been good, but soon the mood changed. Despite his difficulties with his father, Yakov was proud to be Stalin's son and he remained a committed Communist. This led to arguments with Cushing who was a staunch anti-Communist. In addition, there were rows about food, especially the distribution of the contents of Red Cross parcels. It was usual for POWs to share parcels and Cushing claimed to have shared his with the Russians,[22] presumably, though, this generosity ceased when relations soured. Doubtless, language and cultural differences caused misunderstandings: they could only communicate using a German camp patois.

On the fateful day, an argument arose about the state of their shared toilet. Cushing, who had assumed the role of hut superintendent, accused Dzhugashvili of fouling the toilet seat. Murphy, unstable at the best of times, joined in the attack. O'Brien, likewise, needed no urging to get involved. He called Kokorin 'a Bolshevist shit'. Kokorin replied in kind and blows were exchanged.[23] It was hardly an even contest, for it was three, if not four, against two: it's not clear if Walsh joined the affray, for he subsequently claimed to have liked Dzhugashvili and to have been traumatised about what happened. Moreover, the two Russians were smaller men, weakened by inadequate diet, and Kokorin would have been unsteady on his near toeless feet, while the tall Cushing had been a boxer during his time in the US Army. At some point during the fracas, Cushing is alleged to have produced a knife and chased Dzhugashvili down a corridor. To save himself, the Georgian jumped through an open window, which led to him standing outside after curfew time.[24]

Cushing afterwards described what happened as he watched from a window of their shared hut. He said that Yakov 'suddenly rushed outside, sprinted across the compound, scrambled up the wall and attempted to crawl through the perimeter wire'. The Georgian called out to the guard, 'Don't be a coward, shoot me!'[25] Cushing continued, 'A shot rang out, followed by a blinding flash, and poor Jakob [*sic*] hung there, his body horribly burnt and twisted.'[26] This account of Yakov's end is broadly in line with the statement of Konrad Harfich, the SS guard who shot him, during his post-war trial:

> He put one leg through the trip-wire, crossed over the neutral zone and put one foot into the barbed wire entanglement. At the same time he grabbed an insular with his left hand. Then he got out of it and grabbed the electrified fence. He stood for a moment with his right leg back and his chest pushed out and shouted at me 'Guard, don't be a coward, shoot me!'[27]

The guard fired a single shot with the bullet entering just in front of his right ear. Cushing later remarked that 'it was the first time I felt sorry for the poor bastard'.[28] Not the most worthy of tributes, although he went on to say; 'it was one of the saddest events of my life'.[29] Yet, while expressing sorrow, he avoided any suggestion of culpability.

It was a sad end for a young man whose dream of reconciliation with his father were only to be realised posthumously. The 'murderers' did shoot him as Stalin predicted, although he did not have confirmation of this until after the war. Keindl, the camp commandment, was potentially at risk of being disciplined, or worse, for allowing the loss of such a valuable hostage. To minimise blame, it is believed that he conspired with all concerned, including the Irish prisoners, to have the matter portrayed as a straightforward suicide; there was no mention of Stalin's son being chased by a knife-wielding Irishman.[30]

A traumatised Kokorin was transferred to the prison bunker of Sachsenhausen. This was presumably to avoid any further conflict with the Irish. But things didn't get any better for the little Russian. He was put in a cell with another Russian officer who attempted suicide by cutting his wrists one night when Kokorin was asleep. When an air raid alert sounded during the night, Kokorin got down from the top bunk and stepped into a pool of the man's blood. Payne Best who was housed in the same prison bunker at that time was told about Kokorin and his abject state by one of the wardens he was friendly with. The Englishman claimed that he used his influence with the guards to have him moved to an adjoining cell where, although he was not permitted to have direct contact with the Russian, he was able to cheer him up somewhat by having some of his allocation of tobacco sent to him, and by turning up the volume on his radio whenever cheery music was being broadcast.[31]

The Irishman, Murphy, was also transferred, in this instance to another camp entirely, although it is not clear if this had anything to do with the events just described. He was one of many prisoners of war who lost their mind. He survived the war, but died soon after in Netley, a mental institution for servicemen near Southampton.[32] His place in the hut was filled by an Irish-born Liverpudlian, John Spence.[33] As we will discover, Spence was to prove an unpopular and suspect figure within *Sonderlager* 'A'. Later arrivals included a group of British officers, survivors of the 'Great Escape' from Stalag Luft III, one of whom was Major Johnnie Dodge, an American who was a relative of Winston Churchill through marriage.

Soon after the end of the war, the Americans uncovered an SS report about Yakov Dzhugashvili's death which they passed on to the British. The contents created a dilemma for the British Foreign Office. It was initially thought that they might present Stalin with a copy of the file at the upcoming Potsdam Conference in July 1945, presumably while tendering their condolences. However, when the contents were perused, the 'unpleasant' and embarrassing fact that Yakov Dzhugashvili's suicidal action was preceded by an argument with a British fellow prisoner – Cushing – was discovered. The mandarins therefore advised that it would be distasteful 'to draw attention to an Anglo-Russian quarrel' in connection with Stalin's son's death. Consequently, Stalin was not told of the discovery.[34] On 3 January 1951, the *Daily Telegraph* published an intriguing article by a 'special correspondent':

Quest for news of Stalin's second son: Offer of reward
News of a curious quest by Russian agents in Germany has reached London. They are seeking information about the fate of Capt. Dzhugashvili, M. Stalin's second [*sic*] son.

A reward of a million roubles for details of his whereabouts is offered. The Kremlin had hitherto accepted the general view that Capt. Dzhugashvili did not long survive his capture by the Germans in 1941.

His elder brother [a mistaken reference to his younger half-brother Vasilli] Lt.-Gen. Dzhugashvili is commanding general of an important Soviet Air Group. The sons retained their father's family name.

Capt. Dzhugashvili was first reported in an officers' prisoner-of-war camp in the province of Holstein. Here he showed complete unconcern about his fate and refused to submit to ordinary camp discipline.

It was reported of him that he would never address a German officer by rank, or rank and name, which is the usual custom. He would use the officer's surname.

In Concentration Camp

Towards 1942 he was transferred to the notorious Oranienburg [Sachsenhausen] concentration camp near Berlin. It was from that camp that the German Army was informed that he had died, though the cause of death was not specified.

No reason for the sudden revival of interest in the young man has been given, but it has been stated in Russian Army circles in Europe that M. Stalin himself might have issued the order for the search. This theory is advanced to support a report that M. Stalin is ill.

Even if that were so, no Government department in Moscow could question the Marshal's orders, however, strange.[35]

Major Johnnie Dodge, who had survived captivity, read this report and, shortly afterwards, arrived at the Foreign Office in London with a proposal that he and a fellow former resident of *Sonderlager* 'A', Colonel Jack Churchill, be sent to Moscow to meet Stalin to tell him what they knew about his son's death in Sachsenhausen. Both had only arrived in the compound after Dzhugashvili's death, so their information could only have been obtained second hand. In support of his proposal, Dodge bizarrely suggested that hearing about his son's sad end might somehow 'soften Stalin's heart towards the West'. As Dodge's version of events has Stalin's son being pursued by a British soldier, with a knife shortly before his death, it defies reason that Dodge should think that this information would soften Stalin's heart towards anyone, least of all the British. Perhaps Dodge's real motivation was the reward mentioned in the newspaper article; in other words, what he may have wanted was, not so much to soften Stalin's heart, as to lighten his pocket. Needless to say, the Foreign Office declined his offer. A Foreign Office staffer, who happened to have spent some time in the company of Dodge as a POW, advised, with compassionate understatement, that he was 'not entirely dispassionate in judgement'.[36]

It seems, though, that Stalin, the 'man of steel', who was prepared to have millions sacrificed to maintain his hold on power, had in the end, begun to feel remorse for his 'fool' of a son, conceding, finally, that the boy had in fact been 'a real man'.[37]

CHAPTER FOUR

TRAITORS

Sachsenhausen, March 1944

In the months following Stalin's son's death, a number of new prisoners arrived in *Sonderlager* 'A'. They included two Polish RAF men and a group of former Red Army officers. They were joined later by an extraordinary group of British officers, a number of them survivors of The Great Escape. The first British arrival was Captain Peter Churchill, a Special Operations Executive (SOE) officer who had been captured in the company of his French fellow operative and lover, Odette Sansom, while attempting to build a resistance network in the south of France. In the hope that it would save both of them, they conspired to tell their Gestapo interrogators that he was related to Winston Churchill and that they were married. Despite initial German scepticism and repeated gruelling interrogations, the deception worked, at least for Churchill, and now considered a potential hostage, he was given the status of a special prisoner. Sansom, however, continued to be treated by the Gestapo as a French Résistant and spy. She was tortured and sentenced to be executed, although fortunately this was never carried out.

Churchill, on the basis of his assumed relationship with the British Prime Minister, was dispatched to Sachsenhausen. He must have feared what was in store for him given the reputation of that camp, but he was relieved when shown his new abode. He later described the *Sonderlager* he was escorted to as a 'haven' set within the desert of suffering that was Sachsenhausen. As he was admiring the tree-enclosed compound, a tall person with unruly red hair approached and saluted. 'Sergeant Cushing at your service, Sorr [*sic*] and welcome to Sonderlager 'A'.'[1]

Cushing introduced Churchill to his roommate Andy Walsh and to the two other Irish prisoners in an adjoining room, Patrick O'Brien and John

Spence. Cushing asked if Churchill would like tea or a cigarette, to which the bemused officer quipped 'both'. Within minutes, he sat on his allotted bunk, a teacup in hand, enjoying the first cigarette he had smoked for quite some time. The Irishmen were anxious to please. Churchill was the first British officer they had encountered since Friesack. How would they explain their presence here, and more particularly in Friesack? Would they be regarded as traitors? Since Stalingrad and the Allied invasion of southern Italy, it had become evident that the tide of war had turned in favour of the Allies and, with the prospect of victory, the thoughts of the former Friesack men would have begun to focus on their post-war reputations. The reaction of these officers to their tale of officer-sanctioned feigned collaboration would be important. It could make the difference between joyous liberation and court martial at war's end.

First impressions were important and, as the Captain was made comfortable, Cushing and Walsh told him about their time in Friesack. Churchill was given to understand that it was their commanding officer, John McGrath, who suggested they enrol for training with the Germans in order to double-cross them. This of course was misleading, for, as we have learned, Cushing had already volunteered before McGrath's arrival in that camp, but a little muddling of the timescales would help to deflect suspicion. No matter, Churchill was charmed by the two Irishmen. Following months of solitary confinement, he delighted in their brogue-infused storytelling. He believed them, although his confidence in them was not to be shared by later British arrivals.

A number of the recently arrived Russian prisoners were now sharing a hut with the Irish quartet. They had been placed there following the death of Stalin's son and Kokorin's departure. The group included generals who had apparently turned traitor and allied themselves with the Nazis. In the rapid encircling movements that characterised the 1941 German invasion, almost 900,000 Soviet troops were taken prisoner. (In total, 5.7 million were captured by the Germans or their allies during the war, more than half of whom died in captivity.[2]) Nazi racial theory, and the excuse that the Soviet Union had not ratified the Geneva Convention, contributed to mass murder, cruel exploitation and the fatal neglect of Russian prisoners. Nevertheless, the Nazis were always on the lookout for prestigious prisoners, including high-ranking officers, who might prove to be useful to them. Subsequently, when the German military began to experience serious manpower losses themselves, consideration was given to the recruitment of Russian prisoners into the German war machine. The most significant collaborator was Andrei Vlasov, a decorated Red Army General, who was allowed to establish a 'Russian Liberation Army', recruited from Russian prisoners of war. Another important General to agree to work with the Germans was Ivan Bessonov, who now shared accommodation with the Irish group in Sachsenhausen.

Bessonov, a stocky, crude, arrogant, but clever man from the Urals, had been a senior NKVD general. (The NKVD was the Soviet Secret Police, later rebranded as the KGB.) When captured in July 1941 he faced summary execution as Hitler had ordered that all captured political commissars be shot. To save himself, he immediately adopted an anti-Stalinist stance and volunteered to work for the Nazis. The tactic worked and he became an important Nazi collaborator. He had inside knowledge of Stalin's military and security apparatus and he was more than willing to share all he knew with the Nazis. He also had first-hand knowledge of the terror wrought by the arrests and executions in Russia in the years preceding the war: first-hand because he, as a NKVD general, would have been an agent of that terror. He would also have feared becoming a victim, for the secret police themselves were not immune from being purged. Thousands of NKVD personnel were arrested in the late 1930s after the arrest and execution of two secret police chiefs in 1936 and 1939. The wily Bessonov escaped these purges, just as he managed to escape execution after his capture by the Germans.

Even judged against the standards of the NKVD, Bessonov was an obnoxious individual. He is believed to have been instrumental in having his Red Army commanding officer arrested in order to take over his command.[3] Later, while working for the Germans, he was implicated in the execution of a fellow Russian POW who tried to escape.[4] Although he refused to become involved with General Vlasov's 'Russian Liberation Army', this was because he believed he should have been put in charge of it.[5] The role he was assigned by the Germans was to recruit Soviet POWs into anti-Communist partisan units that would be trained to operate behind Soviet lines. For a time, the Germans appeared to have considered him as a potential Russian Quisling, appointing him head of 'The Political Centre for the Struggle against Bolshevism'.[6] In this role he was fond of imagining himself as the ruler of a new Russia, but he ran afoul of his German bosses when, according to himself, he was overheard declaring 'as if I'd give the Ukraine to these bastards'.[7] Despite this, he may have continued to advise the SS on their anti-partisan tactics while in Sachsenhausen.

Bessonov, learning of Churchill's presence and believing that he was a cousin of the British Prime Minister, used Cushing and Walsh as emissaries in a bizarre scheme that he wanted put to the Englishman. As conveyed by the Irishmen, he suggested that Captain Churchill allow himself to be parachuted back to England in order to try to convince his 'cousin' Winston to allow British paratroopers to accompany Bessonov's renegade recruits in a parachute drop near one of the large Soviet gulags. The idea was that they would release the prisoners and recruit the fittest into an anti-Stalinist force that could eventually overthrow the Stalinist regime. Self-survival was almost certainly Bessonov's primary motivation for suggesting this absurd plan: liberation by the Red Army would lead to his certain execution, so his only hope was that the Western Allies might change sides also. Peter Churchill listened to this proposal with mounting incredulity before declining the offer.[8]

One could be forgiven for seeing Bessonov's intrigues as nothing more than the delusional ravings of a renegade officer. His proposal had no chance of being put into practice, but it was not entirely implausible. There were close to three million prisoners in Soviet Gulags at the outbreak of the war and Bessonov knew the location of many of these forced labour camps. Before his fall from favour, a dozen of his men, wearing NKVD uniforms, had been parachuted into the Komi region of Siberia, but they were quickly captured and executed.[9] It's doubtful that he would have had the proposal put to Peter Churchill without some level of encouragement from the SS, on whom the plan would depend. Of course, it was delusional to think that when victory seemed assured the British, and more especially the Americans, would ever consider allying themselves with Germany against the Soviet Union. But it was a delusion shared by many in the Nazi leadership, not least by Himmler, virtually to the war's end.[10] It is largely for this reason that some of the characters depicted in this book became hostages; to be used as leverage in negotiations with this in mind. Peter Churchill, as we will see, was not the last of the British Officers to be presented with an offer of a flight out of Germany in an attempt to achieve a cessation of hostilities on the Western front.

Bessonov had another reason for attempting to involve Churchill in this scheme. It provided him with the chance of reviving his standing with the Nazi authorities. But why did Cushing and Walsh agree to get involved? It seems from Peter Churchill's account that they were disappointed with his rejection of the proposal.[11] As noted in the previous chapter, Cushing, was anti-Communist, but it's likely his motivation had more to do with his own self-survival. He might have been considering a contingency plan, in the event that their story about pretend collaboration wasn't believed. An alliance between Germany and Britain, were it ever to come about, would remove any prospect of them being accused of collaboration, for then the Germans would no longer be the enemy. Certainly, it is not beyond the ingenuity of Cushing to have considered the fail-safe benefits of such an unlikely eventuality.

Major General Pyotr Privalov, another of the Russians present, was very different to Bessonov. A refined and decorated officer, commander of the 15th Rifle Corps of the Red Army, he had been seriously wounded before being captured in December 1942 when his car was ambushed in Eastern Ukraine.[12] Under interrogation, he indicated a willingness to work for the Germans, although in his case this seems to have been nothing more than a stratagem for escape. Following one unsuccessful escape attempt, he was transferred to Sachsenhausen. Privalov was a cultured man, although taciturn and hampered by his lack of German which was the lingua franca among the different nationalities in the camp. Although he was the ranking officer, it was Bessonov who was dominant among the Soviet prisoners: his burly physique and over-bearing manner allowed him to maintain his fearsome NKVD status, notwithstanding the changed circumstances. The other Russians present were Lieutenant Colonel Victor Brodnikov, who is believed to have worked for the Germans under Bessonov,[13] and Lieutenant Nikolay Russchenko, a former reserve office who was captured during fighting near Leningrad. He claimed to have escaped and led a Russian partisan group in actions behind German lines. When recaptured, he was tortured, but kept denying any involvement with the resistance.[14] Acting as orderly to the officers was a Soviet soldier, Fyoder Ceredilin, who had spent time in a Soviet gulag before the war.

In uncomfortably close proximity to the Russians were two young Polish RAF officers, Jan Izycki and Stanislaw Jensen. They were flying a Wellington Bomber when it was shot down over France a year previously. Jensen, the pilot, managed to crash land the plane in a field and they both managed to drag themselves clear of the burning wreck. Izycki, the navigator, suffered serious burns to his face which his full beard now only partly obscured. His hands were also badly burned. When captured, they sought medical attention, but Izycki's wounds didn't save him from a severe beating.[15] The Poles tended to keep to themselves in the *Sonderlager*. They both shared the Polish national prejudice against Russians and tried as far as possible to avoid contact with their Soviet neighbours.

A group of Italians had also entered the special compound in late 1943. They had been stationed in the Italian embassy in Berlin when the post-Mussolini Italian government changed sides and they, like hundreds of thousands of Italian servicemen, were imprisoned. The officers among them were soon transferred out of Sachsenhausen, leaving behind two orderlies, Amechi and Burtoli, who assumed the roles of cook and servant for the growing number of British officers in the compound.

At some point, Cushing and Walsh approached Peter Churchill again in conspiratorial fashion. They had come to tell him that they had an informer in their midst. They were referring to Lance-Bombardier John Spence, their fellow Irish POW who had taken Murphy's place within their section of the hut. If, as Cushing and Walsh suspected, Spence was, for whatever reason, currying favour with the Camp Commandant by informing on others, there was a risk that they would be tarnished with the same brush, hence their interest in isolating him and distancing themselves from him. The crimes and betrayals attributed to Spence were numerous. For one, it appears he had volunteered to work on a German Radio Service (*Irland Redaktion*) that directed propaganda broadcasts to Ireland.

Early in the war, the Germans established propaganda radio stations directed at different countries. The Irish service, which transmitted for only a few hours weekly, directly after Lord Haw-Haw's talk, initially confined its broadcasts to the Irish language. This was an extraordinary constraint on a propaganda service given that only a very small percentage of the Irish population spoke the language and, as most of those lived in what were then relatively poor communities along the western seaboard, few of them would have owned a radio and the few that did would have had difficulty in picking up the signal.[16] The radio talks were delivered by a number of German academics specialising in Irish studies. In charge of the service was Adolf Mahr, who was technically on leave from his position as Director of the National Museum in

Dublin. When the radio service expanded in 1941 to include nightly English transmissions, new recruits were sought. Frank Stuart was one of the first to contribute in English.[17] Spence was probably recruited around this time also and he operated under the alias 'Brennan', although there is no record of him broadcasting under that name.[18] Nevertheless, he was a willing collaborator, and the charges against him go much further.

Peter Churchill in his book *The Spirit in the Cage* didn't refer to Spence by his real name, using the alias 'Judd' in his descriptions of these incidents,[19] but there is no doubt that 'Judd' was Spence.[20] By far the worst accusation made by Churchill is that 'Judd', while working at the station and living in Berlin, betrayed some Jewish people who had befriended him by reporting their undercover existence to the Nazis, resulting in their arrest and deportation to an 'extermination camp'.[21] No sources are indicated, but it is probable Churchill heard of this from Cushing or Walsh, who likely came into contact with Spence during their time in Berlin. Another collaborator in the radio centre, Patrick Joseph Dillon, who broadcast under the alias 'Cadogan', painted a less dramatic, but no less reprehensible, picture of Spence's betrayal.

In late April 1943 Dillon, Glasgow-born of Irish background, was a merchant seaman who was captured when his boat was sunk in the Atlantic.[22] After disclosing pro-German sympathies, he was taken to the Radio Centre in Berlin in April 1943. In the *Irland Redaktion* office he was introduced to a Mr Brennan whose real name he later learned was Spence. Spence was assigned to look after Dillon and took him to his lodgings. Dillon claimed that the landlady didn't want the two men to share a room for some reason and lodged Dillon downstairs in rooms occupied by a German woman, Charlotte Greger. Dillon began a relationship with Greger whose husband, a Jew, was incarcerated in a concentration camp. Dillon, who was anti-Semitic, claimed to have changed his views under her influence and says they had made plans to escape to Switzerland. He says he made the mistake of confiding in Spence, who betrayed him, leading to the Gregers' arrest. Dillon claimed he then refused to continue with his radio talks unless his lover was freed and she was subsequently released, but soon after five women 'who used to keep company with Spence' were arrested following another disclosure to the Gestapo by Spence.[23] According to Dillon, Spence then disappeared for a time, but ten days later the Gestapo again came to the house, having been informed by the Irishman that there was a Jew hiding in the accommodation. A Jewish girl, possibly a relative of the woman's husband, had been secretly living in the house, but was now elsewhere, having been warned to stay away after the earlier arrest. However, this time Dillon and Greger were both arrested; the implication being that this was on suspicion of their joint collaboration in hiding the fugitive.

Although purportedly a witness to, and victim of, Spence's treachery, Dillon's testimony must be treated with caution. He gave this account when he was facing post-war charges of renegade activities, so any story that portrayed him as undergoing a 'road to Damascus' conversion and helping a Jew to avoid capture is most likely a self-serving invention. His broadcasts, under the pseudonym 'Cadogan', were invariably replete with anti-Jewish demagoguery and this continued until at least June 1943, after his supposed conversion by Greger.[24] It is even possible that Dillon was attempting to put the blame for his own actions on Spence. Whatever the truth of the matter, the story about Spence betraying some Jewish person or persons had wide currency and, for this reason, and because he was believed to be acting as an informer in Sachsenhausen, he was disliked, distrusted and shunned. It is not clear why Spence ended up in *Sonderlager* 'A'. Dillon says that he was told that he had been arrested near the Swiss frontier, which would suggest that he was attempting to escape Germany.[25]

Spence didn't help his cause in Sachsenhausen, for it seems he was rude and disagreeable. He refused to comply with the rudimentary disciplinary codes applying to the lower ranks in the camp, refusing to salute Churchill or obey his orders. As indicated, he was believed to be a stool pigeon who informed the Camp Commandant, Anton Keindl, about fellow prisoners and even SS guards who were sometimes incautious in what they said to prisoners. He was suspected of reporting a young SS guard who told Andy Walsh that he listened to the BBC in the guard room at night and advised Walsh how he might do the same.[26] Listening to enemy broadcasts, although not uncommon towards the end of the war, was a serious offence and encouraging a prisoner to do so could have led to the guard being shot. The Camp Commandant launched an investigation during which prisoners were asked if they had listened to the BBC. All denied it of course; Churchill was notified in advance by one of the guards of Keindl's visit and he sent Cushing and Walsh on a mission to alert all the prisoners. The guard was exonerated.[27]

Peter Churchill, who was at this time the only British officer present, decided to take action against Spence. He told Cushing and Walsh to summon Spence, but he refused to leave his quarters. Accompanied by the two gleefully expectant Irishmen, Churchill marched officiously to confront Spence. Churchill demanded he explain why he refused to obey his order. Spence deigned to remain blasé and seated until Churchill hoisted him up by the lapels, slapped a cigarette from his month and struck him with such force that he sent him 'spinning into the corner of the room'.[28] A further assault followed before the subdued Spence had his lance corporal's insignia torn from his tunic. According to Churchill, Spence promised to conform, but later complained to Keindl that he had been assaulted. Churchill was shown a copy of the complaint by a friendly SS guard. In retribution, the Englishman ordered that there was to be no social contact with any of the other prisoners. After three weeks, Spence, again according to Churchill, was remorseful and sought an interview. He was ordered, as a penalty, to surrender his next Red Cross parcel to the Russians, and, more ominously for him, sign a confession drawn up by Churchill. This document dealt with his German propaganda work, his snooping on fellow prisoners and, most damning of all, it contained an admittance that he was 'instrumental in the apprehension of over a dozen Jews, who in all probability have been murdered in the Extermination Camps to which I knew they would be sent'.[29] Churchill promised him that, in the event of Spence behaving properly during the remainder of the war, he would destroy the papers. Spence apparently signed the document and Cushing, Walsh and a recently arrived Free-French RAF captain, Ray Van Wymeersch, witnessed it.

It is difficult to believe that anyone would confess to treason and complicity in murder on the basis of no more pressure than that of social isolation. In his book, Churchill portrays Spence as having rowed with everyone in the camp before his (Churchill's) arrival, with the result that 'no one would have him as a room-mate'.[30] Isolation, therefore, was nothing new to him. A greater level of 'persuasion' would surely have had to have been applied. And, if Churchill really believed Spence was implicated in such a heinous crime, why would he (Churchill) conditionally promise not to mention it after the war was over? Churchill clearly over-egged the story for his book, for although he would have known about the 'extermination camps' when wrote his story, he was unlikely to have knowledge of them as a prisoner in 1944.

Soon after these events, Peter Churchill was joined by other British officers, four of them survivors of The Great Escape from Stalag Luft III POW camp at Sagan. The first to arrive was Wing Commander Harry Day, generally known as 'Wings'. He had been captured after being shot down while leading a squadron on a reconnaissance mission over western Germany only a few weeks into the war. He was badly burned and was the only member of his crew to survive. Middle-aged, tall and slim, he was respected and liked by fellow inmates in the various camps he was placed in, despite having a tendency to be abrupt at times.[31] Immensely brave, he had been decorated when, as a young marine officer during the First World War, he repeatedly went below the deck of his torpedoed ship to rescue two trapped and injured crewmen. He made light of his gallantry by claiming he had only gone below to retrieve the ship's store of liquor.[32] The other early arrival was the previously mentioned Major Johnnie Dodge. The American-born Dodge, from a privileged background, was the only one among a British contingent that subsequently came to include two Churchills who was actually a relation of Winston Churchill: the connection was through his mother's second marriage. Like Day, he was a decorated veteran of the First World War. The next to arrive was Flight Lieutenant Bertram James, usually called 'Jimmy'. A handsome man, he had been shot down while flying his Wellington Bomber over the Netherlands in June 1940. After being greeted on entry into the camp by Day, James asked who else was in the *Sonderlager*. Day replied: 'Well, there are a few renegade Irishmen who played the part of collaborators for a while – we're still not sure which of them can be trusted.'[33]

James was, according to Dowse, with whom he was to share a room in the compound, 'reserved, shy and quite'.[34] Flight Lieutenant Sydney Dowse, a fellow escaper from Stalag Luft III, arrived soon after James. Blond, tall and handsome, and known as the 'Laughing Boy' for his cheerful good humour,[35] his Spitfire had been shot down while on a reconnaissance mission over the French coast near Brest in August 1941. He had managed to ditch his plane in the sea and swim ashore without attracting attention, but must have been charmed and dismayed in equal measure to find a group of young French women waiting to greet him on the beach calling out excitedly '*l'Aviator Anglais.*'[36]

These four, plus the previously mentioned Frenchman, Van Wymeersch, were among the seventy-six prisoners who escaped from Stalag Luft III on 24

March 1944. All but three of the escapees were recaptured and fifty of these were murdered by the Nazis. The Frenchman was almost certainly destined to be among the victims, but through good luck and ingenuity he managed to evade execution. While awaiting transport from a prison in Berlin after his recapture, he observed a group of civilian prisoners being marched elsewhere and joined up with them without being noticed. He ended up in Buchenwald before the resulting confusion led to his transfer to Sachsenhausen.[37] At the time of their arrival in Sachsenhausen, none of the Sagan escapees knew about the murder of their colleagues. They only learned about it when they read a report in *Deutsche Allgemeine Zietung* which they were regularly supplied with. The newspaper did not refer directly to the crime, but it was evident from a comment that mocked a statement by Anthony Eden, the Foreign Secretary, condemning the killings.

Day was especially shaken by the news. Although he wouldn't then have known the list of victims, he would have assumed they included some close friends. Roger Bushell, with whom Day had planned the Sagan escape, was one. Day's escape partner, the Polish RAF officer Pavel Tobolski, was also among those murdered. So was his close friend Mike Casey. He had first known the Irishman Casey from 57 Squadron which Day commanded and they had met again in captivity.[38] They had a lot in common; both were sons of the Empire. Day, whose father was a senior administrator, was born in Sarawak in Borneo, while Casey had been born in India where his father was a high-ranking officer in the Indian police force. They were both shipped home as children to be educated. Day went to Haileybury, a public school in Hertford in England, while Casey was sent to Clongowes Wood in Ireland before moving to Stonyhurst in Lancashire.[39]

For Dowse, the terrible news would have reminded him of the harrowing scene that occurred when he and his escape partner Stanislaw Krol, a Polish RAF Officer, were being separated after their recapture. Krol had appealed to Dowse 'Don't leave me! I've had it if you leave me! I'm finished!'[40] Dowse had no choice in the matter; he was being escorted to Berlin for Gestapo interrogation. He tried to reassure Krol, telling him they would take him back to Sagan, believing at the time that that was likely. Dowse, after reading the report, would have guessed that Krol's worst fears were borne out. He was, in fact, shot shortly after Dowse's departure.

A sixth British officer, the last to arrive in *Sonderlager* 'A', and by far the most eccentric, was Lieutenant Colonel Jack Churchill. Although from Surrey with no obvious Scottish connections, he had assumed a Scottish identity and included in his battle kit a Scottish claymore sword, bagpipes, a longbow and set of arrows. A commando officer, he was the stuff of comic strip legend. He is said to have been the last British soldier to kill an enemy with an arrow; his son claims he killed a German soldier with an arrow near the village of L'Epinette, east of Paris in 1940.[41] It would not have been beyond his capabilities for he had previously represented Britain in pre-war archery competitions. He led commando actions in Norway, France, Sicily and Yugoslavia for which he would be awarded the Military Cross. He would sometimes lead troops into battle playing Scottish martial airs on his bagpipes. The Claymore sword was not just for show either; in the Sicily landings he led an assault with his sword drawn using it to subdue a platoon of German soldiers. He was captured after being rendered unconscious by a grenade explosion while leading a group of Titoist partisans and a platoon of British commandos in battle on an Island off the Croatian coast.[42] Like Peter Churchill, the Germans assumed him to be a relative of Winston Churchill, although, in his case, he never pretended to be so.

Life in the *Sonderlager* was not unpleasant most of the time. The prisoners were reasonably well fed. They were on SS rations, being provided with the same quality and quantity of food as their gaolers. They did better when Red Cross parcels arrived. Occasionally, the two Italian orderlies, Bartoli and Ameche, who shared their accommodation – Ameche was a cousin and look-alike of the then famous Hollywood actor Don Ameche – would prepare a communal meal using the contents of the parcels. The Russians were sometimes invited. Bessonov would wolf down his food, spitting out whatever bits he found disagreeable, much to the silent disapproval of his fellow Russians.[43] During the day, the occupants could wander about within their compound. There were German newspapers and books to read. German language lessons were provided by Peter Churchill. Card and board games were played and sing-songs occupied many evenings, with Cushing to the fore. Bessonov gave lectures in which he critiqued the Soviet Union and expounded on his formula for a constitutional framework for a 'free' Russia. Rather surprisingly, these were attended by Harry Day and John Dodge, with Peter Churchill translating

Bessonov's poor German. Dodge was acquainted with the Soviet Union, having been arrested by the Cheka – forerunners of the NKVD – and detained for a week in December 1921 on suspicion of using a trade visit as cover for spying,[44] an experience that must have contributed to his subsequent staunch anti-Communism.

A large wall map was fashioned from several sheets of paper on which Cushing regularly marked up the progress of the war, based on information gleaned from newspapers and radio broadcasts. An outdoor running track was marked out and a long jump pit was dug. A ball was made from rags and paper for netball games. Such exercises allowed the inmates to become fit and bronzed over the summer months.[45] None of this could compensate for isolation from family. No communication was permitted with the outside world. They could not write or receive letters from home. They were all *Nacht und Nebel* ('Night and Fog') prisoners. Not knowing if their parents were alive or dead, how wives or children were fairing, and knowing that their families were left to wonder if they were alive or dead all contributed to bouts of depression. This was more problematic for the older prisoners like Day and Dodge, both of whom were married with children. For Day, there was the added difficulty of knowing from earlier letters that his marriage was in difficulty. Depression and mental breakdown were common in the POW camps[46] and Day himself had a breakdown while in Sagan in 1941.[47] The Irish orderly, O'Brien, is rarely mentioned in memoirs, leaving the impression that he had withdrawn into himself after his arrest and interrogation in Berlin.

There were frequent reminders of the contrast between the relative benign conditions enjoyed by the *Sonderlager* inmates and the privations endured by ordinary Sachsenhausen camp prisoners. Once a week the group were escorted to the main compound of the camp for a shower, which involved them passing a large *Appell Platz* ('roll call square') with its ominous gallows. Here they could see half-starved figures in their striped camp uniforms being marched continuously around the square carrying heavy backpacks loaded with stones. The purpose of the exercise was to test new designs for army boots.[48] The marches were continued to the point of the collapse of the prisoners or the footwear. Suicides within the main camp were common. Often during the night the special prisoners would be awoken by machine-gun fire, an indication that some poor soul was suffering the same suicidal fate as Yakov Dzhugashvili.

During the day, smoke from the crematorium was a constant reminder of the murderous nature of the camp.[49]

They had been told on entering Sachsenhausen that there was no possibility of escape. The trustee's they encountered told them the only way out was via the crematorium chimney. Such warnings only spurred on the serial escapers; they had attempted numerous escapes prior to the mass breakout from Stalag Luft III and they were spoiling to attempt another. They had to try to escape again, it was their duty to attempt to they told themselves. And it served another purpose, it relieved the boredom of captivity and allowed them to dream of an early homecoming.

CHAPTER FIVE

BREAKOUT

23 September 1944

Dowse and James emerged from the tunnel into the wet night, about four feet outside the perimeter wall of the camp. To their relief there was no sound except the pounding rain in the darkness. The two of them had spent months digging the narrow tunnel which was just big enough to crawl through, and their slim frames and their familiarity with it allowed them to get out without too much difficulty. They were followed by Harry Day, for whom it was an ordeal; his knee was swollen and causing great pain. Jack Churchill's was the next head to emerge. His stocky frame got him stuck in the exit hole for a time and he had to be pulled free by the others. With Dodge, the last to appear, the situation proved near impossible. His lanky, gangly physique made his passage through the tunnel extremely difficult and slow. When he eventually reached the exit hole and tried to squeeze through, he got completely stuck. He could only manage to get his head and one arm partially out. It took ten minutes of strenuous pulling before the others could drag him free. Raising his dishevelled frame into a standing position he blurted out 'Ah! Free at Last!' to the alarm of the others who threw themselves to the ground expecting a burst of machine-gun fire from the guard towers.[1] Fortunately, due to the heavy rain, the guards didn't see or hear anything. The inveterate escapees were about to make another dash for freedom.

Sydney Dowse and Bertram James had started to plan the escape in the early summer of 1944. Preliminary work had begun on a tunnel, but it needed the approval of Harry Day as the senior officer, and he was slow to give it.[2] This was untypical of Day who had taken a leading role in five escape attempts in his previous camps. He hesitated because he was concerned about the trustworthiness of some of their co-inhabitants in the *Sonderlager*. He wasn't sure he could trust the Russian Bessonov, or the Irish orderlies, especially Spence. News of the Normandy landings in June complicated matters further. Would it be best to wait for liberation rather than risk death in a further, almost certainly futile escape attempt? As senior officer, Day bore a weighty responsibility for the lives of the younger men, especially after news of the murder of their fellow escapers from Stalag Luft III. It was only after an angry confrontation with the Camp Commandant that he finally made up his mind and sanctioned the escape attempt.

Dowse had been the cause of the row. Left alone in the compound while the others were taking their weekly shower, he took it upon himself to reverse all the skull and crossbones signs, the death's head symbol of the *SS-Totenkopfverbände,* the unit responsible for the concentration camp security, so that they all faced away from the prisoners. Dowse may have seen this as a mere prank, but it was a foolhardy act and one that he could have paid for with his life. When the guard on duty, known as 'Jim', realised what Dowse had done he was livid, not just because Dowse had tampered with the macabre insignia of his unit, but out of fear for his own future for allowing it to occur on his watch. A shouting match ensued, with Dowse giving as good as he got. When Day returned to the compound he managed to calm things, but he was shortly afterwards summoned to see Kaindl, the Camp Commandant. He proceeded to admonish Day for Dowse's action, warning that severe action would be taken if anything of this nature happened again. Relations between the English officer and the Austrian SS Commander were already strained. Kaindl, knowing the reputation of the RAF group, considered them a liability and likely to make more trouble for him. Day had previously enjoyed a friendly relationship with the commander of his earlier place of confinement in *Dulag Luft*, Major Theodor Rumpel of the Luftwaffe. There the prisoners were allowed to go on long country walks on condition of parole, meaning that they gave their word not to use the privilege to escape. Rumpel even invited Day and some of the other senior officers to dine in his house on occasions. Kaindl's attitude was in stark contrast and Day disliked him intensely. In the confrontation over Dowse's actions, Day considered that he was being treated with contempt.[3] He returned in high dudgeon to the *Sonderlager* where he immediately sanctioned work on the tunnel. He had reverted to his long-held view that the war remained to be won and that it was their duty to contribute by attempting to escape.

It was decided that the project would be known to as few people as possible. The two Italian orderlies who acted as batmen in the British Officers' quarters would have to be trusted, but the officers decided not to confide in the Russians, or in the four Irish who shared accommodation with them. However, Andy Walsh possessed information that might allow some of them to make good their escape from Germany. Walsh, who Day considered to be the most balanced of the four, not much of a compliment, had spoken about his friendship with a German named Hans Fullert whom he had met during his *Abwehr* training days in Berlin in 1941.[4] From something that was said to him, Walsh came to the conclusion that Fullert had anti-Nazi leanings. He lived in the eastern Berlin suburb of Mahlsdorf and was employed by the giant Todt organisation that provided logistical support to the military. His work involved him driving a truck loaded with equipment and supplies to German fortifications in northern France and he often brought back goods for sale on the black-market.[5] Walsh said that Fullert had offered to take him to France anytime he wanted.[6] Day hoped that he might be prepared to repeat this offer to one or more of the escapers if they could make their way to Berlin. This would allow them to make their way to France where they could make contact with the Resistance and, through them, allied forces. Walsh had disclosed information about Fullert in general conversation and was later questioned on the details by Day. The address was obtained without the purpose being disclosed, but it can be assumed Walsh would have guessed what was afoot, knowing Day's reputation. Besides, he and Cushing would have had a good idea that a tunnel was under construction for, as Peter Churchill observed, the Irish boys were 'as bright as they make them and always first to sense the least thing wrong in the camp'.[7]

Given that Walsh and Cushing probably knew, or at least suspected, that an escape plan was being hatched, the fact that they kept this knowledge to themselves tells us that Cushing, who had been an informer in Friesack, was no longer playing that role. He, and the other Irishmen, now needed to focus on their standing within their own soon-to-be victorious army. Cushing and Walsh may have been offended by being kept out of the loop, but keeping quiet was in their best interests. If the tunnel was somehow discovered, suspicion was likely to fall on them if they were known to be aware of it.

The tunnel began under James's bed. The digging work was assigned to the younger men – Dowse and James – with Jack Churchill joining them after his arrival in the *Sonderlager*. To begin with, their only digging tool was an adapted table knife, although this was later supplemented by a small saw secured from a guard, possibly through bribery.[8] Tactically, it was wise not to involve Day in the tunnelling work as his absence for long periods would be noticed. The soil was sandy which made things easier, but increased the risk of collapse. The floor of their timber hut was raised above the ground with an outside skirt which proved perfect for secretly disposing of the excavated soil. While the tunnel was underway, they heard news that seven Russian POWs from the main concentration camp had been hung after an attempted escape. This shocked, but didn't deter, them.

One difficulty they had was calculating how far they would need to burrow to reach a safe distance beyond the perimeter of the camp. For this they needed to see over the wall of their compound. Day had a brainwave. He asked the camp authorities to provide them with a gymnastic pommel horse to aid their athletic recreation. To everyone's surprise, the apparatus was delivered. Standing on the horse, while making it seem like an exercise routine, they could see the layout beyond their compound which bordered the outer perimeter of the camp. They noticed that, behind the wall beyond their huts, there was a compound in which there were some unoccupied huts with others under construction. Only an outer wall, with no electrified wiring or guard tower, separated this area from open countryside, so this compound was chosen for the projected tunnel exit point.

The work progressed slowly over the summer. Dowse and James had worked for only a few hours each day to avoid lengthy, suspicious absences. Peter Churchill decided to take no part as he believed, given his SOE background, and the fact that he was not in uniform when captured, that he was certain to be shot if caught escaping. Johnnie Dodge was anxious to help but, as he had been billeted in the hut where Spence and the other Irishmen and Russians lodged, it was decided that his involvement in tunnel work might compromise security. The dig was arduous and risky. To minimise the amount of earth to be disposed of, they kept the tunnel dimensions just large enough for one man to wriggle through at a time. There was no light and little air in the tunnel and there was a constant fear that in a collapse they would suffocate. Increasingly frequent bombing raids nearby increased this risk. However, it held up and was eventually deemed of sufficient length to reach their intended exit point in the unoccupied compound.

The tunnel took almost four months to complete, after which the would-be escapers needed to wait for a suitable night to breakout. Two conditions were deemed essential. First, it had to be raining hard. This would make it less likely that the guards and their dogs would spot their emergence from the tunnel. The second condition related to which guard would be on duty. It was not unusual for prisoners to categorise their guards as either good, or bad, Germans and the *Sonderlager* prisoners had decided views about the two SS men who alternated on night duty.[9] The oldest, an SS conscript whom they called 'George', was considered a kindly and helpful individual, while 'Jim', the guard who had reported Dowse for his tampering with the death head insignia, was viewed as a Nazi bully.[10] They knew that whoever was on duty during the night of a successful escape would be disciplined and the British were determined it would not be 'George'. It wasn't until late September that both conditions were met. 'Jim' was on duty and it had begun to rain heavily on the evening which happened to coincide with Jack Churchill's thirty-seventh birthday. The noisy celebrations that night provided added cover.

When the five eventually extracted themselves from the tunnel, there remained the one outer un-fenced wall to clamber over, but this was easily negotiated for, as they had hoped, a builder's ladder had been left in the yard. They located it after fumbling about in the dark and clambered over the wall. They had made their escape from Sachsenhausen, but now faced the more difficult task of making their way out of Germany. There was sand in their every pore and caked to their uniforms which they had altered as best they could to look like civilian clothes. In pockets they had stuffed some bread for the journey. None had false identification papers.

They then prepared to set off in separate groups. It had previously been decided that their chances of success would be enhanced if they went singly or in pairs. Day and Dowse were to make their way together and Churchill and James likewise. Dodge was the odd one out. It wasn't just the luck of the draw that caused the American to travel alone. Despite his 'Dodger' nickname, he was seen by the others as something of a liability. His height and awkward posture made him conspicuous and he was not, to put it kindly, intellectually gifted. Although he, like the others, had been tutored by Peter Churchill in basic German, he was a poor student and hadn't even mastered the basics of the language. Also, he made little or no preparations and was considered to be impulsive. His approach was to put his trust in fate and his easy-going charm.[11]

Day and Dowse made their way to an 'S' Bahn Station in Oranienburg, about two kilometres away. They had obtained a timetable and an 'S' and 'U' Bahn map from a trustee in the camp. However, due to the delay in emerging from the tunnel they missed the last train. They hid and waited for the first early morning train and, using some of the Deutschmarks they had acquired, they were able to make it to Berlin without attracting anyone's attention. At Friedrichstrasse station they changed to a train for Mahlsdorf. The Germans among the early morning commuters didn't seem to notice a thin trail of fine sand being deposited by the two as they moved about; or if they did notice, they paid little heed. Berlin was full of dirty and bedraggled conscripted foreign workers who were best ignored.

The two were able to find the location of the house where Walsh had told them Fullert lived but, to their dismay, they discovered that the house had been destroyed by bombing. They decided to try to get some rest at the rear of the ruins as Day's knee was still causing him great discomfort. There they were spotted by a resident of a nearby house who took them for looters and called the police.[12] They were arrested and taken to various locations in Berlin before being escorted back to Sachsenhausen. They were deposited in the prison bunker, where they were manacled and left in solitary confinement in between interrogation sessions. They had been free for less than twenty-four hours.[13]

Churchill and James had located a canal and continued along its banks hoping to reach a west- or north-bound railway line and 'jump' a goods train. For four days they tramped over fields in darkness and slept in woods during daylight until they reached a railway marshalling yard. There they found wagons loaded with timber with a notice attached to each indicating delivery destinations. Churchill changed a number of destinations around as an act of sabotage. They then took cover in a nearby wood where they could observe train movements. They were hoping they could be transported to France or Belgium where they might make it to the advancing allies, or to a port where they could stow away in a ship bound for a neutral country. During the night, they observed engine activity which indicated that the wagons were about to be moved. They ran and crouched on the tracks behind a trailing wagon waiting to jump on as it moved off. However, instead of going forward, the train went suddenly into reverse over them as they lay between the rails. They had enough clearance from the axles, but it was a long set of wagons and near the end, they could see, to their horror, the dark crimson glow of the steam engine's furnace approaching, its underbelly lower than the rest of the train. It seemed certain to hit them. They endeavoured to press their bodies further into the sleepers as the hissing of escaping steam grew louder. Then they felt the heat of the engine on their prostrate bodies before, to their great relief, they felt the cool air and rain as the engine passed over them. With a screeching of brakes, the train came to a halt and, as they raised their heads and looked back over their shoulders, they were dazzled by the headlights of the train which now illuminated them. To their surprise, they didn't appear to have been spotted, so they got up and walked, as casually as they could manage under the circumstances, back to the end of the series of wagons to again lie in wait for the train to move out. Despite a railway worker almost stumbling upon them, they remained unobserved and, when it seemed the train was finally on its way, they hoisted themselves onto a wagon-load of logs. But the marshalling of wagons was still not complete and the train once more went into reverse at speed. With the two men scrambling to locate secure hand-holds on the wet timber, the buffers slammed into those of another wagon. The sudden halt caused Churchill to become dislodged and he fell onto the track below. Although he injured an ankle, he managed to climb back onto the wagon with the help of James without being spotted. Eventually, to their relief, the train began to move forward, although Churchill's ankle made for an uncomfortable night's journey.

After a few hours, the train approached a station and the pair, fearing discovery in the approaching daylight, got down from the wagon, Churchill gingerly because of his injury. After narrowly avoiding capture on a few occasions, they came across a group of Russians working in the fields. James, who had learned some Russian from the Soviet inmates in Sachsenhausen, approached and told them they were escaped RAF officers. The Russians, who were slave workers assigned to a local farmer, invited them to make their way to their sleeping quarters after nightfall. James and Churchill approached their hut in the dark and were not disappointed. The Russians shared their food with them and made them warm and welcome around their fire. After some days they departed from their hosts, hoping to board another northbound freight train. When this didn't prove possible, they continued on foot until they were eventually spotted and despite initially avoiding capture they were finally surrounded by armed soldiers.[14] They had been at liberty for fourteen days and had travelled about 170 kilometres. When recaptured they were only thirty kilometres south of the Baltic port of Rostock.[15]

John Dodge had set off alone, knowing he had to avoid human contact because of his lack of German. He, too, located a railway line and walked along it in the darkness. At a station he encountered a German who challenged him. Unable to recall any appropriate German words, he mumbled incoherently. Fortunately, the German assumed him to be a French labourer who had lost his way and directed him to a labour camp that happened to be nearby. Feigning to follow his directions, Dodge made his way back to the railway line and managed to jump onto a passing coal wagon. Seeing the train was about to stop at a station he jumped off and took to the fields hoping to catch another train later. He was spotted but he managed to outrun his pursuer; although nearly fifty years old, the fitness exercises in the camp stood to him. Later, he came across some French prisoners assigned to farm work – in total 600,000 French people had been conscripted to work in Germany under the *Service du Travail Obligatoire* facilitated by the Vichy regime – and they agreed to help. They hid him in the loft of a barn and supplied him with food. He stayed there for a number of weeks. Accidentally discovered by a Polish worker, news of his presence spread and it was decided he must be moved. He was first brought to a village bar in the evening where he joined a large group of French forced labourers spending their meagre earnings on beer. He was told not to worry about the German proprietor as he was deaf and that the only policeman in the area was a sympathetic Luxembourger. As the night wore on, Dodge, who had acquired some French at school, was in his element in the bar. Beer followed beer in noisy revelry until silence was called for in order to hear the BBC news. Dodge was called on to translate into French news of the progress of the Allies. Every mention by him in his halting French of an allied victory was cheered to the rafters.[16] It might have occurred to him that he was more popular with these Frenchmen than with the voters of the Mile End Constituency of London where he unsuccessfully ran for election as a Tory Party candidate in 1924. For the conscripted French farm workers, some of whom had risked their lives to hide him, he represented something altogether more radical. The presence of a British officer in their midst was a portent of a victory that would soon set them free.

Aided by French and Polish farm workers, Dodge lay hidden in a succession of lofts until one morning he was confronted by a German farmer who had climbed into his hiding place and pointed a gun at his head. The Luxemburg policeman was sent for and he was taken into custody, reluctantly on both men's part. The policeman confirmed that he'd known all about his presence in the area for the last few weeks and regretted that some idiot must have given him away.[17] Dodge was, like the others, returned to the prison bunker in Sachsenhausen. Deemed by his colleagues the least likely to escape, it was exactly a month since he had, with some difficulty, emerged from the tunnel. He was the last of the five to be caught.

On their return to Sachsenhausen, the would-be escapees were placed in solitary confinement in punishment cells in the prison 'bunker'. They were handcuffed and shackled at night and endured numerous interrogations. A special court was ordered by Ernst Kaltenbrunner, head of the powerful SS Reich Security Main Office, to try them.[18] Day, as the senior officer, was the prime target. He was hauled before the court repeatedly and accused, along with Dowse, of spying on military installations. This may have been because of where they were picked up. Why would they have made for a suburb of Berlin, instead of towards the border or a port? They demanded to know who their outside contacts were. They appeared to suspect that Day had some German opposition contacts. Any evidence that he was conducting espionage or consorting with anti-Nazis meant certain execution. Day must have wondered if Walsh had said anything about their destination in Berlin, or if Spence had overheard anything. He was near breaking point when an interrogation began early one morning. For weeks he had had little sleep, his knee was still painful, he was exhausted and in this condition he knew he was in danger of being tripped up by his relentless interrogators. He was facing five interrogators that included SS and Gestapo officers and Peter Mohr of the Criminal Police (*Kripo*). Under pressure, he allowed his anger and frustration to surface. He stood up to address them, reciting his rights under the Geneva Convention and pointing out that, as a RAF officer, it was his duty to try to escape. His voice rising and trembling, he pleaded that he was not a spy or a saboteur, but simply attempting to escape. He went on to point out that German POWs, who were, he believed, possessed of the same spirit, would not sit passively in captivity any more than he was prepared to do. Day slumped back in his chair. His speech may have begun as a stratagem, but it seems to have become a *cri de cœur*. There was silence. Then Mohr said quietly, 'We understand, Wing Commander.'[19] What Day had said, and perhaps the passion of his appeal, seemed somehow to touch a residual core of human empathy. Maybe it was his overstated allusion to a shared chivalry among soldiers. It may also have been that he had an unlikely ally in Mohr. An orthodox professional policeman, he had been involved in the Stalag Luft III escape investigation and had been appalled to learn of the murder of fifty of the escapers. He may well have wanted to ensure that no more would suffer the same fate. Whatever the reason, the ordeal was over. On the morning of 15 February 1945, Day, Dowse, James and Churchill were escorted back to the *Sonderlager*. The news of their imminent return had become known to the others and a motley guard of honour awaited them. With Peter Churchill acting as drill master, in no order of rank or nationality, Russians, Irish, Italian, Poles and a Frenchman, stood at attention, as presentable as their tattered uniforms would allow, to honour and welcome them back.[20]

John Dodge never returned to *Sonderlager* 'A'. Under intense interrogation he agreed to be flown to England where he promised to lobby his cousin Winston Churchill to conclude an armistice which would prevent the Communists from penetrating further into Germany. By the time he made it home the war was virtually over and it's unlikely that he ever broached the subject with the Prime Minister. Although Dodge had allowed himself to be used by the Germans, there was little likelihood that, with his powerful connections, he would be rebuked. Sydney Dowse had been similarly propositioned about a homebound peace mission but, like Peter Churchill earlier, he declined.[21]

CHAPTER SIX

GATES OF HELL

Late February 1945

About a week after Day and his comrades were returned to *Sonderlager* 'A', Payne Best, who still knew nothing of their existence, walked outside to inspect his little garden plot. With the wind coming from the east, he could hear the faint sound of artillery fire. The Red Army had now reached the Oder River about fifty miles away. He was not enthusiastic about being liberated by the Russians. Aside from political aversion, he had reason to fear that the Soviets would take an unwelcome interest in his British intelligence work. Preoccupied with this prospect, he didn't notice the Camp Commandant until he strode up to him. Anton Kaindl, a small man with a receding hairline above his large round spectacles, warmly greeted the tall, gaunt Englishman. After the niceties were completed, Payne Best asked if it was likely that he and the other prisoners would be evacuated. Kaindl replied that he had asked to be relieved of responsibility for the more important prisoners in his charge, but he had not, as yet, received a reply.

In contrast to Day, Payne Best liked the Camp Commandant, whom he credited with improving conditions in the camp. When Kaindl took charge of Sachsenhausen in August 1942, he did order some improvement, not out of any humane consideration on his part, but because he was under instructions to improve slave-labour productivity and emaciated prisoners made poor workers. He often visited Payne Best in his cell, sometimes canvassing his opinion about the conduct of the guards assigned to the prison bunker. The Commandant admired Payne Best for, what he called, his 'impeccable attitude'.[1] As compared to the British prisoners in *Sonderlager* 'A', Payne Best was no trouble. He made no attempts to escape – a breakout could cause great trouble for a commandant – and he was a cultured English gentleman, one who spoke German fluently and appreciated German culture. Since it had become apparent that the war was lost, there was a further reason to treat Payne Best with consideration; he might return the favour when he, Kaindl, was called to account. What is perplexing is Payne Best's reciprocated affection. He could not have been entirely unaware of the wanton cruelty and murder still taking place in the camp. There was no end to summary executions. As in camps elsewhere, as the productiveness of prisoners diminished, so did their chances of survival.

The order for Payne Best's evacuation came through only a few hours after his conversation with the Camp Commandant. Kurt Eccarius, the burly prison bunker commander, told Payne Best to pack his belongings and be prepared to leave within the hour.[2] There was quite a lot of packing to be done and, with the help of the guards, Payne Best filled a suitcase and five boxes containing his belongings, which included only part of his extensive wardrobe. As he departed, Payne Best's retinue of block guards lined up to bid him goodbye. It was as if a cherished guest was departing. Kaindl and Eccarius were also there to bid him a fond farewell, displaying a courtesy and sentimentality entirely at odds with their savage approach to most prisoners.[3]

When Payne Best approached the camp gate accompanied by his SS porters, he was disappointed to find a *Grüne Minna*, the German equivalent of a 'Black Maria', waiting to transport him. He dolefully viewed it as 'a great come down' after his pampered life in the prison bunker.[4] Already inside the van, locked into cages, were his Russian cell block neighbour Vassily Kokorin and a British officer Payne Best had not previously known of. He turned out to be Squadron Leader Hugh Mallory Falconer, the last British officer to join the hostage group.

Falconer, in his mid-thirties, had also been a prisoner in the bunker. A Special Operations Executive (SOE) officer, he had previously served with the French Foreign Legion. He was captured in January 1943 while taking part in an undercover mission to organise resistance in Tunis to coincide with the Allies advance into Tunisia. He and two Free French agents had disembarked from a submarine during the night off the Tunisian coast before rowing ashore in kayaks.[5] They made their way to Tunis on foot, but, unfortunately for them, a night curfew was still in operation and they were spotted and arrested for curfew violation. The Germans soon realised they had captured a British agent and Falconer was intensively interrogated over a three-week period by the Gestapo with some sessions lasting twenty-one hours. At one stage he was told he was about to be shot. He was put up against a wall in front of a firing squad before being reprieved at the last minute.[6] It's probable the Germans intended only to unnerve him at this point, hoping to get him to disclose information, although as the Englishman would have known, as a captured SOE operative he was always likely to be shot. By then the Allies were rapidly advancing on Tunis and the Germans were forced into a hasty evacuation. Falconer was flown to Italy for further interrogation, but his dossier, compiled by the Gestapo in Tunis was, with other files, loaded onto the last German ship to leave the port and that vessel was lost at sea, presumably a casualty of an Allied air attack. When he realised that his new interrogators had no information on him, Falconer tried to convince them that he was a regular British officer captured during the Allied advance into Tunisia and that therefore he should be treated as a POW. Although not convinced of his story, in the absence of records, the Germans could only speculate about his true identity. It seems they formed the view that he was an important prisoner, possibly related to somebody important.[7] For this reason, he was sent to the prison bunker in Sachsenhausen where he was held in strict isolation while enduring some pretty rough treatment.[8]

On the journey from Sachsenhausen Payne Best was, as usual, treated with more consideration than the other prisoners. He was not placed in a cage in the van, but was allowed to sit beside the guard near the open rear door. Their initial destination was the partially destroyed Gestapo headquarters in Prinz Albrecht Strasse in Berlin. After some sleepless nights there in cold, dark cells, their sleep interrupted by bombing raids, the prisoners were driven to Buchenwald Concentration Camp in the company of a number of important German prisoners who had also been under interrogation by the Gestapo. On arrival at Buchenwald, confusion reigned. The Camp Commandant was not expecting them and a row developed between him and the SS guard assigned to deliver the prisoners to the camp. Eventually, a place of detention was found for them outside the camp in a barrack building for SS personnel in which part of the cellar complex had been converted into holding cells.

The German special prisoners who had accompanied them from Berlin included General Franz Halder, one of the most senior *Wehrmacht* officers of the early war years. Halder had been Chief of the Supreme Command (OKH) of the German Army until September 1942. As with most of the other high-ranking German officers we will encounter among the *Prominenten*, he was arrested following the 20 July attempt on Hitler's life. Although he had been involved in earlier oppositional intrigues, he had no role in that plot. His wife Gertrude, who had volunteered to join him in captivity, now accompanied him. Another *Wehrmacht* officer present was General Alexander von Falkenhausen who had been Governor General of occupied Belgium until his arrest. As with Halder, it was a suspicion that he had been part of an oppositional conspiracy, rather than evidence that led to his arrest. Two other military personnel were present who were directly involved in the plot to kill Hitler, both of whom had served in the *Abwehr* and were part of an oppositional conspiracy within that organisation. Franz Leidig was a former naval officer and his colleague, Ludwig Gehre, wore an eye patch. Following news that Hitler had survived the bomb placed by Clause von Stauffenberg, Gehre, expecting imminent arrest and torture, had entered into a suicide pact with his wife. He shot her and then attempted to shoot himself, but the bullet went through his eye and he survived.

A second married couple accompanied the Halders – Erich Heberlein, a diplomat, and his wife, Margot. Prisoners were anxious to share their stories and the account of their arrest involved a particularly cruel subterfuge involving the Gestapo and Spanish secret police. Erich Heberlein had been First Secretary in the German Embassy in Madrid when, in January 1943, he was ordered to return to Berlin. A career diplomat who disliked and distrusted the Nazis, he declined to travel back to Germany and offered his resignation instead. When this was refused, he declared himself on sick-leave and he and his wife retired to an estate they owned in Toledo. On 17 July 1944, in the middle of the night, the couple were awoken by loud banging on their door. The caller, dressed in the uniform of a Spanish policeman, told them that they should immediately travel to meet the Governor of Toledo who had news of their only son who was a *Wehrmacht* soldier stationed on the eastern front.[9] They left immediately without dressing, but on reaching the city they were greeted, not by the Governor, but by a group of Gestapo agents who bundled the couple, still in their night attire, into separate cars. Erich Heberlein was beaten before being taken to an airfield and flown to France and later Germany. His wife had a revolver pressed against her ribs while she was driven over the border to France, before being taken to Germany.[10] The couple had spent months in separate prisons before being reunited in a chalet in *Sonderlager* 'B' in Sachsenhausen.[11] Margot Heberlein proved to be a formidable woman within the *Prominenten* entourage. While her husband remained always formal and polite, as befits a trained diplomat, the 'Grey Mare' as Payne Best called her, the product of an Irish mother and Spanish father, 'was undoubtedly the better horse'.[12] Now in middle age, she had once been a noted opera singer and society beauty in Madrid.

The enlarged group was held in the barrack building at Buchenwald for a number of weeks, during which time they were joined by an incongruous fellow prisoner who had, until shortly before, been an SS doctor in Dachau. Sigmund Rascher was a man who rivalled the infamous Dr Mengele in his odiousness. As the head doctor in Dachau Concentration Camp, he was responsible for cruel experiments on prisoners. A fanatical Nazi without scruples – he is believed to have denounced his own father – he had sought Himmler's permission to be allowed to conduct experiments on prisoners on behalf of the Luftwaffe. Himmler encouraged him and took a great interest in his work thereafter. In Dachau, Rascher conducted high-altitude experiments that involved putting prisoners in a decompression chamber, frequently until their lungs ruptured. He also supervised experiments involving prisoners being immersed in icy cold water to determine how long a man could survive before freezing to death. To conduct tests on blood coagulation he had numerous prisoners shot. Hundreds endured terrible tortures and died as a result of his experiments.[13] He and his wife were arrested, not for these crimes, but because it was discovered that children they claimed as their own had been kidnapped.[14] We can safely assume that most of the special prisoners felt disgust at being forced to endure the company of such a despicable individual, but Payne Best continued to be non-judgemental when it came to Nazis. Bizarrely, he found him to be a 'good comrade' and 'the life and soul of our party'.[15] In contrast, two other prisoners who had joined the group in Berlin exemplified the moral courage of the small proportion of German civilians who actively opposed Nazism. One was Dietrich Bonhoeffer, a Lutheran pastor and theologian, who had been involved in oppositional activities before his arrest. The other was Josef Müller, a lawyer and former leading member of a Bavarian Catholic political party, who had worked in partnership with Bonhoeffer in attempts to gain support from the Vatican and the Anglican Church in England for a planned coup against Hitler. Details of their extraordinary collaboration is contained in Addendum II of this book.

The group remained in their place of detention near Buchenwald until early April, when an order came for them to be moved on again to ensure that they did not fall into enemy hands. The front was approaching – here it was the Americans who were close. They were now to be transported in a prison van powered by a wood-fuelled generator. The van moved off in convoy with a bus containing a larger group of prisoners. These were *Sippenhaft*; relatives of German officers and civilians implicated in the 20 July plot to kill Hitler.

They were taken to Flossenbürg concentration camp where the authorities, in a repeat of what happened earlier, told their SS escorts that they couldn't accommodate these prisoners. This time the convoy continued further south west. However, a police car overtook them and waved down the van. Three prisoners were ordered out – Müller, Gehre and Liedig – all of whom had been connected to a high-level opposition group within the *Abwehr*. The three were transported back to Flossenbürg where it was feared that they would be executed. Müller's co-conspirator, Bonheoffer, due to some confusion, was not among those removed from the van at that time and it seems that Liedig may have been mistaken for him. The SS rectified their mistake a few days later. During a Sunday service that Bonheoffer was conducting for the other prisoners in a camp near the Bavarian village of Schoneberg, two plain-clothed Gestapo agents entered the room and hustled him away. Sensing he was doomed, the pastor passed Payne Best a note and asked him, if he ever got back to England, to give it to his friend George Bell, Anglican Bishop of Chichester. Bonheoffer was hanged the next day in Flossenbürg, along with the head of the *Abwehr*, Admiral Canaris, Gehre and others involved in the plot against Hitler. They had been subjected to a drumhead trial, humiliated by being stripped naked and marched to their place of execution. At the time these executions took place, the British officers and their Irish orderlies, the former inhabitants of *Sonderlager* 'A' in Sachsenhausen, were also in Flossenbürg although they knew nothing then of Payne Best and his travelling companions. Before recounting their experiences in that dreadful camp, we will describe their final days in Sachsenhausen.

***

Perhaps because they were judged to be of less importance than Payne Best and his entourage, the British and Irish contingent, with their Russian and Italian neighbours from *Sonderlager* 'A', were kept in Sachsenhausen until early April 1945. In their final days there they experienced a bombing raid at uncomfortably close quarters. Bombing raids were almost a daily occurrence at that time; by day the Americans, by night the British, both on their way to bomb Berlin. The air raid siren would set in train a now familiar routine within the *Sonderlager*. The SS guards would make for their underground air raid shelter where they could still observe the prisoners' hut through a slit, while the prisoners inside gathered at the windows to watch the spectacle. It was reassuring confirmation that the Germans were facing ruin. The Russian Bessonov would leap about excitedly cheering on the bombers as they roared past.[16] Often the thud of the explosions could be heard thirty-five kilometres away in Berlin and the resulting cloud of dust and smoke seen by the camp inmates. Whereas previously they could watch fighter planes engaged in dogfights, the RAF Mosquitos and USAF Flying Fortresses now went unchallenged except for anti-aircraft flak.

But one day, shortly before their departure from Sachsenhausen, the target of the raid was the nearby town of Oranienburg. In a crescendo of noise, the huge flotilla of planes flew directly over their camp.[17] The raid lasted half an hour and the huts shook as the bombs landed. They mostly fell on the Heinkel aircraft factory nearby, causing blinding flashes and deafening explosions. A night raid followed. These were generally more spectacular with clusters of marker flares and anti-aircraft fire lighting up the sky, but it was anxious viewing for those in the camp. The bombs were landing nearby and there was a greater risk of misdirected bombs at night.

For the residents of the town, and for prisoners in the main part of the Sachsenhausen camp who had been sent to work there, there could be no elation. Thousands of camp inmates worked as slave labourers in Oranienburg, and hundreds of them were killed that day, with many more injured. The camp hospital could not cope with the hundreds of wounded Germans taken there. Prisoner slave labourers, severely wounded during the bombing of the factories, were either shot or left to die. Although they were not to know it at that time, the bombing of German cities also imperilled the lives of the British airmen.

Hitler, enraged by the relentless bombing, and even more incensed by reports of large numbers of German solders surrendering and deserting to the

Western Allies, wanted to renounce the Geneva Convention which he believed contributed to the latter. He was urged on by Goebbels who suggested that all Allied airmen in captivity should be shot. When some officers present pointed out the risk of reprisals on German POWs, Hitler's anger only increased. 'To hell with that!' he is reported as bellowing. 'If I make it clear that I show no consideration for prisoners but that I treat enemy prisoners without any consideration for their rights, regardless of reprisals, then quite a few will think before they desert.'[18] What Hitler was saying was that retaliatory executions of German POWs were needed to discourage the surrender of German troops.[19] Admiral Doenitz was tasked with evaluating the proposal. Fortunately for Day, James, Dowse and countless other captive airmen, no action ensued.

It had become evident that the ground war was daily approaching Sachsenhausen as the rumble of artillery fire was becoming ever more audible. Marshall Zhukov, commander of the First Belorussian Front of the Red Army, was attacking the last significant obstacle to the advance into Berlin, the Seelow Heights.[20] It was obvious that the camp would have to be evacuated if the prisoners and guards were not to fall into Russian hands. The SS guards had become noticeably edgy. One approached Thomas Cushing and asked if he would write a commendation that could be proffered if and when he was captured. Cushing, regarding the supplicant as an undeserving bully and, knowing that he was unable to read English, claimed he wrote: 'To whom it may concern. – Should this son-of-a-bitch fall into Allied hands alive, it is the wish of the undersigned that he be dispatched forthwith, as painfully as possible.'[21] This wording may have been an invention on Cushing's part, but there is much evidence of guards seeking such commendations from allied prisoners. By then morale had sunk and the SS, originally viewed as an elite force, were now greatly disliked by both the regular army and civilians.[22]

It had become apparent that preparations for evacuation were underway: files were being incinerated and most of the Sachsenhausen population had been dispatched, dead or alive. Four British servicemen were among the victims. They had been captured in 1943 in Crete while on a sabotage mission led by Lieutenant Commander Mike Cumberlege of the Royal Navy Reserve and SOE.[23] Both Harry Day and Jack Churchill had managed to exchange some written notes with Cumberlege during their period of incarceration following their last escape attempt. The four unfortunate men were taken to the execution area, cynically known as Station Z, where the method of execution generally involved a pretend examination by a 'doctor' during which the prisoner was asked to stand against a wall for a height measurement. A slit would open in the wall behind the victim and he would be shot upwards through the back of the neck. Cumberlege and his comrades were almost certainly executed in this way.

When the British, Irish, Italian and Russian contingents in *Sonderlager* 'A' were finally told that they were to be evacuated, Bessonov and his colleagues must have been relieved, for they would have feared a reckoning with their perilously close erstwhile comrades. It wouldn't have been any consolation for Bessonov to have known that his great rival in collaboration, General Vlassov, had been in action with his 'Russian Liberation Army' not far away on the river Oder. Two coaches took the *Sonderlager* prisoners to Oranienburg where they boarded a train for the long journey to the south of Germany. They were part of a larger group which included five Greek generals with two soldiers serving as their batmen. They had been resident in *Sonderlager* 'B', a compound of chalets adjoining *Sonderlager* 'A' but walled off from it. The British contingent had been only vaguely aware of who the occupants of these houses were. What struck them initially when they saw the Greeks was how well dressed they were and the large amount of luggage they had with them.[24]

The most senior of the Greeks was General Alexandros Papagos who had been Commander in Chief of the Greek Army before its surrender to the Germans. A royalist and a conservative – he participated in a successful coup in 1935 which abolished the Greek Republic and restored the monarchy – he had achieved hero status for his role in repulsing the Italian invasion in 1940. The subsequent German attack could not be resisted and he and other Greek generals were taken into captivity. They were provided with comfortable chalets, and in all other respects were well cared for. It is not entirely clear why Papagos and his entourage received such privileged treatment in captivity. It may have been because he and his military colleagues had strong anti-Communist sentiments and they may have been viewed by the Germans as potential allies after the war, although, with the German withdrawal from the country in September 1944, this issue had become redundant. In this matter, and in the selection and treatment of *Prominenten* prisoners generally, it is impossible to know for sure. Decision-making in the Nazi state was unpredictable and inconsistent. Hitler had sole overarching authority, but, as he could not decide on everything, decisions about who should live or die, and how they should be treated in the interim, were subject to arbitrary decisions by increasingly chaotic bureaucracies, each trying to outdo the other in anticipating or working towards the Führer's will.[25] Orders made for reasons that had long become obsolete tended to remain in force in the absence of countermanding instructions.

Flossenbürg, 4–15 April 1945

When, after long train and bus journeys, Harry Day and his fellow *Sonderlager* prisoners arrived at Flossenbürg Concentration Camp, they were initially refused entry. They had been placed under the charge of Peter Mohr of the German Criminal Police, the man who had been involved in Day's trial in Sachsenhausen after his recapture. Day regarded him as a humane man who made clear his dislike of the SS.[26] Mohr's task now was to escort these prisoners and ensure their safe detention. The Camp Commander of Flossenbürg, the thuggish Max Koegel (he had previously commanded an extermination camp in Majdenek in Poland) announced that the camp was overcrowded and he couldn't accommodate them. He told Mohr that he could instead arrange to have them executed. Mohr explained that they were not to be killed, telling him 'they could be of great importance to Germany in any negotiations with the Western Allies' and suggesting that there would be great difficulty, not least for him, if they were liquidated.[27] This settled the matter. While the others were taken to accommodation outside the camp, the British group were, after some delay, marched inside to a section of the camp hospital that had been hastily cleared of patients, possibly by way of a selection of the feeblest for execution. The Camp Commandant, knowing the reputation of some of the arrivals, warned them that escape was out of the question. Day, Dowse and James were specifically warned of the consequences. As if to emphasise the warning, a few days later, another group of British arrivals in Flossenbürg, thirteen captured SOE officers, were executed.

Even judged by the standards of German concentration camps, Flossenbürg was a dreadful place. Inmates were forced to work to exhaustion and slow death in stone quarries.[28] The camp was located on top of a hill, recessed into a bowl, the result of past quarrying at its summit. There were no perimeter walls. Instead, a double line of electrified wire fences surrounded a complex of crudely built wood and some brick barracks. Although technically a forced labour camp, prisoners died daily from exhaustion, disease and execution. The death tally was so high that the incinerator could not cope, resulting in bodies being stacked in the open.

The camp was overcrowded with thousands of recently arrived prisoners, many of them Jewish evacuees from other camps, including Auschwitz. There were around 50,000 prisoners held either in the main camp or in sub camps. The condition of the camp prisoners shocked the British. Although they had some knowledge of the plight of the general camp inmates in Sachsenhausen, their isolation within a special enclosure shielded them from much of its horrors. Here they could see close up the awfulness of the Nazi camp system. There was continuous smoke from the crematorium and prisoners resembled walking skeletons. Stretcher parties could be seen with blanket-covered remains of those who died of overwork and starvation. As Peter Churchill later recalled:

> Our toilets were shared by those who were dying in the next ward. Men weighing no more than five stone would come in wearing short-length shirts hardly covering their nakedness and would look at us over the next stall with the eyes of those who had not long to live.[29]

The British group were later moved from the hospital to the prison section of the camp where they were allocated cells, almost certainly those vacated by the executed *Abwehr* plotters, including its head, Admiral Canaris. Other victims included Ludwig Gehre and Dietrich Bonhoeffer who had been removed from the group accompanying Payne Best. Josef Müller was not among those executed. Shortly after the move to the prison bunker, Peter Churchill, while attempting to discover the identity of other prisoners in the nearby cells, encountered him. The Bavarian, after identifying himself, called from behind his cell door: 'Yesterday they took me to the hanging shed and I refused to be executed without a court martial.'[30] He may well have believed then that his argument had stayed the executioner's hand, but, as he was subsequently to learn, what actually saved him was a decision by Ernst Kaltenbrunner, second only to Himmler within the SS hierarchy, that Müller was more valuable alive than dead.

Müller had been involved in an extraordinary conspiracy in which he liaised with the Pope in an attempt to secure British support for a planned coup against Hitler. Why was Müller allowed to escape execution rather than his co-collaborator Pastor Bonhoeffer? After all, the Bavarian was the more deeply involved in the international intrigues facilitated by leading figures in the *Abwehr*. It can only be because the Catholic Church was judged by Kaltenbrunner to have greater potential to influence end-of-war events as compared to the divided and less internationally well-connected Lutherans. With his strong links to the Vatican, Josef Müller might prove to be helpful in lobbying the Western Allies for a separate peace, or if that failed, increasing Kaltenbrunner's chances of survival.

A few days after these events, Harry Day was looking skyward at a large formation of American bombers in the distance when he became aware of a young SS man near him also observing their flight. He was startled to realise that he was the same man who had been pointed out to him as being the prison block executioner. Gesturing towards the planes he said to the SS man, 'You see! The Americans will be here very soon now.' The SS man made no reply as they continued to watch the planes. Day decided to risk another line of conversation. 'The Americans do not like the SS, nor things like the Cell Block, nor that building there': Day was nodding in the direction of the execution shed when he said this. He continued: 'Perhaps if things go well for us, we might be able to say a word for you – when the Americans come.' This finally provoked a response. The executioner looked at Day and, with a shrug of his shoulders, told him that he did not like doing what he had to do, but duty was duty.[31]

On 15 April the group were told to prepare for another move. A van and a canvas covered truck awaited them. It was now dusk; transports, wherever possible, were scheduled for the hours of darkness to avoid allied air attacks. Artillery could be heard in the distance as twenty-one special prisoners were squeezed into a van designed to carry nine. Joining the British and Irish was Josef Müller and a number of new faces including that of a Croat, Hinko Dragic. He had been an officer in the Yugoslav army and had been arrested after the German occupation when it was discovered he had been responsible for uncovering a German spy in 1935.[32] Two German aristocrats were also bundled into the prison van. One was Prince Philip of Hesse, a former aristocratic supporter of Hitler who had fallen out of favour. He was related to many of the royal families of

Europe and his wife was a sister of the King of Italy. The other aristocrat was the elderly Count Wilhelm von Flügge, a businessman with associations to the anti-Nazi opposition. The count had been a director of IG Farben, the most important chemical company in the world before the war, and the most enthusiastic employer of slave and concentration camp labour during it. Flügge, though, played no role in this. Even before the war he had associated with the opposition. During the war he became linked to the conspiracy within the *Abwehr*. Based mainly in Beirut dealing with his company's interests in the Middle East, he used this base to liaise with diplomats from various states on behalf of the opposition. Flügge's links to the *Abwehr* plotters came to the attention of the Gestapo and was lured back to Germany and arrested in April 1944.[33]

The vehicles took off into the night. It was a long and uncomfortable journey for those crammed into the van, relieved only by the stories of Flügge, a cultured gentleman with impressive knowledge of world cultures, languages and the arts. When they finally reached the gates of Dachau Concentration Camp, with its cast-iron arched sign falsely declaring *Arbeit Macht Frei* ('work makes you free') there was a lengthy delay while the SS argued about accommodation. As the prisoners waited in the cramped van, Cushing, Peter Churchill and Dragic began a singsong. They harmonised a 'deep-throated chorus of nostalgic songs'[34] including 'Boulevard of Broken Dreams',[35] then a popular melody. Peter Churchill recalled that 'Dragic had a lovely voice' and Cushing, who, as he noted, 'had soldiered over half the world, knew all the tunes and could hold them to our harmonising'.[36] Cushing and Churchill had sung together many nights in Sachsenhausen. Singing played an important part of prison camp life and good singers were appreciated. The sessions helped enliven the long winter curfew nights. The songs could sometimes be melancholic or, at times, rousingly defiant. They evoked memories of home, of happier times, and they let their captors know that their spirits remained unbroken.

The quality of the singing in the van outside the Dachau gates made an impression on Josef Müller. He seemed to have heard it as his requiem. It seems he judged his recent reprieve from execution most likely to be only a deferral. As they disembarked from the vehicle, he grasped Peter Churchill by the hand and declared: 'If this is the end for me, as I fear, I shall think to the last of the lovely singing that you and your friends performed as we entered this infamous camp.'[37]

PART II
THE *PROMINENTEN*

In April 1945, Dachau became the assembly point for scores of special prisoners who had been evacuated from other camps to prevent them falling into enemy hands. They were collectively known as *Prominenten* and included a number of renowned political and military figures. They were being held as hostages in the hope that they could be traded for some advantage to the regime, or for the benefit of particular SS leaders.

CHAPTER SEVEN

THE BUNKER PRISONERS

A rhyme learned by German children in the 1930s went: '*Lieber Gott, mach mich fromm/Dass ich nicht nach Dachau komm*', which roughly translates as 'Dear God, make me good/Do not make me to Dachau come.'[1] The fact that children were made to fear Dachau, situated about thirty kilometres north of Munich, as an earthly hell indicates its early and continued notoriety. It was the first Nazi concentration camp and became the prototype for other lesser known, if no less hellish camps, including Sachsenhausen.

9 April 1945

Yet when Payne Best, Kokorin, Halder, and the rest of their convoy, arrived at Dachau, the Camp Commandant, the portly Eduard Weiter, welcomed them in a manner so unctuous that it must have astonished the prisoners and bemused the SS guards present. Among the former was Kurt von Schuschnigg, the former Chancellor of Austria, who was accompanied by his attractive wife and their young daughter. Payne Best described the scene, as Weiter greeted them:

> With a most obliging air he made us a regular speech of welcome, even gallantly attempting, but failing, to kiss Mrs. von Schuschnigg's hand. He was very sorry that we had been kept waiting for so long, but Dachau was very crowded and it had really been most difficult to find suitable accommodation for such distinguished guests.[2]

The effusive greeting was no doubt intended to create a favourable impression in the hope that, should they survive, these important prisoners would bear witness to his hospitable conduct after the war.

Weiter had been given command of the camp in November 1943, but frequently absented himself, leaving his subordinates to manage things. This occasion, however, required his presence due to the arrival of some celebrity prisoners, and because a Berlin SS Headquarter officer accompanying the prisoners was known to be carrying special orders for his attention. The orders were stated to be from the Reichführer, Heinrich Himmler, although the contents were more likely to have been written by his subordinate, Heinrich Müller, the head of the Gestapo who had been involved in the interrogation of Georg Elser, Hitler's would-be assassin. Elser had been transferred to Dachau from Sachsenhausen about eight weeks previously. After stipulating how certain of the other special prisoners should be treated, the document went on to deal with him:

> The question of our prisoner in special protective custody, 'Eller' [the SS code name for Elser] has also been discussed at the highest level. The following has been decided:

> On the occasion of one of the next 'Terror' Attacks on Munich, [meaning an Allied Bombing raid] or, as the case may be, the neighbourhood of Dachau, it shall be said that 'Eller' suffered fatal injuries.

> I request you therefore, when such an occasion arises to liquidate 'Eller' as discreetly as possible. Please take steps that only very few people, who must be specially pledged to silence, hear about this.[3]

Elser must have anticipated execution from the day he was captured and his transfer to Dachau didn't offer hope. Nevertheless, as it became evident that the Allies were approaching Munich, he must have begun to hold out some prospect of survival. As in Sachsenhausen, he was held in conditions of strict isolation with only his guards for company. Two guards were in constant attendance in his cell, with another posted outside. He continued to do carpentry work for which he was supplied with tools and materials. He often played melancholy tunes on a zither he had made for himself. Although well supplied with food, he ate little but smoked his full allocation of forty cigarettes a day.[4]

On the day his execution order was received, Elser was finishing his evening meal of semolina pudding when a guard told him he was required for interrogation. Elser must have immediately suspected the worst. He hadn't been interrogated for years so why would they recommence it now? One of Elser's SS minders escorted him to the Guard House. From there, in darkness, he was taken to the execution shed. The camp commander had decided not to wait for an air raid, perhaps in order to free up the two cells to make way for some of the treasured new arrivals.

It seems strange that the SS should seek to cover up Elser's execution. In a camp where it wasn't unusual for scores of prisoners to be killed in a single day, why would the execution of one prisoner, particularly one who had confessed to attempting to kill Hitler, need to be kept secret? One reason was that they wanted to blame the Allies for prominent concentration camp deaths. When Ernst Thälmann, the leader of the German Communist Party, was executed in Buchenwald in August 1944, the Nazis announced that he had been killed in a bombing raid. The aim was to demonstrate that Allied bombing was killing their own. However, another factor may have influenced the need for subterfuge; SS leaders didn't wish to be identified with such deeds when it was clear they would soon have to answer for them in the near future.

SS First Lieutenant Edgar Stiller, assigned to take charge of the *Prominenten* in Dachau, was an ethnic German originally from the disputed Sudetenland in Czechoslovakia. Now in his early forties, he had been a policeman in pre-war Austria where he had joined the Nazi party in 1933. He must have given the direct order for the killing of Elser, although the actual deed was carried out by the camp executioner.[5] Harry Day described Stiller as having 'a long face, deep grey eyes under a high forehead, and a narrow, thin lipped mouth, tight and cruel'.[6] He was present when the RAF special prisoners later entered Dachau and he singled out Day for particular attention, no doubt aware of his reputation for planning escapes. He approached Day to inform him that, '[here] an order is an order. There will be no complaints,' while stroking his pistol holster for emphasis.[7]

Payne Best and the other newly arrived special prisoners, who at that time knew nothing of Elser's killing, were relieved to discover that they were to be housed in relatively good conditions within one wing of the prison bunker.[8] Their concrete cells had high windows, which, although barred, could be opened from the inside. The cell doors were unlocked during the day and the privileged inmates had access to an outside narrow garden, in which they were provided with a bench and some chairs where they could relax and mingle. An air raid shelter was located nearby to which they were required to make haste to on a number of occasions, although the prison bunker was never directly hit.

Two prisoners from the main camp, trustees, were assigned to act as general factotums to the special prisoners. Wilhelm Visintainer was assigned to work mainly as a gardener. He was to become a popular and indispensable member of the group from then on. Formally a circus clown with the Krone Circus, one of the largest circuses in pre-war Europe, he was nicknamed '*Kohlenklau*' ('coal pincher') because he resembled a villainous cartoon character that featured in a Nazi press publicity campaign against pilfering. The crime that resulted in his incarceration was smuggling food to prisoners housed in a concentration camp in France. Visintainer had by then spent over four gruelling years in Dachau. On one occasion he was beaten into unconsciousness while suspended from a rafter for some misdemeanour. Another time he had all his teeth knocked out and spent six months in a dark cell, fed only three days in every week.[9] Despite these experiences, he somehow managed to maintain a sense of humour and occasionally acted the clown to amuse. But, as those who got to know him came to appreciate, this 'clown' was highly intelligent. He could converse in most of the many languages of the camp and became an unofficial translator. He also was a source of information about the horrors of Dachau. He told the new arrivals that the grassy area where they could relax was formerly an execution yard. He told Payne Best that when he had earlier dug the soil to lay a flower bed, he removed a 'hundredweight and a half of pistol bullets'; indicating that the nearby wall as the place of execution.[10] He also pointed out the hooks on the wall from which prisoners had previously been suspended by their manacled wrists.

The other trustee assigned to the bunker was Paul Wauer, a Jehovah's Witness. The persecution of Jehovah's Witnesses began soon after the Nazis came to power, in part due to their refusal, on religious grounds, to be conscripted into the army. Thousands were arrested in the mid-1930s and sent to prisons or concentration camps. Wauer witnessed the cold-blooded murder of many of his co-religionists and was himself tortured.[11] After 1941, conditions improved as the SS realised that Jehovah's Witnesses could be good workers, provided they were reasonably fed and were not required to do anything in conflict with their religious beliefs.[12] Wauer's own situation improved when, in December 1941, he was assigned to work as a barber in the prison bunker in Sachsenhausen. In that capacity, he had serviced some of the British special prisoners housed there.

The prisoners in the Bunker were free to mingle and enjoyed the opportunity to meet new companions. They included the aforementioned Kurt Schuschnigg and his wife and daughter. They had managed to retain a radio they had been provided with in Sachsenhausen and every afternoon most of the special prisoners would gather around the radio to listen to the German war bulletin. Three former high-ranking German officers, now prisoners, listened with expert attention to the broadcasts, Generals Falkenhausen, Halder and Thomas.

Alexander von Falkenhausen had been Governor General of Belgium from May 1940 to July 1944. Occupied Belgium was unusual in retaining a semblance of self-rule under German military occupation and this contributed to it having a somewhat less repressive regime as compared to other German-occupied territories. Falkenhausen, who was never a Nazi, became part of a circle plotting against Hitler, although it was mere suspicion of this that led to his arrest. He was greatly admired by his fellow internees in Dachau. Payne Best, not the best judge of character, held him in particular high regard[13] presumably not knowing that during his governorship of Belgium, thousands of Jews were deported from Belgium to the gas chambers of Auschwitz.[14]

Franz Halder, the former Chief of the Army General Staff, we have also already encountered accompanying Payne Best and the others on the Journey to Dachau. At one time, this high-ranking *Wehrmacht* officer was considered the most able of the German generals.[15] Before the war, he had been the leader of a group of generals plotting to depose Hitler, but the Munich agreement undermined this conspiracy. On a number of occasions, he had carried a loaded hand gun into meetings with Hitler, but couldn't bring himself to use it.[16] He was regarded by a fellow oppositionist as 'a weak man with shattered nerves'.[17] Hitler, contemptuous of career officers and increasingly irritated by Halder's Cassandra-like warnings about the war against the Soviet Union,[18] dismissed him during an acrimonious encounter.[19] He remained in semi-retirement in a reserve role until he was arrested following the 20 July 1944 attempt on Hitler's life, although by then he was no longer an active conspirator.

The other *Wehrmacht* general present was Georg Thomas who had been chief of procurement at the Combined Armed Forces Supreme Command before resigning when Albert Speer assumed most of these responsibilities. Like Halder, he grew pessimistic about the prospects of defeating the Soviets, although he had played a significant role in the planning of Operation Barbarossa; a plan that, from the start, envisaged a savage exploitation of the captive populations. He was, however, repelled by the systematic murder of Jews.[20]

The three generals were usually joined by another *Wehrmacht* officer, Colonel Bogislaw von Bonin, to listen to the daily news bulletins. Von Bonin was never an oppositional plotter but was interned after he ordered a tactical retreat near Warsaw, thereby disobeying Hitler's orders. The four officers would gather to listen to the radio news and then mark up what they judged to be the latest frontline positions on a large map spread out on a table. They would go on to discuss the possible success of an Allied attack, or the likely strength of German defences, almost as if they were attending an operations command session. This fascinating drama was played out in the presence of the other special prisoners who were anxious to learn about the progress of the Allies.

This was probably the only time during the day when young Sissi Schuschnigg would not be the centre of attention. Vera von Schuschnigg had volunteered to join her husband in captivity and their daughter was born when he was still in the Gestapo prison in Munich. Little blonde Sissi had never known life outside a concentration camp, although she was spared the horrors experienced by other children in the camps. Her previous home was in *Sonderlager* 'B' in Sachsenhausen, which, although not uncomfortable, meant she had only her parents and their guards for company. Now she was enjoying the relative freedom of her new abode and revelling in the attention of her many new admirers. Kohlenklau was a favourite, not just because he was funny, but because he sometimes managed to find chocolate for her, a scarce and treasured luxury in wartime Germany.

A restriction placed on the movement of the special prisoners was that they were forbidden to have contact with prisoners housed in the other end of the bunker who were not part of their group. Richard Stevens and John McGrath were housed there and had shared a cell since their transfer from Sachsenhausen in 1943. It seems though, that the pair didn't get on well during their enforced cohabitation. Lengthy cell sharing can be trying even for compatible detainees, and these two were never likely to be that. Their backgrounds were very different. Stevens was the product of a classical education and had mastered a number of European and Asian languages while McGrath, the son of an Irish farmer, had had only a modest secondary school education. He had, however, compensated by inventing for himself a middle-class persona (see Addenda I), one that the suave colonial officer may have challenged at some point during their uneasy close confinement. McGrath, though, had more substantive reasons to dislike and distrust his companion.

Not unlike Payne Best, Stevens seems to have enjoyed particularly favourable treatment and, uniquely, he had been allowed to leave Dachau and travel to Munich, where, according to McGrath, he visited a paramour.[21] To leave the camp, Stevens would have had to give his word not to attempt to escape, an honour system known as 'parole'. McGrath suspected that the privileges granted to Stevens were a reward for providing valuable information to the SS. He may have been right in his assessment, for it is believed that both Stevens and Payne Best 'provided plenty of information' to the Germans.[22] There may also have been another reason for the latitude shown to the Englishman. As noted in Chapter 1, Stevens seems to have become depressed in Sachsenhausen and it's possible he may have come close to having a breakdown. This would have alarmed Himmler. His detention was part of Hitler's project to conduct a show trial, related to Elser's assassination attempt, one that would demonstrate Britain's culpability for the war. It would therefore be important to maintain in Stevens at least a semblance of sanity. Facilitating a sexual liaison might have been intended to achieve this.

In his three years in Dachau, the only other contact McGrath had with a British Army colleague occurred in late 1943 when a Sergeant Llewellyn Edwards smuggled him a note. Edwards, who had been captured in Italy, was detained for a period in the main camp in Dachau. On learning that two British officers were detained in the prison bunker, he managed, presumably by way of a trustee, to make contact. He later received a hand-written note from McGrath, which Edwards memorised as follows:

Sergeant Edwards I am sorry to hear of your plight. Col Stevens and myself have been here ten months. I was taken prisoner in France, wounded twice, was in charge of a prisoner of war camp and reported something which caused an international row, and was moved to Mauthausen Concentration Camp. Here I was kept for 10 months. In the past 18 months we have had two Red Cross parcels between us. The food situation is bad as you know, hardly enough to keep body and soul together, but if I can manage to get a little extra I will send it to you. Be careful what you say and warn the others. Keep your chin up, everything is going our way. I will try, if possible get your particulars to the Red Cross but it is as you realise very difficult.[23]

McGrath had given instructions that his note be destroyed after reading, so it is likely Edwards was reciting from memory which would explain Sachsenhausen being mistaken for Mauthausen. He did manage to supply Edwards with some bread, but the sergeant later contracted malaria and was transferred to a hospital in Switzerland where he got a message to the British embassy in Berne alerting them to McGrath and Stevens's presence in Dachau. As a result, the British asked the Red Cross to make enquiries, but the reply from the Germans was a flat denial; these prisoners were not in Dachau. As regards McGrath, they claimed that he had taken part in an escape from his POW camp and had not been heard of since. As a *Nacht und Nebel* ('Night and Fog') prisoner, he was intended to be invisible to the outside world.

Payne Best's arrival along with the German generals and the other distinguished prisoners would have very quickly become known to Stevens and McGrath. The Irishman knew of Payne Best from 1939 newspaper reports, for the Venlo incident had received worldwide publicity, and he had caught a glimpse of him while both were in the Sachsenhausen bunker. He was anxious to meet him when he learned of his presence in Dachau, but was hampered by the order preventing contact between himself and Stevens and the new arrivals. In any event, he learned that Payne Best was ill as a result of food poisoning acquired during his journey south.

However, the captain must have soon recovered for we find him celebrating his birthday on 14 April in the company of friends. It might have surprised McGrath, although it will not shock the reader at this stage, to learn that Payne Best celebrated the occasion in the jovial company of some of his SS guards, Stiller having provided the company with bottles of wine. The celebrations continued into the next day when a keg of beer was procured and one of the SS guards entertained the company with songs, accompanying himself on a lute. Towards the end of the night, as the others headed for their quarters, a guard whispered to Payne Best to 'stay back a bit', whereupon Stevens was ushered into the room. This was a breach of orders to keep them apart, but it seems the guards felt the risk was worth taking as a birthday gift for their good friend. Stevens, who rivalled Payne Best sartorially – it's possible the Germans retrieved his wardrobe after their invasion of the Netherlands – threw his arms around his erstwhile companion and they shared experiences of their years of separation over a bottle of wine.[24]

It may have been news of this reunion that provoked McGrath into making contact with Payne Best, for he may have feared that Stevens would have portrayed him in a poor light. He was in possession of a Red Cross parcel, a relatively rare treat, and, having hidden a note among the contents, he arranged for a guard to deliver it to Payne Best. The note began:

Dear Capt. Best,

Only this afternoon have I heard that this is your Birthday and I hasten to send you my best wishes and Happy Return to home. I was at Sachsenhausen for 10 months while you were there and while I think that I saw you once or twice, I never got the chance of passing you a line, as much as I wanted to. They never let me out of sight for 10 months I was there. I hear that you are not feeling very well and I am sending you a few things that I hope will be useful, including a little English Tea.

In confidence I should tell you that I have absolutely no use for the man who was taken with you, Stevens. I think that he is the biggest Rotter that I have ever heard of. It is a long story and goes back to 1941 when I was taken to Berlin on my way to the Irish Camp just outside the City. There I met a young German officer [Clissmann] who was married to a girl in Ireland and who was at Trinity College, Dublin for 5 years. He was in the background of your case and knew everything. He was very willing to talk as his wife wished to return to Ireland to live and he wanted a job there. He knew that I was connected with a lot of companies and could probably assist him. He asked me if I knew Stevens and gave me some of the facts.

There can be no doubt that Stevens talked and talked and gave away everything he knew and of course as a result they continued to work on him. It appears that they failed to get anything worthwhile from you and more or less gave up as a bad job. When Stevens came here he was given almost complete freedom, out all day and go where he wished, even supplied with a bicycle, in fact he had everything a man could wish for. They again had him on a string as under expert direction of the Gestapo he was allowed to go to Munich and visit a girl there and stay out even to 2 a.m., and so this rotten story goes on from bad to worse and is too long to put on paper just now. I do not know if this man is man or just a dangerous fool.

Further traducing his cell mate, McGrath went on to inform Payne Best that Stevens had recently managed to enter the cells of 'some working girls' that had been accused of stealing 'and had intercourse with them'. McGrath went on:

He got caught and it all came out. I have felt the situation very much. It is such a disgrace, and the man is such a liar that I do not speak to him more than I have to. I simply give him hell over these things, but I am afraid he has gone so low that he is beyond everything. I felt you should know the position and I know that you will respect my confidence.[25]

Such a damning account would normally only be shared with a known ally. McGrath could not have known how Payne Best would react to such invective directed against his erstwhile colleague, and the Irishman was taking a major leap of faith in sending it. Payne Best was delighted with the present of Red Cross delicacies and, as it became clear subsequently, he was not at all put out by McGrath's description of Stevens. Indeed, in hindsight, McGrath's missive was welcome, particularly as it was to provide support for Payne Best's case that it was Stevens, not he, who told all to the Germans. The importance of this to Payne Best is demonstrated by the fact that he kept a copy of McGrath's note throughout his remaining detention.

Despite their affectionate reunion, Stevens began to irritate Payne Best, who feared that his habit of entering his cell to talk to him, disregarding SS orders, would have negative repercussions. And his fears were justified, for Stiller, on learning of their meetings, ordered Payne Best to prepare to depart. Aware by then of what had happened to Elser, Payne Best conveyed his anxiety about what was in store for him to one of his new friends, Martin Niemöller. The pipe-smoking pastor promised to try to discover what the SS had in mind for him. Soon, he was in a position to reassure: 'I have found out about it – you are only being moved to the brothel where other foreigners are.'[26] Payne Best's immediate reaction is not recorded.

Martin Niemöller is best remembered today as the composer of the lines that begin 'First they came for the communists and I did not speak out because I was not a communist' and reiterating the stance in respect of socialists, trade unionists, Jews and others, until the last line, 'Then they came for me and there was no one left to speak for me.' A U-boat commander in the First World War, he had led a Friecorps unit during the revolutionary upheavals of 1919 and 1920, but later followed in his father's footsteps by becoming a pastor of the Lutheran Church. He was an opponent of the Weimar Republic and applauded Hitler's rise to power. His break with the Nazis was provoked by the Aryan Paragraph, which restricted membership of all public bodies and organisations, including the churches, to certified Aryans. In 1934 he, along with other Protestant dignitaries, met with Hitler in an attempt to dissuade him from interfering with the churches who had in membership and ministry individuals of Jewish ancestry. Hitler used the occasion of the meeting to berate Niemöller after it was revealed that a compromising telephone conversation of his had been recorded. This contributed to him establishing the Confessing Church along with Bonhoeffer. He was arrested in 1937 and housed in Moabit prison and later Sachsenhausen, before being transferred to Dachau. As an internationally known figure, there were many appeals made on his behalf, mainly by Protestant dignitaries.

Payne Best, presumably put at ease by Niemöller's information about his new abode, bade farewell to his friends in the prison bunker before being escorted to the brothel hut.

CHAPTER EIGHT

THE BROTHEL PRISONERS

In 1942, Himmler had ordered that a brothel, referred to as a *Sonderbau* ('special building'), be built in all the major concentration camps. While brothels had already existed for SS personnel, these were for use by slave workers within the camps. The SS owned a vast economic empire, largely dependent on slave labour, and Himmler sought ways of incentivising labour productivity. In his mind, it was sex that male prisoners most craved. He envisaged a graduated reward system, which would include a visit to a brothel, for 'star performers'.[1] The race laws would, however, still apply and only Aryans could receive this reward. Women, inmates of female concentration camps, were cajoled or cohered to occupy the brothels.[2] Mostly classed as 'anti-socials', they were promised release if they stayed there for six months, a promise that was never kept.[3] In Dachau, some of the women were used by Dr Rascher in his cruel medical experiments.[4]

By the time Payne Best and other special prisoners occupied the *Sonderbau* in late April 1945, it was no longer operating as a brothel, although it still retained much of its gaudy decorations. The Englishman was obliged to share accommodation with a French Catholic clergymen, Monsignor Gabriel Piguet, Bishop of Clermont-Ferrand. Payne Best was taking the place of General Delestraint who had been taken for execution the previous evening. The General, a devout Catholic, had been a close friend of the Bishop. Delestraint was executed along with three other French prisoners and eleven Czech officers.[5]

A supporter and friend of Charles de Gaulle, Delestraint had been asked by the General to head his underground *Armée Secréte* (secret army). He was arrested after being betrayed by an informer in July 1943.[6] He and the bishop had been imprisoned together in Nazweiler Concentration Camp in Alsace before being taken to Dachau, where they arrived 'exhausted and in great pain'.[7]

Placing them in the brothel was probably a deliberate attempt to humiliate Piguet in particular. The evening before Payne Best's arrival, Delestraint had been serving at a Mass being celebrated by the Bishop, when, without warning, the General was whisked away. His execution may have been in revenge for the advances of the Free French army, which, at that time, was involved in the capture of Stuttgart. But, for the prisoners, it was another reminder of the capricious evil hiding behind the mask of civility sometimes worn by the SS in their dealings with the special prisoners. It must have seemed to them that the Nazis determined, in an entirely arbitrary manner, who should live and who should die.

Bishop Piguet was himself a former soldier; he had been badly wounded in the First World War and was awarded the *Croix de Guerre*. Like almost all of the French clergy, he was initially a supporter of Marshall Pétain. The Vichy regime imposed Catholic moral standards and adapted corporatist governance arrangements. Piguet only changed his political stance after the occupation of *zone libre* (Vichy France) by the German army in November 1942. He then began to assist those on the run from the Germans and the Vichy French Milice. He also arranged for a number of Jewish children to be sheltered in schools in his diocese, saving them from deportation and likely extermination. For this, he was to be posthumously declared to be Righteous Among the Nations by Yad Vasham, the Shoah Martyrs and Heroes Remembrance Authority in Israel. The authorities never knew of the bishop's role in hiding Jewish children; his arrest in May 1944 was for sheltering priests wanted for resistance activities.[8]

There were less pious occupants of the *Sonderbau*. Sante Garibaldi, the grandson of the famous Italian patriot, was one of them. An émigré in France, he had assisted the French Resistance despite his advanced years. He was arrested in 1943 for suspected espionage and, although never convicted, he remained in captivity. When he arrived in Dachau, he was assigned to the most demeaning job in main camp, cleaning out latrines. He seems to have been selected for particularly harsh treatment and was the victim of unprovoked assaults; on one occasion his arm was broken by a guard who hit him with his rifle butt. Later assigned to the brothel, presumably to further degrade him, he somehow managed to remain there after the transfer of its previous inhabitants. Although still dressed in the blue and grey striped prison uniform, he managed to impress the other special prisoners.[9] He was almost always in the company of Colonel Davide Ferrero, another Italian with French connections. Ferrero was said to have had a distinguished military career in the French Foreign Legion before becoming involved with the Italian partisan movement. All were struck by his tall, athletic physique and his commanding presence. However, some may have wondered why he was accorded relatively favourable treatment by the Nazis when summary execution was the normal fate of a captured Italian partisan.

Payne Best, the epitome of an English gentleman, who had enjoyed the friendship of members of the Dutch royal family before his enforced departure from their kingdom, would have been pleased to be placed in close proximity to three Princes. He may, though, have been somewhat underwhelmed when he first met with Prince Friederich Leopold of Prussia. Leopold, a descendent of the first Kaiser, Wilhelm, was, like Garibaldi, dressed in the garb of an ordinary prisoner. He had been living on his estate in Austria when the *Anschluss* took place. Unlike many of the old German nobility, he was not favourably disposed towards the Nazis. He was arrested in May 1944, having been accused, he claimed in his post-war debriefing, of listening to foreign radio broadcasts.[10] In reality, his detention had more to do with his homosexuality and his partner, Baron Cerrini, nominally his private secretary, was arrested at the same time. In October 1944, both were transferred from their prison in Salzburg to Dachau and placed with other special prisoners. When Leopold contracted diphtheria, he was sent to the ill-equipped and dangerously overcrowded camp hospital where four or five shared a bed, most of them gravely ill, suffering from typhus, TB or other infectious diseases. Cerrini loyally accompanied him to the hospital and both were lucky to survive the experience. When Leopold recovered somewhat, he was sent to work as an ordinary prisoner in the kitchens of the main camp, despite his weight having fallen to just forty-three kilograms. Notwithstanding his misfortune, Leopold managed to retain a sunny disposition and, known to all as 'Pat', he had become a popular figure among the ordinary camp prisoners in Dachau. Later, it must have been decided that he had value as a hostage, for both he and Cerrini had their special status restored and they were billeted with other *Prominenten* in the *Sonderbau.*

The other German aristocrat present, Prince Philip of Hesse, we have already encountered in the company of Payne Best on the journey to Dachau. He was nephew of Kaiser Wilhelm II and a great-grandson of Queen Victoria and had married Princess Mafalda of Savoy, daughter of the King of Italy. His brother, Prince Christoph von Hessen, had married the sister of Prince Philip, the future Duke of Edinburgh. Unlike Leopold, Philip had been an early and enthusiastic supporter of the Nazis. He had joined the Nazi party in 1930 and was made president of his home province of Hessen-Nassau when Hitler came to power. He became a particular friend of Hermann Göring and was, for a time, 'a glittering member of Nazi high society'.[11] Through Göring, Philip became intimate with Hitler and acted as his art advisor, while still providing a similar service for Göring. More significantly, using his wife's contacts, he helped Hitler forge an alliance with Mussolini. Things changed suddenly for him in 1943 when he was arrested while present in the Führer's headquarters and taken to Flossenburg concentration camp.[12] Philip was bewildered, he couldn't understand how he had suddenly changed from being Hitler's friend to being his enemy. Shortly before, on 24 July 1943, Mussolini had been removed from office by the Grand Council of Fascism and the King of Italy had ordered his arrest. This greatly alarmed Hitler, who feared the possibility that something similar might be thought of as possible in Germany. Damningly for Philip, Hitler had come to suspect that he and his wife Mafalda, due to her connections to the Italian throne, were implicated in the plot against Mussolini.

Princess Mafalda was in Bulgaria attending the funeral of her sister's husband, King Boris. On her return to Rome, realising she was being tailed by the SS, she sought refuge in the Vatican and was given shelter by Monsignor Giovanni Montini, later to become Pope Paul VI, who allowed her to stay in his residence with three of her children. The following morning she received a message from the German embassy telling her that her husband wished to speak to her. She made her way to the embassy to take the telephone call after being told that this was the only way to ensure a secure line. On arrival, she was told her husband was due to land at an airport in Rome and that she was to be taken in a car to meet him. When she arrived at the airport she was kidnapped and flown to Berlin where she was interrogated by the Gestapo. Treated more harshly than her husband, she was falsely told that her children were all dead and she was sent to Buchenwald concentration camp. She was housed there at the same time as other special prisoners, but did not receive comparable treatment. She died in Buchenwald in August of 1944 as a result of injuries sustained in an Allied bombing raid. Philip was not informed of his wife's death and only learned of her fate when he was told about it in Dachau by Martin Niemöller, who had also been in Buchenwald at that time. Philip had revelled in the glory of contributing to Hitler's new order, and had been quite prepared to ignore what it entailed for its victims, until he and his wife became victims themselves.

The other aristocrat present was Prince Xavier de Bourbon, the Carlist pretender to the Spanish throne who, like Philip, was also related to many of the royal houses of Europe. He had been the titular leader of the traditionalist and avowedly anti-democratic Carlist militias, known as the *Requetés*, who fought on the Nationalist side in the Spanish Civil War. Xavier was expelled by Franco when he objected to his militia being integrated, along with the Falange, into a unified Francoist party.[13] He returned to Belgium where he had been previously exiled and re-enlisted in the Belgium army with whom he had fought during the First World War. When Belgium surrendered to the Nazis, he joined up with the French Army, leading to his arrest after the German occupation.

Fritz Thyssen, a leading pre-war German industrialist, was another important prisoner housed in the *Sonderbau*. He was one of the richest men in pre-war Germany, having inherited a huge coal and steel conglomerate. He had been acclaimed within Germany in the 1920s for his strident opposition to post-First World War reparations and to the French and Belgium occupation of the Ruhr, having led an employer boycott of French attempts to sequester coal in lieu of monies.[14] He was impressed by Hitler and joined in lobbying President von Hindenburg to appoint him as chancellor. He viewed the Nazis as a bulwark against the communist revolution he greatly feared, having being taken prisoner for a time by revolutionaries in 1918. He joined the Nazis in 1933 and his firm became the party's most significant financial backer. For his support, Thyssen was made a Councillor of State and became a member of the Reichstag after the Nazi takeover. A conservative nationalist, his political philosophy was Corporatism, a doctrine that had support among some elements within the early Nazi Party.[15] Hitler, though, had no time for any institutional structures that could interfere with his dictatorial powers. Thyssen, like other industrial magnates and members of the aristocracy, had foolishly believed that his presence within the party would have a moderating effect on Hitler. If he had reservations about the Nazis' racial policies, it didn't deter him from implementing them in his own companies, for his Jewish directors and employees were dismissed. It troubled him, though, that the regime was hostile to the Catholic Church, to which he belonged. His break with Nazism became manifest when he telegrammed Göring, with whom he had been on friendly terms, to declare his opposition to the invasion of Poland. Realising that this was likely to lead to his arrest, he made haste for Switzerland. When he later left there to visit his dying mother in Brussels, he was arrested by Vichy secret police while travelling through France. He was transported to Germany where he and his wife were detained in an asylum in Potsdam for over two years. He was later moved to various concentration camps before ending up with the *Prominenten* in Dachau.[16]

Meanwhile, a French VIP, the most prestigious of the *Prominenten* hostages, had been installed in the Dachau prison bunker.

CHAPTER NINE

OLD FOES MEET

Like other special prisoners we have encountered, Léon Blum, a former French prime minister, was accompanied by his wife who had volunteered to join him in captivity. Having been transported by car from Buchenwald, the pair were kept waiting at the gates of Dachau. They had arrived in darkness, but now dawn was breaking and they could hear the sound of marching feet approaching. As the gates opened and columns of prisoners paraded past, Blum managed to roll down a window of the car to get a better view. The prisoners were being marched in rows of five. Many had a red triangle sewn onto their garments indicating they were political prisoners. Blum saw misery etched on their faces. There were men of all ages, from seemingly quite elderly to children. Each group of one hundred were accompanied by a number of armed SS guards or by members of the *Volksstrum*, a recently formed militia of mostly elderly German men. The prisoners were being marched to their work assignments in factories and farms in the district. Most wore uncomfortable wooden clogs for footwear. Blum, thinking it possible that he might recognise some French political prisoners among them, leaned his head out the car window. He didn't see anyone he knew, but some of those passing recognised him. With his full drooping grey moustache and round glasses, he was instantly recognisable. One of the prisoners reached out to shake his hand, whereupon he was savagely kicked away by one of the guards. Blum was dismayed that he had inadvertently caused such trouble and injury to the man.[1] It was another reminder of the awfulness of a regime, and of an ideology he had bitterly opposed during his time as leader of the French Socialist Party.

Surprisingly, the conditions of his detention up to then had been comfortable. Blum had been allocated a former hunting lodge annexed to the Buchenwald Concentration Camp which he shared for a time with Georges

Mandel, a leading French conservative politician. They were even assigned a camp inmate to act as servant. Later Janot, Blum's former secretary and lover, who had bravely volunteered to join him in captivity, became the third resident. Their relatively benign treatment was all the more remarkable given that all three were Jews. More strangely still, Léon and Janot were allowed to marry in captivity. Janot, a handsome woman, twenty-seven years younger, was devoted to Blum. She was born Jeanne Levylier Humbert to wealthy Jewish parents in Paris in 1900. The couple were married on 8 October 1943 in a ceremony that involved nothing more than them signing a marriage contract drawn up by a German notary.[2] This was her third marriage (she was divorced from her first husband and widowed by her second). Léon Blum was also a widower and both he and Janot had adult children. He had two sons; one, Robert was a prisoner of war and the other René was a hostage like his father, but detained elsewhere. Despite the absence of ceremony, their wedding was a unique event. A year previously, the Nazis had declared Germany to be 'Jew-Free', for by then all Jews, except those in hiding, were either dead or in concentration camps. Their marriage was almost certainly the only officially sanctioned marriage of a Jewish couple held in a concentration camp in Nazi Germany. Why were they treated with such consideration? Pierre Laval, the arch-collaborationist and second in command to Pétain in the Vichy French administration, may, as he claimed, have intervened on their behalf, but the more probable reason is that Himmler considered Blum as a prize hostage and judged it advantageous for himself to spare this elderly and distinguished prisoner the ordeal of normal concentration camp life, even to the extent of allowing the marriage. It was certainly not due to any humane considerations; with the exception of Hitler, he was the most culpable for the Holocaust.

At seventy-two years old, Blum was the oldest and, by common consent, the most prominent, charming and erudite of the *Prominenten*. Before he entered French politics he had been a distinguished lawyer, a literary figure of stature and a member of the prestigious French Council of State. He came to politics relatively late in life: he had reached middle age before he was first elected to the French National Assembly. It was the *fin de siécle* Dreyfus Affair that obliged him to take a stand. Captain Dreyfus, was, like himself, an assimilated Jew with Alsatian roots and Blum could not remain aloof while a cruel injustice was being inflicted on the officer who had been framed on a charge of treason. Nor could he ignore the concurrent rise of political anti-Semitism that threatened the very existence of the Republic and the enlightenment values he cherished. As a *Dreyfusard* he met his political mentor and inspiration, the Socialist leader Jean Jaures. From Jaures he inherited his democratic socialist ideals; a fusion of French republicanism and Marxism. Blum became leader of the Socialist Party and went on to head the first elected left government in France, the *Front Populaire*, during 1936 and 1937. Following the surrender to the Germans in 1940, he was arrested by the collaborationist Vichy government and tried, along with the Radical Party leader Edouard Daladier, Blum's successor as Prime Minister, and General Gamelin, French Commander-in-Chief during the Battle of France. They and two other lesser figures were charged with being responsible for the defeat. Blum was accused of encouraging strikes and failing to properly equip the French armed services which, it was claimed, left the country criminally unprepared to defend itself. Marshal Pétain, in an absurd piece of theatre, declared the defendants guilty before their trial had started, sentencing them to life imprisonment.[3]

The trial went ahead regardless, with the Vichy regime no doubt expecting that the defendants would be publicly humiliated and their despised Third Republic discredited. However, Blum conducted a stunningly successful defence, turning the tables on his accusers.[4] The Nazis, appalled that a Jew could be allowed such latitude, demanded a halt to the proceedings. In any event, Hitler wanted the French to focus on their guilt for the war, not their unpreparedness for it. Also, to the annoyance of the Germans, the presence of foreign journalists meant that the trial received international coverage. Blum's stature was enhanced. He was the subject of a feature in *The New York Times* and American trade unions organised a huge rally in his honour in New York.[5]

He and other leading pre-war French political and military leaders were transferred to camps in Germany in April 1943. Blum and Mandel were separated from their former cabinet colleagues because they were Jews. When, in June 1944, the Résistance assassinated Philippe Henriot, a leading figure in the Vichy regime, the Nazis demanded that a prominent French politician be executed in reprisal. Mandel, Blum's co-detainee at Buchenwald, was chosen. He was taken back to France and handed over to the Malice, the thuggish Vichy militia of which Henriot had been a leader. Mandel was murdered on 7

July 1944 in Fontainebleau forest. Another prominent Jewish member of Blum's Popular Front government, the Radical Jean Zay was also murdered around the same time.

The question remains as to why Blum, by far the most illustrious French Jew in captivity, did not suffer the same fate, especially as Henriot, a strident anti-Semite, had been an unrelenting enemy of his. Laval, during his post-war trial, again claimed to have been instrumental in saving Blum, but this lacks credibility, for by that stage Laval's influence had greatly diminished. Here again, with the Allied breakthrough in France, it is likely that Himmler decided that Blum had more value to him as a living hostage than as a dead martyr.

When Blum and his wife were eventually admitted into Dachau that morning, they were escorted to the prison section where they were assigned a narrow cell. The tall and frail Blum was assisted to a cot by his wife. He was tired and suffering from severe back pain after their long journey. He was about to rest when they heard the bolts of their cell door being opened. A tall, thin figure entered, bespectacled and well dressed, with a stiff, winged shirt collar, his reddish brown hair parted in the middle. He approached a nonplussed Blum and he asked, 'Do you not know me?' Blum peered at him through his round-rimmed glasses, but didn't immediately recognise him. The visitor gestured towards himself. 'But look, I am Doctor Schacht!'[6]

Hjalmar Schacht had been an internationally renowned figure in the Weimar Republic. In 1923 he was appointed President of the Reichsbank and is credited with ending hyper-inflation and transforming the German financial system 'from chaos to stability in less than a week'.[7] He did this by the simple, but far from painless, expedient of waiting until the mark hit a low of 18,000 billion to the pound, and then issuing a new *Rentenmark*, making it equivalent to one trillion old marks. By the early 1930s, he had become a supporter of Hitler. More than that, he played an important role in his rise to power. Schacht's support allayed the fears of the moneyed elite concerning the Nazis' economic policies. He lobbied President Hindenburg to appoint Hitler as Chancellor and, working with Franz Thyssen, he organised a petition among major industrialists, to bring added pressure on the ageing statesman.[8] By way of reward, he was appointed Minister of Economics in the pre-war Nazi government. In that role, he was responsible for a major public works programme; most notably the building of the autobahn network. This won him further acclaim and raised his profile internationally. At first, he co-operated with a massive rearmament programme at Hitler's behest, but later he began to voice concerns at the impact huge military spending was having on German foreign currency reserves. The depletion of the reserves caused food shortages due to a lack of foreign currency to purchase imports. As a result, he fell out of favour with Hitler and was dismissed from his economic ministerial role in 1937. He remained a minister without portfolio until January 1943, but this counted for little, as the cabinet ceased to be convened after 1937.[9]

Like most of the assembling German *Prominenten*, Schacht was arrested after the 20 July attempt on Hitler's life, on suspicion of involvement in anti-Hitler conspiracies. In reality, other than some early contacts with oppositionists, he had played no part in the conspiracy. On the contrary, at least up until 1941, he seems to have harboured hopes of being restored to Hitler's affection, a suspicion that caused a leading anti-Nazi conspirator to disdainfully refer to him as 'His Majesty's Most Loyal Opposition'.[10] When it became clear that Germany faced defeat, Schacht relinquished all such ambitions, although he remained aloof from the opposition. His ego allowed him to believe he could be head of a post-Hitler government.[11] Ironically, during the period of his early involvement with the Nazis, he once wrote fawningly to Hitler, assuring him of his undying loyalty and pledging that, 'even if someday you should see me imprisoned in a fortress, you can always count on me as your loyal supporter'.[12] It was no more than the sycophantic scribbling of an ambitious opportunist. Schacht was never a convinced Nazi – he never actually became a member of the party – and it didn't take him long to regret this declaration of fidelity.

Blum then realised who his visitor was. They had met in 1936 and in 1937 when he was Prime Minister and Schacht was still German Minister for Economics in Hitler's cabinet. These were significant encounters, for they were about the possibility, or so it seemed at the time, of preventing war. Their first meeting took place on 25 August 1936 in Paris. Blum was then only a few months into his term as Premier. Under the guise of meeting with the Governor of the Bank of France, Schacht sought a confidential meeting with Blum, at which he intended to submit a proposal that, he claimed, could facilitate a restoration of friendly relations between France and Germany.

When they met in Paris, Blum had teased Schacht about the incongruity of an emissary of Hitler seeking an accord with, not just a Marxist, but a Jew.

Schacht responded as if there was no dilemma; he complimented Blum on meeting him while insisting that their meeting illustrated Hitler's sincere desire for peace.[13] The proposal that Schacht had come to make, for which he had received only lukewarm approval from Hitler, was that former German colonies, such as the Cameroons, then under French jurisdiction, be returned to Germany, or at least made available for its economic needs. Hitler at that time also had in mind the possibility of deporting German Jews to the French colonial island of Madagascar, but this wasn't included in Schacht's brief; his mission was purely economic. Renewed German exploitation of its former colonies could help relieve the food and raw material shortages afflicting Germany. The incentive for France was that Germany would agree to return to the League of Nations and the Disarmament Conference, thereby dangling the prospect of peace and security in Europe.[14]

What Schacht was proposing in 1936 were unilateral concessions by France, offering only in return the doubtful possibility that Hitler might be pacified. Blum, though, was at that time favourably disposed to concessions that could ensure peace. His Popular Front Government had been elected on the slogan *Pain, Paix, Liberté* ('bread, peace, freedom'). Besides, France was in chaos. A wave of strikes and factory occupations had followed the Popular Front's election victory as close to two million workers defied their employers in an atmosphere of euphoria and revolutionary fervour.[15] Although this had moderated following the *Matignon* accords, which secured for workers the then unprecedented forty-hour working week and two weeks of paid holiday, reactionary forces were now on the streets. The proto-fascist *Action Française,* although banned, had reconstituted itself and mobilised hundreds of thousands of activists.[16] Charles Maurras, their loathsome leader, had earlier called for Blum 'to be shot in the back'.[17] In February 1936, a right-wing mob had dragged Blum from a car and brutally attacked him. He might have been killed except that construction workers at a nearby building site came to his rescue.[18] Blum continued to be the target of poisonous anti-Semitic attacks by the opposition and the right-wing press. The cry was 'better Hitler than Blum'. A military coup and civil war similar to Spain's seemed a possibility. For Blum, progress on disarmament could offer the best prospect for restoring calm, as resources could then be directed into economic and social improvements. He agreed to favourably explore Schacht's proposal while making it clear that

Britain would have to be consulted. That sealed the matter as Anthony Eden, then British Foreign Secretary who was opposed to appeasement, dismissed any suggestion of Germany regaining their old African colonies.[19] Britain had acquired control over some of them and any concession by France would have implications for the Empire. Prime Minister Neville Chamberlain was prepared to buy peace, but only with other nations' territory, as the Munich Agreement was to demonstrate. Schacht had anticipated this response from Eden and tried in vain to persuade Blum to consult with other, more conciliatory, personages, of which there were many, within the English establishment.

Blum and Schacht had met again in March 1937, but by this time attitudes had hardened. Germany had signed the Anti-Comintern Pact with Japan 'to defend Western civilisation' and tensions over the Civil War in Spain changed Blum's priorities. It was becoming clear that *paix et liberté* ('peace and freedom') were incompatible. He told Schacht that political *détente* must precede economic concessions. He rhetorically asked, 'how can a country be expected to contemplate economic agreements capable of increasing the strength of another country which it fears may be an aggressor?'[20] Schacht was having his own difficulties with Hitler and this response was not going to help his cause. By the end of that year he was no longer economics minister.

Blum, while recalling these events, did not choose to debate them with his visitor in Dachau. He merely asked, 'If someone had predicted that we would meet again in the prison of Dachau; who would have been more surprised, you or me?'[21] Schacht didn't respond, but welcomed Blum to the prison community and left. Blum had little time to ponder this encounter before another visitor entered, Kurt Schuschnigg, the pre-*Anschluss* Chancellor of Austria. Blum instantly recognised the gaunt, silver-haired, bespectacled Austrian. They, too, had been adversaries. They had led opposing movements within the polarised politics of pre-war Europe. Blum was the leading proponent of democratic socialism while Schuschnigg was an opponent of democracy and, more especially, of socialism. Although Blum sometimes referred to himself as a Marxist, his socialism was never doctrinaire or reductionist, and he remained steadfast in his opposition to communism. For him parliamentary democracy, freedom of thought, assembly and debate, the products of the enlightenment, were sacrosanct. Even in the heady aftermath of the Russian Revolution in 1919, while excoriating the capitalist system, he argued against the Bolshevik concept of the dictatorship of the proletariat, declaring that, for him, the proletarian revolution 'will not be opposed in any way to the idea of democracy or the democratic ideal'.[22]

Schuschnigg had become Chancellor of Austria in 1934 after his predecessor, Engelbert Dollfuss, was assassinated by Austrian Nazis. The regime followed a variant of fascism, Austrofascism or Clericofascism as it is alternatively labelled. The Chancellor held dictatorial powers in an Austrian Corporate State (*Ständestaat*) that operated from 1933 to 1938. Corporatism was the guiding philosophy, as it was in a number of pre-war Catholic countries, continuing post-war in the case of Spain and Portugal. Under corporatist theory, parliamentary democracy and free trade unions were to be outlawed and replaced by sectoral or vocational corporations, representative of employers and workers, overseen – controlled – by a single ruling party. The stated aim was to eliminate dysfunctional parliaments and force an end to class conflict. It was an economic and social structure that had the support of the Vatican. Schuschnigg's Austrian version was influenced by Mussolini's Italian Corporate State, but modified to address Pope Pius XI's mild criticism of it as expressed in his 1931 encyclical *Quadragesimo Anno*, to which Dollfuss and Schuschnigg piously professed their adherence.[23]

Schuschnigg received support from the Austrian Hierarchy for his corporatist programme although their support was conditional on their interests being addressed.[24] Indeed, the Church was to be well represented on the embryonic corporate structures: embryonic because the system was not fully operational before the German takeover.[25] Notwithstanding the nod to Catholic social doctrine, the Austrian system of government was no less authoritarian than Mussolini's. Thousands of communists, social democrats and Nazis were detained in concentration camps, although Schuschnigg's regime never descended to the Nazis' level of barbarism. Racial theory and anti-Semitism was not a feature of Austrian state policy, prior to the *Anschluss*, a redeeming aspect of Schuschnigg's rule not likely to have escaped Blum.

Schuschnigg's attempt to rebuff Nazi demands for absorption into the Reich became untenable when he lost Mussolini's protection due to the faltering Italian invasion of Ethiopia and the Duce's consequent need for Hitler's support. On 12 February 1938, Schuschnigg was summoned to the Berghof, Hitler's Alpine retreat in Berchtesgaden, where he was forced to appoint the leading

Austrian Nazi, Seyss-Inquart, as Minister of Public Security, thus surrendering control of the police to the Nazis.[26] He was also required to release all Nazis from detention. A month later the Germans took over in a bloodless and largely popular invasion. Schuschnigg was arrested and detained in a small room in the Hotel Metropole in Vienna where he was abused and humiliated. He was given just one towel with which he was forced to clean a toilet the guards deliberately soiled.[27] Despite his Aryan bloodlines, his treatment was much worse than that of Blum, a measure of how he had infuriated Hitler by his imprisonment of Austrian Nazis and by his attempts to resist a German takeover. He was visited by Himmler in his seventh month of confinement. Himmler was evasive in response to the former Chancellor's appeals, but his conditions did improve subsequently. Soon after war was declared, Schuschnigg was transferred from Vienna to a Gestapo prison in Munich where he was kept in solitary confinement before being transferred to Sachsenhausen in 1942. There he was allocated a comfortable chalet in *Sonderlager* 'B', where his wife Vera volunteered to join him. (Schuschnigg was allowed to marry while a prisoner, albeit by proxy.)

Blum recalled that Schuschnigg 'had once been a most ruthless enemy to my friends among the Austrian socialists'.[28] What Blum was referring to was the role Schuschnigg played in putting down a workers uprising in 1933, when he was Minister for Justice. In the aftermath of that uprising, which only ended when the army threatened to shell a working-class housing complex in Vienna, Schuschnigg demanded the execution of the socialist leaders involved. Nine were killed; most summarily by the *Heimwehr*, a right-wing militia not dissimilar to the German Brown Shirts.[29] Blum decided to put aside past differences and he greeted him warmly, although he reminded Schuschnigg that he had once warned against relying on Mussolini.[30] Schuschnigg responded: 'History will judge which of us was right. Both of us wanted peace, and now, we both have the same adversaries.'[31] The Austrian was not prepared to concede the point. Although he admired Blum as a person, he saw little difference between democratic socialism and communism and had imprisoned supporters of both when in power. However, although his regime was labelled 'fascist', Schuschnigg was at heart a Catholic conservative of the old school. In an ideal world, he would have preferred the restoration of the Habsburg monarchy in a society where rank and religion reigned supreme. However, that option had been precluded by the Treaty of Versailles.

The Blums were reverently attended to in their Dachau cell by most of the *Prominenten* over the next week, despite many of the visitors being hostile to their politics. There were about a dozen politicians present with decidedly rightist backgrounds. These included Richard Schmitz, a former mayor of Vienna, and a colleague of Schuschnigg's, and Johannes van Dijk, a former Dutch Minister of Defence, and a member of the Anti-Revolutionary Party, along with a number of Greek and Hungarian political prisoners with similar right-wing pedigrees. Capricious fate had placed political foes in close confinement in Dachau. But for now, all past differences were to be set aside. What would bind them now was their anti-Nazism and their shared hopes for survival.

CHAPTER TEN

HOSTAGES FOR FORTUNE

For some time the British had been receiving information about an apparent desire by some senior Nazis to discuss a bargained release of hostages. On 12 March 1945, Sir Alexander Cadegan, the Permanent Under-Secretary at the Foreign Office, arranged a meeting in his room to discuss this issue. The meeting was attended by Lord Drogheda, Director General of the Ministry of Economic Warfare; Sir Claude Dansey, the deputy head of MI6 and by a number of other officials. The immediate purpose was to discuss matters related to 'the removal of monies from Germany and their possible secretion in neutral countries'.[1] The participants were told that a Monsieur Musy, a Swiss national, was acting as middleman for the Germans in negotiations with American Jewish organisations for the release of Jewish concentration camp prisoners in exchange for large sums of money. The issue of hostage bartering had also been the subject of newspaper reports. 'Will they attempt to barter with the lives of two kings?' asked a *Sunday Express* headline.[2] The kings being speculated about were Christian of Denmark and Leopold of Belgium. The article went on to mention 'blackmail' proposals in respect of Kurt Schuschnigg and Léon Blum, among others.

Dansey informed the meeting that Monsieur Musy, a former Swiss prime minister and Catholic right-wing politician, was anxious to have more clients bartered and Léon Blum's name was mentioned. If Dansey had any inkling that Payne Best and Stevens were likely to be in the company of Blum, he doesn't appear to have made this information available to the meeting. The committee concluded that Musy was not a reputable person and that he was involved in a lucrative racket and personally benefiting from ransom payments. There were also fears expressed that much of the ransom monies were going into a special Gestapo war chest either for current or post-war underground activity.[3]

Nevertheless, the meeting went on to consider 'what kind of persons could we try to get out through his services'. Three categories were identified: (i) 'the Leon Blum type'; (ii) 'men who could give us information of various kinds, e.g. industrialists, engineers, etc.'; and (iii) 'refugees'.[4]

Léon Blum himself had foreseen the dilemma the British now faced. While in Buchenwald, aware that he was being kept as a hostage, he had reflected in his journal on how his captivity was likely to be exploited by the Nazis:

> But what use is made of a hostage, however precious? One tries to exchange him for an appropriate equivalent value, and that kind of negotiation necessarily involved a threat – blackmail in which the life of the hostage is at stake. When you say: 'I offer to exchange Mr. so and so, who is in my hands, for this other,' it necessarily means: 'if you refuse to bargain, I will do away with Mr. so and so.' We knew perfectly well that if I was being kept with such care, this was for a last-minute bargain. We were convinced the Allies would reject it, and we approved their situation in advance: we understood very well that rejection would bring about the natural consequence, for me as well as for my wife, who had come to join me voluntarily and whose fate was inseparable from mine.[5]

He was right; the British did reject the offer. The consensus of the Foreign Office meeting was against using the services of Musy. In respect of 'the Leon Blum type' of prisoner, the minute of the meeting concluded: 'The price for such important persons would be very high and it was doubtful if we would get them anyway as the Germans were keeping them back as hostages, possibly to be exchanged for a guarantee for the lives of important Nazis.'[6]

The committee was right in its assessment of Musy as a shady character. Politically, he was a creature of the extreme right. He had got to know Himmler personally from his visits to Germany in the 1930s when he was a leader of a Swiss fascist group participating in anti-communist rallies. Towards the end of 1944, he had initiated contact with Walter Schellenberg, Himmler's most trusted subordinate and the man who had kidnapped Stevens and Payne Best in 1939. Schellenberg, now head of Foreign Intelligence in the SS, had been encouraging Himmler to open negotiations with a view to ending the war and he considered Musy a possible conduit for talks with the Western powers. Prisoner release was meant to be the bait in Schellenberg's scheme.

A meeting involving Himmler and Musy, with Schellenberg in attendance, had taken place on 3 November 1944 when Himmler offered to release some prominent Jewish and French prisoners in return for equipment and materials in short supply in Germany. Musy suggested that payment in foreign currency might be more feasible,[7] and doubtlessly more remunerable for him. In the event, Heinrich Müller, the head of the Gestapo, refused to allow any releases, most likely because the request was made by Schellenberg rather than Himmler, for the Reichsführer remained wary of being seen to be personally involved. A second meeting between Himmler and Musy had taken place on 12 January 1945 when it was agreed that 1,200 Jewish prisoners would be released every fortnight on payment of five million Swiss francs for each transport.[8] One trainload of Jewish prisoners from Theresienstad camp in Czechoslovakia arrived in Switzerland on 7 February 1945. Hitler was told about it after the event by Ernst Kaltenbrunner,[9] the thuggish Austrian, who before the war had worked for the SS in Vienna to undermine Schuschnigg's government. Kaltenbrunner was now head of the RSHA (the Reich Main Security office within the SS), and, having built an alliance with Martin Bormann, Hitler's influential private secretary, he felt secure enough to conspire against Himmler, still nominally his boss.[10] Hitler was furious and ordered an immediate stop to all such releases and forbade, under threat of death, any release – not just of Jews, but of any prisoners, including British or American POWs.[11] That put an end to the ransom transports and to Monsieur Musy's gravy train.

Two days after the Foreign Office meeting, a telegram was received from the British Military Attaché in Berne who had learned from Swiss sources that General de Gaulle had asked Professor Burckhardt, President of the International Red Cross, to help to secure the lives of French deportees in Germany. The communiqué continued: '[T]he idea apparently was that Himmler would facilitate the departure of French women and children and possibly others in return for Allied promise not to bomb certain areas in which German women and children would be concentrated.' The Attaché went on to say that he understood from American intelligence in Switzerland that:

Burckhardt is meeting someone, possibly Kaltenbrunner in S(outh) Germany or Austria today. They tell me that apart from the above proposal it is likely that Dr. Burckhardt hopes to rescue certain important persons in Germany, including Niemoller. They consider the question of peace feelers being put out is not excluded.[12]

The meeting between Burckhardt and Kaltenbrunner had, in fact, taken place two days earlier, on the same day as the Foreign Office meeting to discuss Musy's activities.[13] Kaltenbrunner was pursuing his own secret channels. It seems his meeting with Burckhardt was his attempt at making contact with the Allies, while name-checking Martin Niemöller to incite interest.

There was an element of competition among some high-ranking Nazis in their frantic attempts to broker a truce near the end of the war. Most still held out hope that Britain and America would allow the German army to concentrate their remaining resources in resisting the Soviet advance. It was even thought by some that Britain and America could be persuaded to join the fight against the Soviet Union. With so little leverage, they needed anything that might make an impression on the Allies and Himmler and Schellenberg, and separately Kaltenbrunner, would have seen the release of prisoners as a means of achieving this, as well as providing cash that might aid their escape if all else failed.

There is little evidence that the allies had any interest in separate peace negotiations, although a fear of retribution plagued Stalin. His suspicions had been heightened when his demands for a second front kept being delayed and it was largely to allay his worries that the Casablanca declaration of February 1943 was issued, confirming that nothing less than unconditional surrender would be acceptable. Within the Nazi mind-set, such declarations were, just like the pre-war Molotov Ribbentrop pact, merely tactical and could be reneged on at any time. Guderian, the *Wehrmacht* Chief of Staff, was among those who suggested capitulation in the West in order to concentrate on stopping the Russian advance. He too believed that Britain and the US would acquiesce to prevent post-war Soviet domination of east and central Europe. It was a view widely held among the Nazi regime that the British and Americans would eventually take fright at the rapid Soviet advance. They weren't entirely wrong, for, just before the end of the war, Churchill ordered his chiefs of staff to work on a plan to dislodge the Russians from Poland. When Truman heard of this he thought the old man had gone mad.[14] But, in any event, this would have been too late for the Nazis to benefit.

Hitler never positively supported moves to try and secure separate terms with either the Soviet Union or the Western Allies, although he sometimes considered the possibility. In 1942, Mussolini had urged him to make peace with Stalin and the Japanese offered to be a conduit for such negotiations. Goebbels also encouraged him to think in this direction. Hitler vacillated, first stating that it would be easier to deal with the British, then deciding that no compromise was possible with either side. This didn't stop attempts by others within the Nazi hierarchy to encourage the Allies into talks. Göring had Swedish contacts. Ribbentrop put out feelers to the western allies via Stockholm, Berne and Madrid. Hitler sometimes half-heartedly permitted such feelers, although he never had confidence that they would work. He insisted, not without reason, that a major victory was needed to permit reasonable terms to be negotiated. He must have known though, that if ever negotiations got underway, the first demand would be for his removal. As defeat loomed, he lost all interest in such ventures; 'If the war should be lost, then the nation too will be lost,' he told Albert Speer who had pleaded that the country's industries and infrastructure should not be destroyed so that Germany would have some hope of a future revival. Hitler's response demonstrated his total disdain for survivors: 'Those who remain alive after the battles are over are in any case only inferior persons, since the best have fallen.'[15]

Himmler didn't see himself as unworthy of survival or salvation. Realising in 1944 that the war was effectively lost, he repeatedly tried to open discussions with the British. Schellenberg was his emissary in a number of these attempts. One involved Coco Chanel, the Parisian couturier and enthusiastic collaborator, with whom Schellenberg is believed to have had an affair.[16] The SS man arranged for her to travel to Madrid to meet with her old friend, Sir Samuel Hoare, the British Ambassador, and through him, to convey to her other old friend, Winston Churchill, the veracity of Himmler's desire to make peace.[17] Of course, nothing came of this or other initiatives and by March 1945 Himmler was desperate. He was by then out of favour with the Führer. After Hitler had given him his first field command, putting him in charge of the Army Group Vistula in an attempt to stop the Soviet advance, his limitations as a battle commander had become obvious and he was relieved of his command on 20 March. Hitler's paranoia did not allow him to view the Reichsführer's failure as simply due to incompetency: he suspected treachery. The SS had failed him in his hour of greatest need and its leader was being accused of direct disobedience, and even 'secret sabotage'.[18]

Himmler, now fearing for his very survival, allowed Schellenberg to try again to establish contact with the West. This time the chosen conduit was Count Folke Bernadotte, head of the Swedish Red Cross and a close relation of the Swedish monarch. Himmler met with Bernadotte and signalled to him that he was prepared to free thousands of Jewish concentration camp prisoners. At one point, he indicated that he would consider surrendering all the German forces on the Western Front. His suggested actions were treasonable: he was, in effect, offering to usurp Hitler. However, he procrastinated, constantly changing his mind, despite Schellenberg encouraging him to defy Hitler. The talks with Bernadotte did have a positive outcome for thousands of prisoners, for Schellenberg won Himmler's approval for the transport out of Germany of 20,000 Scandinavian concentration inmates during the final days of the war.[19]

For some time, Himmler had been arranging for groups of prominent prisoners to be gathered together for hostage purposes. There were a number of different such hostage groups. A group of Jewish prisoners who were believed to have rich and influential relatives in the United States were assembled in a special section of Bergen-Belsen with the hope that they might be traded for foreign currency.[20] Castle Schloss Itter, near Innsbruck, held important French political and military prisoners whom Blum had not been allowed to join because of his Jewish identity. Buchenwald had a special compound holding prominent German political prisoners.

The *Prominenten* who are the subject of our story, although likely assembled at the behest of Himmler, came to be under the direct control of Kaltenbrunner.[21] As we have seen, many of them were not at all prominent or influential and it is difficult to understand what possible bargaining value Kaltenbrunner considered them to have. It would seem that he wanted hostages from as many countries as possible – there were seventeen different nationalities represented within the group – but we can only guess at what rationale, if there was any, influenced the selection of particular individuals. Chance probably played a part. The Irish soldiers were placed in Sachsenhausen because they knew too much. When the British officers arrived in the *Sonderlager* the Irish men offered themselves as their batmen. The concept of officers having soldiers as servants was commonplace in most armies and it was the practice to assign NCOs or private soldiers to *oflags* to tend to the needs of officers at the ratio of about one orderly to every ten officers. It may be that local SS officers facilitated the entry into the convoy of some others out of favouritism, or as informers. Edgar Stiller, who was in direct charge of the *Prominenten*, probably had leeway to add individuals. Two former Italian fascist police chiefs, Tumburini and Apollonio, were late additions to the group and, as no Allied government was likely to be interested in negotiating for their release, one can only speculate as to the true reason for their inclusion. A few seem to have managed, through subterfuge, to integrate themselves into the group. When Harry Day and the other British officers were awaiting transport at Flossenbürg, an inmate of the main camp managed, with their help, to infiltrate himself into the Group. His name was Wadim Greenwich, a Russian-born British Secret Service operative who had worked in the British embassy in Prague. He had been abducted in Bulgaria during February 1941 near the Turkish border, while travelling on a train bound for Istanbul.[22] Hinko Dragic, the former Yugoslavian officer, also linked up with the group at that point, although how he managed this is less clear. It may have been due to disorganisation, connivance or the bribing the guards.

Chaos could have contributed. Ian Kershaw, one of the foremost authorities on the Nazi period, refers to 'chaotic centrifugal tendencies' existing within the regime.[23] There was no functioning system of state governance during the war. The Nazi party had usurped the state and its civil service, but the party had no centralised system of decision-making. Different party bureaucracies pursued their own, frequently competing, interests. Hitler, true to his twisted take on Darwinism, let rivals within his entourage fight it out among themselves. Even when forced to arbitrate, he seldom put anything in writing so his decisions usually had to be relayed through third-party communiqués. As defeat loomed, and the chain of communications was disrupted, decisions had to be taken by low-ranking officers who were contemplating their own post-war prospects. The fate of prominent prisoners was to become a factor in these calculations.

Although Himmler and other senior Nazis were deluded enough to think that the western allies would negotiate a unilateral settlement that would allow the fight to continue against the Soviets, even they could not have believed that the release of hostages would, in itself, secure this. At best, they could be used as a calling card, something that might help establish friendly contact. Emissaries were needed; Sidney Dowse and Peter Churchill had both declined an offer to be flown home to act as such, and although Johnnie Dodge accepted that role, his return was too late to matter.

As all hope of conniving with the Western Allies to the detriment of the Soviets faded, the special prisoners came to have a different possibility for individual Nazis; if it could be demonstrated that they had been saved from extinction and well cared for, the person who could claim credit for this act of humanity might be looked upon, if not with gratitude, then perhaps with some degree of latitude when the reckoning came. The problem for the hostages was that, if their continued existence could not be seen to deliver even this limited benefit, and if they had witnessed events that could incriminate their minders, it might be better that they be liquidated.

Waffen-SS General Karl Wolff, who was to play a part in the fate of the *Prominenten*, was one of those contemplating his future prospects. Formally a member of Himmler's general staff, he was now in command of SS forces in Northern Italy where he also held the position of Chief of Police. Availing of the services of an Italian businessman, he had made contact with Swiss Intelligence, and through them, with Allen Dulles, head of the Swiss station of the Office of Strategic Services (OSS), later to become the CIA. Dulles was receptive to contacts with disaffected Nazis and he himself actually favoured a negotiated end to hostilities.[24] Wolff sought a face-to-face meeting between himself and Dulles with a view to ending the fighting in Italy. The American demanded the release from prison of Ferruccio Parri, head of the overarching Italian partisan administration, the CLN, as a precondition which Wolff arranged.[25] At their meeting in Geneva, the SS General told Dulles that he was confident he could convince Field Marshal Albert Kesselring, to join with him in arranging a general surrender of all German forces in Italy,[26] although Wolff's confidence in this regard was later shown to be wishful thinking on his part. Wolff later confided to Dulles that Himmler had begun to be suspicious of him; having learnt about his trips to Switzerland, Himmler ordered Wolff to cease all contacts and implied that his family would suffer if he didn't do so. Wolff's wife and children were effectively hostages as Himmler had them removed from their lodgings near the Brenner Pass and placed in an SS facility in Salzburg, where, as he told Wolff menacingly, he could take 'better care' of them.[27] What would have concerned Himmler, was not that Wolff was engaging with the enemy, but that he was doing so independently of him and thereby putting to naught his own initiatives.

However, the surrender plot stalled when Stalin got wind that something was going on. The Soviet leader reacted furiously to news of negotiations in Italy. His paranoia, fuelled by Goebbels propaganda about an imminent rift between east and west, caused him to view it as evidence of treachery on the part of the Americans. President Truman, who had just succeeded the deceased Roosevelt, came under pressure to have 'Operation Sunrise' (the code name for Dulles's secret talks with Wolff) halted, and it was, temporarily.

Ernst Kaltenbrunner, a bitter opponent of Wolff within the Nazi hierarchy, had also been attempting to make contact with the Americans in Berne. He asked an Austrian industrialist to convey the information that he and Himmler were anxious to end the war and were contemplating the liquidation of unnamed 'war mongers' (which presumably meant Hitler and his close entourage).[28] It's possible he mentioned Himmler to add weight to his initiative. If so, he miscalculated, for as far as Dulles was concerned, Himmler was a pariah with whom no deals could be contemplated and, in any event, Kaltenbrunner's own reputation was little better.

Himmler, Schellenberg, Kaltenbrunner and Wolff were all walking a metaphorical tightrope in their attempts to establish contact with the West. While trying to curry favour with the enemy to enhance their post-war survival prospects, they ran the risk of being shot as traitors. They needed to maintain the appearance of loyalty to Hitler, while betraying him. Kaltenbrunner was even prepared to betray his erstwhile colleagues in order to garnish his reputation for loyalty. For him, the *Prominenten* were post-war indemnity cover, if only he could find a buyer for his assets. In the end, it was Wolff, not Kaltenbrunner, who would stand to benefit after the *Prominenten* moved into his area of control.

PART III

ALPINE ODYSSEY

With a compact army of young SS and Hitler Youth fanatics, they will retreat behind a loyal rearguard cover of Volkgrenadiere and Volksströrmer, to the Alpine massif which reaches from Southern Bavaria across western Austria to Northern Italy. There immense stores of food and ammunition are being laid down in prepared fortifications. If the retreat is a success such an army might hold out for years.

Time, 12 February 1945

Rumours of the Nazis preparing to retreat to an Alpine fortress were widely believed inside and outside Germany. The decision to evacuate the *Prominenten* hostages into the Alps was, almost certainly, based on the assumption that their final place of detention would be within the Nazis' last redoubt.

CHAPTER ELEVEN

EVACUATION

Dachau, 17 April 1945

Harry Day and his group of fellow prisoners had been the last to arrive in Dachau, but were among the first of the special prisoners to be evacuated. They were less than two days in the brothel block when Stiller ordered them to prepare for another move. Day was troubled by this. He had observed that things were chaotic and it was clear that the SS guards were anxious to be elsewhere when the Americans arrived. Could it be that they planned to liquidate the prisoners? Ten days earlier, the Americans had liberated Ohrdruf, a sub-camp of Buchenwald, and, just two days previous, British and Canadian soldiers had entered Bergen-Belsen. The Allies encountered horrific scenes in both camps. In Ohrdruf the bodies of prisoners were strewn everywhere and a mass of charred corpses was found, where the SS had tried to obliterate evidence of their crimes.[1] In Belsen, SS guards opened fire on prisoners who left their huts to celebrate their imminent liberation. When the British eventually entered, they had to bury 23,000 bodies.[2] News of these atrocities reached Dachau, increasing the prisoner's fears that their SS guards were planning to kill them.[3]

Harry Day and Sidney Dowse planned not to join the exodus. The two serial escapers determined, on this occasion, not to break out of the camp, but to hide within it and await the arrival of the Americans. In the hut assigned to them, they had discovered a trapdoor in the ceiling of the communal wash room that permitted access to an attic. Having gathered all the bread they could locate, they climbed up and went through the trapdoor into their hiding place shortly before departure hour. When news of their intention filtered through to the rest of the prisoner evacuees, objections were raised by Colonel Davide

Ferrero. The powerfully built Italian argued forcibly that Day and Dowse were bound to be sniffed-out by the SS dogs and, more importantly, their absence would endanger the rest of the party. He urged Peter Churchill to persuade them to come down and join the evacuation. Ferrero said he had obtained information that they were to be taken to the Italian Alps where, he argued, their chances of escape were better because of the presence of Italian partisans. Peter Churchill made his way up to the fugitives to convince them to join the evacuation party. The two were not at all pleased with the suggestion they should abandon their plan, but they acquiesced after an appeal by Churchill to 'think of the safety of the others'.[4]

Several thousand emaciated concentration camp inmates stood in the assembly square as the special prisoners, including the two airmen, were marched towards the gates. Those watching the departure were weak with hunger and thirst, having been left standing in line for hours without food or water. There were rumours that they were to be marched away from the camp. They knew the front was close, for in the distance they could hear the rumble of artillery. Munich, only fifteen kilometres away, was now a bombed-out ruin. They could sense a change in the attitude of the SS guards, who no longer indulged in their callous cruelties. Many stayed in their guard rooms, fearful of the typhus that was spreading among the prisoners. The meagre food rations had been reduced. Discipline was crumbling and most prisoners could now hold conversations during roll call without fear of punishment. Some talked of imminent deliverance; others said the SS would never allow them to be rescued because they were witnesses to the dreadful crimes that they had perpetrated.

As Peter Churchill dressed in civilian clothes walked towards the gates of Dachau in the company of his uniformed fellow British officers, the name 'Raoul' was called out by someone in the watching crowd of assembled prisoners. Churchill immediately realised the call was directed at him, for it was his *nom de guerre* during his undercover work in France. He scanned the ranks of faces but he recognised none. He was somewhat short-sighted and, in any event, hunger made faces seem dreadfully alike with prominent cheekbones and sunken eye sockets. He made a thumbs-up sign in the hope of identifying the caller, but scores of arms went up to return the gesture. He moved on, troubled. He knew how important it was for prisoners to have information of their continued existence relayed to loved ones.[5]

At the gates, they boarded three grey army buses. Followed by a lorry occupied by some of the SS guards, the buses made their way through the ruins of Munich. There had been a major bombing raid on the city the previous night and virtually no buildings were left intact. To the surprise of the prisoners observing the scenes of devastation, some trams were still running, their windows blown out and replaced with squares of cardboard. Knots of people were observed gathering at points along the rubble-strewn streets where tram stops had once presumably been located.

Flight Lieutenant Bertram James found himself seated beside a distinguished German military prisoner, Count Fabian von Schlabrendorff. The bespectacled German officer told him that he had been a lawyer before becoming a reserve officer in the *Wehrmacht*. He told James that he was involved in the anti-Hitler resistance but didn't elaborate.[6] His reticence may have been because he wasn't sure who could be trusted among those seated around him, but later he told the full astonishing story of his attempt to kill Hitler and his subsequent miraculous survival.

Arrested after the 20 July attempt on Hitler's life, Schlabrendorff was cruelly tortured in the Gestapo cellars in Prinz-Albrecht-Strasse in Berlin: spikes were repeatedly driven into his legs and fingertips, and his head was encased in a metal mask over which a blanket was thrown to muffle his screams.[7] He was then sent for trial by a special 'Peoples Court' presided over by the notorious Roland Friesler. This would have almost certainly been a prelude to his execution, except that the proceedings were interrupted by an air raid alarm. All involved hastily took shelter in underground vaulted cellars during what turned out to be one of the most intensive Allied bombing raids on Berlin. In the midst of the attack, there was a deafening explosion as the building containing the courthouse took a direct hit. Part of the ceiling collapsed and a heavy beam of timber fell upon the Judge, killing him instantly. Schlabrendorff was later told by his council that the judge was found in the rubble with his file in his hands.[8] The Count, a man of strong religious conviction, might have been tempted to see this as an act of divine intervention, but for the fact that he knew that Hitler had similar reprieves, including when he survived almost certain obliteration from a bomb planted by Schlabrendorff himself.

In March 1943 he was acting as a staff officer to General Henning von Tresckow stationed near Smolensk on the Russian front. Tresckow was one of the leading anti-Hitler plotters and he had appointed his relative Schlabrendorff as his staff officer in order to have someone he could trust to liaise on his behalf with others in the opposition. Together they conspired to assassinate Hitler when he was due to visit their section of the front. The method eventually chosen was for a bomb to be placed in Hitler's Wulf Condor aircraft which was to carry him back to Berlin. Schlabrendorff was involved in the design of the bomb which contained plastic explosive concealed in two Cointreau brandy bottles – chosen because of their square shape – and wrapped in a package containing a fuse. The pilot was asked if he would mind taking on board a present of brandy destined for a senior officer in Berlin known to them both. He readily agreed – it wasn't unusual for items to be ferried in this way from the front lines – and as Hitler boarded the plane Schlabrendorff handed over the parcel. He had primed the fuse to set off the detonator thirty minutes into the flight. Following take off, the plotters waited anxiously for news of a mid-air explosion, but it never came. Their contact in Berlin who was to have set in motion a planned military takeover following news of Hitler's death was Captain Ludwig Gehre of the *Abwehr*, the man with the eye patch who was later executed along with Canaris in Flossenbürg. Gehre relayed the news that the bomb had failed to explode and Schlabrendorff now had the task of trying to reclaim the parcel before the bomb was discovered. On some pretext, he flew to Berlin early the next morning and managed to retrieve it. He later discovered that, although the fuse had worked, the detonator hadn't.[9] The Nazis had no knowledge of this threat to Hitler's life and Schlabrendorff had every reason to ensure the SS didn't learn of it now. His former commanding officer and co-collaborator, Tresckow, who had been involved in a number of other attempts to kill Hitler, knowing he would be arrested following the failure of the 20 July plot, blew himself up with a hand grenade.[10] How Schlabrendorff was still alive at that point was miraculous, for, apart from his reprieve after the bombing of the courthouse in Berlin, it seems that the SS had intended to have him executed along with Gehre and the others in Flossenbürg. He realised this when, during the roll call on entry to Dachau, his name was not on the list of those expected. The irritation displayed by the SS confirmed his belief that he was to have been executed in Flossenbürg.[11]

Driving towards the Alps, the convoy stopped a couple of times when allied planes were spotted. The SS guards disembarked for fear of the buses being strafed or bombed. The hostages were left on board; it seems the guards judged that there would be some propaganda value in the hostages being killed in an Allied attack, and it would relieve Stiller, – who was in charge of the transport – of a difficult assignment. Fortunately, the planes passed overhead without incident. After travelling through the night, they reached Innsbruck in the early morning. They were surprised to find the city relatively untouched by the war. Their destination was not after all the high Alps, at least not for now. It was yet another camp, this time on the outskirts of Innsbruck. A sign announced it as 'Police Education Camp – Reichenau', but the title was, as always, misleading; it was a punishment camp for Italian, French and other nationals forced to work in the Reich and deemed in breach of contract for being workshy or for some other perceived violation of SS regulations.

The accommodation provided to the *Prominenten* was the worst the British special prisoners had yet experienced. Outdoor pits served as latrines, their allotted bunks were alive with vermin, and watery soup was all that was on offer by way of a mid-day meal. On their first night a mournful silence descended on the camp as three Austrian resistance fighters were hanged. It wasn't until the following week that the remaining members of the *Prominenten* joined them in Innsbruck.

Hohenlychen, North of Berlin, 22 April 1945

General Gottlob Berger, Himmler's Chief of Staff, having learned that Hitler would be remaining in his Berlin bunker, immediately went to see Himmler to urge him to try to persuade the Führer to leave. News of Hitler's determination to remain had emerged after a meeting in the *Führerbunker* the previous day when Hitler hysterically accused all and sundry of betraying him. Berger, an unsophisticated Hitler loyalist, was appalled. The Russians had broken through the perimeter defence ring to the north of Berlin and soon it would be impossible to escape. Himmler declined to go to Hitler. Unknown to Berger, under Schellenberg's influence, he was in secret and treasonous contact with Count Bernadotte of the Swedish Red Cross. Moreover, he sensed he was out of favour and might even have feared for his life. He did, however, speak to Hitler on the telephone to urge him to leave, without success.

Berger had himself been summoned to the Reich Chancellery in connection with his imminent departure to Munich.[12] When he gained entry into the bunker under the Chancellery ruins, Hitler, in a self-pitying rant, began to complain about how he had been deceived and lied to.[13] In the context of his impending journey to Munich, Berger asked Hitler what was to be done about the *Prominenten*.[14] Before any reply was forthcoming, the conversation moved onto reports of emerging separatist movements in Bavaria and Austria. This evidence of yet more treachery caused Hitler to relapse into frenzied convulsions. According to Berger, 'his hand was shaking, his leg was shaking, and his head was shaking; and all he kept saying was; "Shoot them all! Shoot them all".'[15] Berger could only speculate whether he was referring to the separatists, the *Prominenten*, everybody, or nobody in particular. In all probability, as he might have known, Hitler was prepared to have all concentration camp prisoners liquidated. This may have troubled Berger as he made his way to Munich. Not that he was averse to killing, as head of the SS prisoner-of-war administration, he already had blood on his hands, but he was concerned about the Aryans among the *Prominenten*. Berger shared Himmler's trenchant belief in Nazi racial theory. Just as no mercy must be shown to the racially inferior, racial equals should be protected for their future integration into a Greater German Reich. Himmler had even encouraged his SS recruits to 'behave respectfully towards their foreign racial comrades'.[16]

Berger's arrival in Munich the next day coincided with the evacuation of thousands of ordinary prisoners out of Dachau who were being forced marched towards the Alps. He encountered them and, according to his testimony at Nuremberg, he ordered the officer in charge to have the prisoners returned to the camp. He also claimed that he told the camp commander, Weiter, 'to send no more people by foot to any place but, whenever the Allies advanced any further, to give over the camp completely'.[17] This instruction was, according to Berger, countermanded by Ernst Kaltenbrunner.

As a historian of Dachau states:

It is difficult to say with any precision what orders concerning concentration camps were given in the last weeks of the war, or to what extent they were carried out. Most of the important documents have vanished, and those of the officials responsible who were questioned naturally did not provide exact or complete information on this subject. One can be sure, however, that the desire to exterminate the occupants of the camps did exist. If it could not be done, it was only because of the lack of means and time and because the prisoners had taken such effective counter-measures. Also, when it came to the point some camp authorities did not dare to take responsibilities for crimes which a few months earlier they would have committed without a moment's hesitation.[18]

Evidence was given during post-war trials of high-level orders to have the Dachau prisoners shot or poisoned – with the exception of Aryan prisoners who were nationals of the Western Powers – or, alternatively, to have the camp bombed by the Luftwaffe in an operation code named *Wolkenbrand* ('fire cloud'). What evidence there is points to Kaltenbrunner giving the order.[19] It was also alleged that he ordered nationals of the Western Powers to be transported to the Alps and this is consistent with the evacuation of the *Prominenten*. In the end, the evacuation of all Dachau prisoners to prevent their liberation by the Americans was judged by the local SS as a least-worst alternative, in the context of their own survival prospects.

Preparations to entirely evacuate the camp had been in train for some time. Since the departure of the first group of *Prominenten*, ordinary prisoners continued to be assembled in readiness for evacuation. As days passed without any movement, tension grew. It was evident the Americans were close; maybe they would hand the camp over to them. It seemed that this is what the camp commander wanted, but news had spread that this had been vetoed. The source was a sympathetic SS woman assigned to the camp hospital. She even showed some prisoners a communiqué from SS headquarters which stated that 837 prisoners considered 'dangerous and criminal' must, if necessary, be liquidated.[20] The 'dangerous criminals' were taken to be that number of German and Austrian communists who had fought with the International Brigade during the Spanish Civil War. The 'if necessary' provision meant liquidation to forestall their discovery and rescue. Fortunately, this instruction was never carried out.

Stiller, who had arrived back from Innsbruck, visited some of the remaining special prisoners to inform them that they would be leaving that evening. This second evacuation would include Payne Best, McGrath, Stevens, Frederick

Leopold, Xavier de Bourbon, Schacht, Muller, Liedig, Kokorin and the other Russians as well as a large group of German kin prisoners. By then the situation within Dachau was desperate. Food supplies had dwindled; prisoners, including the *Prominenten*, now had only thin soup to sustain them.[21] Typhus was spreading. Many of the senior SS administrators had deserted the camp and a clandestine international committee of prisoners had been established to maintain order and prepare for liberation. There was increasing levels of Allied air attacks and vehicles in a parking area of the camp were strafed by fighter planes. Some buses intended for the transport of the hostages were destroyed.[22]

John McGrath was not in good health at this time. He was suffering from some unspecified illness for which he had previously been attended to by the notorious Rascher. The Irishman had been instructed to stay confined to bed for fourteen days. He was only in bed for a few days when the evacuation call came and he prepared for evacuation with the others. Before leaving, he resolved to attempt to determine if there were any British prisoners in the main camp. Perhaps recalling the communications from Sergeant Llewellyn Edwards eighteen months earlier, he was anxious to provide a list to the War Office, should he survive. Most likely on the pretext of making a visit to the camp hospital in relation to his illness, he visited the main camp complex. It's not certain if he actually went into the hospital, but if he did, it would have been a dreadful spectacle. Now vastly overcrowded, it was packed with corpse-like, skeletal wrecks of humanity, infected with typhus, tuberculosis or dysentery, or a combination of these and other infectious diseases. The few prisoner doctors and nurses were overwhelmed and so many of their patients were dying that the crematorium couldn't cope.

McGrath managed to make contact with Pat O'Leary, president of the recently formed International (Prisoners) Committee. McGrath must have expected to meet a fellow Irishman, but O'Leary was an assumed name; his real name was Albert Guérisse, a Belgium who had led a resistance network in the south of France that specialised in assisting British airmen to escape. To increase his survival prospects after his capture, Guérisse adopted the persona of an Irish Canadian. He may have confided in McGrath about his true identity for, although McGrath included him in his list of British inmates, he named him as Albert O'Leary, his actual Christian name. In addition, he obtained the names of six other British servicemen interned in the main camp.[23]

Dachau, 26 April 2005

Finally, the wait was over. New vehicles had been secured to replace the buses destroyed. (The requisitioning of scarce vehicles and fuel indicates the priority afforded to this transport by the SS, something that could have only been decided at a high level within that organisation.) Stiller called out urgently to the German kin prisoners, 'Prepare to leave! Bring only what you can carry in your hands!'[24] These *Sippenhaft* prisoners joined with members of the rest of the *Prominenten* in a walk along the central avenue of the camp running between the rows of huts. As previously, thousands of ordinary camp prisoners, still awaiting evacuation themselves, gathered along the route staring in wonderment at the procession of evacuees, some in prison clothes, others in civilian and military attire, some well-dressed, and a few even exotically attired. Some carried their belongings in rudimentary sacks made from blankets. Metal pots, pans, bowls and cups clanged together making the parade look and sound like a gypsy caravan. Others carried suitcases and, ignoring Stiller's order, a wheel cart loaded with cases and bags was being pushed along. The SS guards forced a path through the mass of watching prisoners, curious about this strange parade of disparate and exotic evacuees.

The Schuschniggs walked together; Vera's beauty must have attracted attention, although, on this occasion, her husband, Kurt, appeared the more extravagantly attired in his Tyrolean outfit: knee britches and waist length jacket, and carrying little Sissi in his arms.[25] The Blums were close by, *mari et femme*, Léon walking with the aid of a stick managed to stride along, raising himself on his toe with each step.[26] Both Schuschnigg and Blum were recognised by some of the onlookers. Their names were spoken and news of their presence circulated. Arms were raised in salute by many of the bystanders; some with clenched fist, others, embarrassingly, perhaps out of habit, with a Fascist-style open hand, presumably directed at Schuschnigg. A few proudly called out their nationality and some of the *Prominenten* responded in like manner. It was a terse, but emotional exchange; no one could be sure they would ever see their homeland again. As Léon Blum walked through the ranks of these desperate and emaciated prisoners, no doubt hearing calls from his own countrymen, he tried hard to control his emotions; 'the heart must steel itself or break. I felt mine was about to break.'[27]

Passing through the main Dachau gate they caught glimpses of a train at a halting not far from a number of parked army buses and trucks which they were about to board. Schuschnigg had been told earlier by a Czech SS guard of dreadful scenes when train wagons arrived full of the corpses of mostly Jewish prisoners evacuated from camps to the east. Schuschnigg had told the Blums about this and, as they waited to embark on the buses, Janot attempted to see for herself. It was now dusk and as she moved through the shadows to approach the wagons, a search light illuminated her and she was warned to go back by SS guards.[28] It is perhaps better that she didn't get to see the nightmarish scene. Earlier that day, a train arrived pulling scores of open boxcars each crammed full of prisoners. They had been on route for eighteen days with little food or water. When the side walls were opened, the skeletal remains of about two thousand prisoners were revealed. Some bodies fell to the ground; a few souls, barely alive, managed to crawl away to expire almost immediately. The bodies were left to rot where they had fallen.[29]

It was midnight before the convoy started moving. The few remaining buses were supplemented by army transport trucks. All were overcrowded. Those lucky enough to find a seat were crushed together and obliged to remain in contorted positions; many of the men standing in the truck had to keep their head bent to avoid bumping against the metal struts holding up the canvas covering. Payne Best entered a bus alongside Prince Frederick Leopold, but was ordered off by Stiller because Stevens was already on board and the order to keep them apart, although now nonsensical, was still being enforced.[30] As Payne Best climbed onto the lorry, he was followed by Vassily Kokorin. Payne Best introduced him to the other Russians – he hadn't met them previously – and an excited Russian dialogue commenced. No room could be found for some 'kin prisoners' and they were marched away on foot. They joined thousands of ordinary prisoners who were now being marched out of Dachau. The convoy was held up as column after column marched past, some women and children among them. A break in the ranks finally allowed the buses and trucks to move on. For mile after mile they passed columns of prisoners being force marched to an undetermined location. Fey von Hassell, one of the 'kin' prisoners, described the dreadful scene she witnessed from her bus window:

Thin and worn out, they lurched along in their wooden clogs. Some of the prisoners were too weak to walk any distance, and I could see several of them on their hands and knees. The guards would go over and shout at them, poking them with their rifles. If they couldn't get up, they were shot through the back of the neck.[31]

Whatever discomfort the special prisoners experienced in their overcrowded vehicles was put in perspective by these awful sights.

One special prisoner who had accompanied some of the *Prominenten* from Buchenwald to Dachau was no longer with them. On the day of the departure of the last of the group, Sigmund Rascher, the evil doctor of Dachau, was executed. Himmler would not have wanted his association with his murderous experiments to become known.[32]

Three days after the *Prominenten* left, on 29 April, units of the American army liberated Dachau Concentration Camp. Appalled and maddened by what they found there, they summarily shot twenty-eight SS guards.[33]

CHAPTER TWELVE

COOK'S MUSICAL TOUR

Reichenau Camp, Innsbruck, 27 April 1945

A third convoy of buses arrived in Reichenau carrying mostly kin prisoners, relatives of those implicated in the 20 July 1944 attempt to kill Hitler. Among them was Alexander von Stauffenberg, the elder brother of Clause von Stauffenberg who had been executed for his leading role in the affair. Accompanying Alexander and other members of his family was a young woman, Fey von Hassell, a daughter of the former German ambassador to Italy who had also been executed. Fey, like all the others present on this convoy, had been arrested under the *Sippenhaft* laws for no reason other than the fact a relative had been suspected of involvement in an anti-Hitler conspiracy. Her experience was particularly harrowing as she had her two young sons snatched from her and she had no idea of their fate. Alexander and Fey, in their shared grief, had become close and had fallen in love. Their story is described in Addendum III.

Another young woman arriving with the kin prisoners was to provide some sparkle to the entourage in the days ahead. Isa von Vermehren was arrested along with her father and mother when her brother, a member of the opposition within the *Abwehr*, defected to the British in Istanbul. Before her arrest she had worked as a cabaret artist in Berlin, singing and accompanying herself on the accordion. In that role, she had become a German celebrity, having recorded a number of popular songs and starred in films.

The special prisoners were now gathered together in spring sunshine in the square in the Riechenau camp. It was an incongruously jolly gathering given the grim location. Affectionate greetings were exchanged among those who had been separated during their earlier moves from camp to camp. Precious tobacco was shared and experiences were exchanged with new acquaintances. Each sought news of the war and information about imprisoned relatives and friends. Isa Vermehren was greatly cheered to learn from Sydney Dowse that her parents were still alive and in relatively good health. They had been placed in the same *Sonderlager* in Sachsenhausen as the British, and although it was forbidden to fraternise with prisoners in other sections of the compound, Dowse had managed to make contact by communicating with them from under the window of their hut.[1] Isa was, in turn, able to tell Peter Churchill that his 'wife' was still alive. Vermehren had earlier been in Ravensbruck, a concentration camp mainly for women where Odette was also held. The Frenchwoman was detained under a false name, but her 'Churchill' identity had become known to the other prisoners. Vermehren, though, had no direct contact with her and suggested Churchill talk to Baron von Flügge, who had actually seen her. Von Flügge was the philosophical old gentleman who had accompanied the British airmen and their Irish orderlies on the journey to Dachau. Churchill approached him with a photograph of Odette, but the old man didn't recognise her at first. Churchill asked him to look again. 'Yes, yes ... It might be she ... People can change so much in prison ... Forgive me my dear Churchill.'[2] A far from reassured Churchill took his leave.

In the square, linguistic groups formed, babbling away in German, English, French, Italian, Greek, Hungarian, Russian and other tongues. They were enjoying a level of freedom of assembly unprecedented during their imprisonment. The SS guards didn't interfere, but wandered away to confer with each other, unsure of how to react to the changing circumstances. It was apparent to the assembled prisoners that there was a perceptible change in the power relationship between them and their minders. But, ominously, a new and dour contingent of about twenty SS guards had arrived with the kin prisoners to complement the thirty under the command of Stiller. Led by Lieutenant Ernst Bader, they were composed of SS men believed to have been *Einzsatzgruppen*, members of SS execution squads who had carried out mass murders of Jews, Poles and others considered *untermenschen* behind the front lines in the east. Why, the special prisoners must have wondered, would such hardened killers be assigned to guard them? Many of the younger men and women were, however, distracted, relishing the unusual experience of being in the company of the opposite sex. Among the kin prisoners there were a number of girls and women. For most of the male prisoners, it was the first time since their captivity that they had been in the company of attractive women.

One blonde German woman was attracting particular attention. Her name was Heidel Nowakowski, although all knew her simply as Heidi. Nobody knew for sure who she was or why she was among the special prisoners. She claimed to have worked for an Allied intelligence service, but nobody believed her. It was rumoured that she had been the mistress of an SS officer who may have been arrested. Payne Best disliked her, describing her as a 'short, fair, thickset girl in her early twenties who, but for her stature, might have posed as a model for a youthful Germania'.[3] Bertram James was even more dismissive, seeing her as having the 'nacht oder nie ['tonight or never'] air of a former night club hostess'.[4] Harry Day was less unkind, describing her as a 'classic blonde bombshell'.[5] Her presence certainly had the potential to be incendiary. Heidi was believed to have been the lover, while in confinement, of the recently executed Sigmund Rascher. Regardless of her past association, her current availability made her the subject of much attention. Vassily Kokorin was besotted by her and followed her around like a lapdog. But it soon became obvious that she was looking for a more reliable protector and had set her sights on Captain Ray van Wymeersch, the Free French RAF pilot who had co-signed Spence's 'confession' with Peter Churchill. She wasn't, it seems, the only one to look longingly at the Frenchman. If Harry Day's reminiscences were accurate, someone else was casting admiring glances towards van Wymeersch. The Wing Commander told his biographer, 'the attractive wife of an extremely prominent (Prominentent) had fallen much in love with him'.[6] This could only have been Vera Schuschnigg, although he may have been mistaken and, in any event, there was no suggestion of any impropriety.

Most of the womenfolk and the older males thoroughly disliked Heidi; Isa Vermehren, described her as a 'most unpleasant young lady' and suspected her of being a spy who was 'clever enough to ply her noble profession in the interest of two sides at the same time'.[7] However, one of the older women took a more sympathetic approach to the 'blonde bombshell'. Mrs Heberlein, the Spanish–Irish wife of the former German Ambassador to Spain, tried to shield her from unwanted male attention.[8] It can reasonably be assumed that Kokorin would not have been the only fly to be swatted away by the redoubtable Heberlein. Heidi wasn't of course the only female object of desire. We can only guess at the reaction of Cushing, Walsh and other testosterone-fuelled males at finding themselves in the presence of a number of young attractive women among the *Sippenhaft*. However, most of these girls were well chaperoned by their relatives. All of these families were of aristocratic pedigree and weren't going to let standards slip, not even in the straitened circumstances they found themselves in.

Sidney Dowse and Bertram James, both handsome young airmen, were likely to have elicited admiring glances from some of the young women present, particularly the tall, blond Dowse who had some German antecedents. Their clothing wouldn't have made much of an impression though; years of wear and alterations for their many escape attempts made their RAF uniforms unrecognisable as such. They were stained and holed and, as observed by Isa Vermehren, Dowse wore 'a particularly hideous brown pants and a too short, too small dark blue jacket'.[9]

Vermehren's disapproval of Heidi's assumed lax moral standards may have had been connected to her religiosity. This would not have been readily apparent to her new friends, for it was known that she had worked as a cabaret artist in Berlin. However, she too was from a privileged background, being part of a liberal Protestant family, although she had converted to Catholicism as an adult. During her solitary confinement in Buchenwald, she had experienced episodes of mystical exhilaration. In the Innsbruck camp, she described herself as 'dazzled and intoxicated' by a new found sense of freedom which she attributed to a spiritual presence.[10] To celebrate, she decided to uncase her accordion and commence an improvised *Platzkoncert*. Cushing, never needing any excuse for a singsong, joined in enthusiastically as did the other members of the 'Sonderlager choir'. Vermehren felt that the occasion 'blended the international gathering together' in a prescient imagining of European unity.[11]

Léon Blum's thoughts were darker. In typical florid mode, he categorised the assembled group as representing for their captors,'the filtered deposited residue of the most hated opponents, the most detested adversaries, the subjects and vassals most gravely suspected of treason. We formed the last infantry, the last battalion of enemies and hostages'.[12] Blum's musings were more than kind to many of those present. Only he and Janot, as Jews, socialists and democrats, matched that description, while others, like Philip of Hesse, Hjalmar Schacht, Fritz Thyssen and some of the German generals had been deeply immersed in the Nazi establishment before circumstances, or Hitler's paranoia, made them adversaries.

There was much speculation about whether this was the final destination for the group, or if they were, as some still maintained, destined for an Alpine redoubt. The Brenner Pass, the route into the Italian Alps, was visible from the Innsbruck camp and the prisoners gloomily watched Allied bombing raids on its heights. This would make for a dangerous journey should the rumour of their move in that direction prove true. Hinko Dragic had linked up with two fellow Yugoslavs, one of whom ventured that 'the war could go on and we could be here for months'. Wilhelm Visentainer, the former circus clown who accompanied the group, provided him with some cynical reassurance: 'Don't worry; they will shoot us before that.'[13] Gallows humour, maybe, but that thought had occurred to all. Why else were they being transported to the isolated fastness of the Alps in the company of known assassins?

That evening, just before sunset, the group was told to prepare for another move. This time five buses were awaiting them. Stiller, still determined to separate Payne Best and Stevens, asked the former, who had seated himself beside McGrath, to move to another bus and allow Stevens to take his place. Payne Best objected to being moved and was most likely supported by McGrath who had had more than enough of Stevens's company. To both men's relief, Stiller backed down and moved Stevens instead. It was a small but significant victory. Whereas previously an order was an order, now the SS man's approach was more accommodating and no gesture was made to his holstered pistol. Stevens had earlier suggested to Stiller that he should deliver them to the Allies to avoid future consequences for himself. Although a suggestion of this nature would have been a punishable impudence, Stiller's response on this occasion was a thoughtful, 'Let's see what we come across on the road.'[14] Stiller was obviously weighing up the balance of risks involved. He may have felt confident about a positive reaction by his own men to the overture, but the arrival of Bader and his group of hardened killers changed the equation.

Isa Vermehren, still carrying her accordion, decided to forgo the company of her fellow kin prisoners and boarded what she called 'the Englishmen's bus'. From her earlier musical encounter, she gauged that the journey in this bus would prove to be a livelier affair. As she later described the scene: 'I saw about me in this bus everyone with a cheerful happy go lucky confidence, and under the guidance of Cushing we did the first three hours of the trip with music …'[15]

The convoy of buses moved out of the environs of Innsbruck, preceded by a SS motorcyclist, with a truck carrying most of the guards following to the rear. They began the long climb towards the Brenner Pass in the dark. To avoid being targeted by Allied aircraft, they drove with masked headlights, providing only a glimmer of light to guide them, a perilous precaution as the driver's navigated hairpin bends fringed by barely visible precipices. The buses were overcrowded and overloaded. The guards had crates of material, some of which had been transferred from the accompanying truck to the buses. There was consternation in one of the buses when the prisoners realised that one of the crates contained hand grenades. The road to the Brenner was rutted and a jolt or crash could cause them all to be blown to smithereens. And the prisoners would have asked themselves why the SS would place them on the bus unless they wished to access them quickly. A bus blown up by grenades could be made to look like an Allied air attack.[16]

The buses, overloaded as they were, struggled to maintain momentum on the steeper inclines. One broke down, possibly overheated, just as they reached the Brenner Pass. As a result, the convoy remained parked at a halting spot at the Italian–Austrian frontier for much of the night. It was early morning and now quite cold at the high altitude. In the darkness, the occupants of the buses became gradually aware of a surrounding landscape of utter devastation. The shattered remains of block houses that had hosted anti-aircraft guns and the rubble of other destroyed buildings and railway works lay all around. Against this background they saw the silhouettes of a continuous stream of individuals, many hauling belongings in prams and handcarts. There were even some children among them. Ramshackle carts were being pulled by horses or donkeys, even some cattle and pigs were included in the exodus.[17] The slowly moving horde were Italians making their way home from a Reich now in its final days, each traveller with his or her own terrible tale of forced exile. Ruggero Zangrandi, an Italian political prisoner who spent twenty months in German prisons, described their plight:

Their story became entwined with that of hundreds of others, blended and altered until it became the single story of thousands of Italians who were advancing by every possible means – often on foot – from the four corners of Germany towards a single point – the Brenner Pass. During the months of their journey, during the weeks of forced halts between one major point and another and during the sleepless nights, they, like everyone else, had one great anxiety – the dread of not making it. Although it was now near, unreasonable and insistent hopes and fears made these men feel that the goal was unattainable, antagonistic, treacherous. Failure was no longer due to the opposing will of other men; it was now a matter of chance, of the vastness of the migration in which ones individual destiny, even if different from the others, was submerged-practically annihilated – as by a flood.[18]

Those trudging on foot over the Pass were pitiful and exhausted. The extent of their suffering in Germany possibly exceeded that of many of the occupants of the buses. But they had a singular advantage over the prisoner hostages: they were free.

When the SS guards descended from the buses and truck to confer, the prisoners feared that an air raid was being anticipated, but none materialised that night. The railway alongside the Brenner Pass had been intensively bombed to hinder German transports of supplies and reinforcements to the Italian front, and to prevent the anticipated build-up of German forces in an Alpine redoubt. But fortunately, the Allies had, shortly before, ceased these attacks in order to redirect their air resources in support of a major offensive in northern Italy. As the guards were preoccupied, some prisoners disembarked from their bus and wandered unchallenged about the halt. Day and Churchill, ever on the look-out for escape opportunities, conferred about their chances of disappearing. They decided that, as it was now certain that they were bound for the Italian Alps, it would be best to await opportunities that might present when they were nearer allied lines. Stiller had noticed their *tete á tete* and, walking past, he turned to Day and remarked sarcastically, 'I hope you had an interesting walk, Wing Commander.'[19]

In the 'English Bus' those that had remained on board were still enjoying their sing-song. Their journey into the Alps had taken on the atmosphere of a 'Bank holiday outing to Brighton' as one of the British observed.[20] Or of 'a Cook's tour company,' as Isa Vermehren described it.[21] In the parked bus, she was accompanying Cushing and others in a rendition of 'Boulevard of Broken

Dreams', which had become something of a theme song among this group. The song, written for the first Hollywood film version of *Moulin Rouge*, was popular before the war and it is likely Vermehren had it in her repertoire when performing in Berlin nightclubs. It is a haunting tune with the lyrics telling of the disconsolate existence of a Parisian prostitute. The same song had been sung outside the gates of Dachau, but on that occasion the tone was slow, sonorous and nostalgic.[22] This time the singing had become frenetic and exuberant, perhaps reflecting the accordion player's mood. As performed in the film, the performance concludes with a fast tango reprise. It was presumably at this point, with Vermehren vigorously accompanying him on her accordion, when Cushing frantically began: 'beating out his rhythm on everything that came to hand – suitcases, window panes, saucepans, the heads of the men in front of him, and a variety of other hard objects, but also managed to substitute to a great extent for the missing instruments with an inimitably fine "Babababababa".'[23] How the passing stream of humanity, cold, hungry and exhausted from their long climb up to the Brenner, reacted to hearing the muffled sound of musical revelry coming from the stationary bus can only be imagined.

The singing angered Kurt Schuschnigg. He entered the 'English' bus, scornfully demanding to know 'How can you sing in this grave hour?'[24] It was an anxious time and he possibly wasn't alone in considering the singing unseemly. Irrespective, as an old-fashioned conservative and devout Catholic, he would have disapproved of songs about prostitution. For the singers though, it was their attempt at 'whistling in the dark'; a way of coping with nervous anticipation. Cushing, however, tended always to live in the moment. It wasn't bravado on his part, but his approach to life in general. And his wild exuberance on this occasion would have been further stimulated by his new-found musical relationship with the talented Vermehren, a vivacious young woman. Nevertheless, Schuschnigg's intervention had the desired effect; the spell was broken and silence prevailed as the convoy moved on.

During the descent into Italy, the prisoners began to doze; many had not had a good night's sleep since they left Dachau due to their being attacked by bed bugs during their stay in the Reichenau camp. A few remained awake, feigning sleep while listening to the conversation of the driver and one of his fellow SS men. The two were discussing the allied bombing raids on Berlin when one of them turned to glare at the apparently sleeping passengers and exclaimed, 'If Hitler's killed in the Berlin bombings I'll mow these swine down like ninepins.' On another bus, Bogislaw von Bonin and Wilhelm von Flügge overheard an even more alarming conversation. They listened as one SS guard asked another 'What are we going to do about those who still have to be liquidated?' The response began 'Well we were ordered to put the bomb under the bus either just before or just after the …' The rest of the conversation could not be deciphered by the two eavesdroppers, but it was enough to cause them to believe that some or all of them were likely to be killed unless they could somehow prevent it.[25]

CHAPTER THIRTEEN

A TROUBLED REDOUBT

28 April 1945

Dawn was breaking when the convoy of buses came to a halt. The prisoners were permitted to alight to exercise and relieve themselves while sentries took up position along the road. Stiller and Bader and other members of the SS gathered in animated conversation out of earshot of the prisoners. Their motorcyclist, Fritz, who had scouted the road ahead, was among them and it became obvious that there was a problem. It emerged that the accommodation that had been intended for the prisoners, a hotel high up in the Pustertal Valley, was not available as it was already occupied by some *Wehrmacht* General Staff officers.[1] The SS were clearly at a loss about what to do; they could no longer make contact with headquarters and the vehicles were virtually out of fuel. They had orders to take care of the prisoners while not, under any circumstances, allowing them to fall into enemy hands. Everyone was hungry and tired, including the guards. Stiller, Bader and some of their men decided to walk to the nearby village of Niederdorf to forage for food.

Taking advantage of the confusion and the absence of the SS officers, some of the hostages remained outside the buses. For the first time since their captivity, there was growing optimism that they might soon be free. Contributing to their hopes of liberation was the fact that they had left the Reich and were now in Italy, although it may have surprised some of them to discover that the local population was German-speaking.

Groups again began to coalesce. The German military prisoners converged, with Payne Best joining them. After his five and a half years in captivity, he felt more at ease speaking German than English. The RAF contingent remained close to their *éminence gris*, Harry Day. They were joined by Peter Churchill who was by now an integral part of this group, likewise, his namesake, Jack Churchill. John McGrath was probably on the margins. He was still getting to know his fellow officers and, as the only regular army officer, and, to boot, an Irishman bereft of a public-school background, he was something of an outsider.

The Italians in the group were split between the followers of Sante Garibaldi, which included Colonel Ferrero and the two orderlies, and those with a Fascist background which included Mario Badoglio, the son of Marshal Badoglio who had overthrown Mussolini. He would have been an acceptable colleague, if only for his father's belated move against Mussolini, but there were two other Italians with no claim to political redemption. Tullio Tamburini and Eugenio Appollonio were, until recently, police chiefs of the Republic of Salo, and their inclusion within the group was as surprising as it was suspicious. The small French contingent stayed close to the Blums and the Russians, Danes, Austrians, Greeks, Yugoslavs and Hungarians, had their own national alliances. The largest national group, after the inclusion of the kin hostages, were the Germans, among whom the former generals formed the leading cadre.

They were all now, geographically, within the mooted German redoubt: an alpine fortress – *Alpenfestung* – within which it was believed the Nazis would make their last stand. Unknown to the prisoners, the convoy had passed near the Oetztal Valley, where in underground tunnels constructed by slave labour, the construction of the first jet engine fighter plane, one of Hitler's miracle weapons, was continuing. The Alpine terrain was ideal for defenders. The high jagged peaks, often cloud-covered, would deter low-altitude strategic bombing and the forested hills would provide cover for defenders and prevent the Allies from utilising their advantage in tanks and heavy artillery.

Natural features alone would not have been enough to secure the redoubt so, in June 1944, Himmler belatedly ordered surveys to identify suitable sites for defence fortifications.[2] Goebbels's propaganda ministry later circulated stories of a vast military complex being installed in the Tyrol which became the source of a number of articles in Western newspapers and magazines. Franz Hofer, the Tyrolean Gaulleiter, desperately wanted the fortifications to be constructed and he had written to Martin Bormann in November 1944 quoting a report from the US which warned of high casualty figures and the risk that 'East–West tension will become visible if the war drags on too long.'[3] Hofer knew that Bormann and Hitler would be encouraged by such reports; they were convinced that, given enough time, tensions within the alliance would lead to open conflict.

Work did finally begin on an extension to the Hofer Line, a fortification intended to protect a new railway line due for completion in June 1945 that would have improved access between Austria and Northern Italy.[4] However, the redoubt never became a reality. It was a fable designed to convince the Allies that the war could be continued indefinitely, and it worked: Eisenhower diverted much of his resources south to counter a supposed build-up of fanatical Nazi forces in the Alps.[5] No significant Alpine fortifications were ever constructed. Hitler dithered and only gave sanction for construction work on 20 April 1945 while celebrating what was to be his last birthday. This was far too late to have any impact. The realisation that the last redoubt was nothing more than an aspiration only emerged at the end of the war but, before then, rumours about an impending Alpine last stand were widely believed, not least within German ranks, and it was presumably for this reason that the *Prominenten* had been transported there. The South Tyrol, into which the *Prominenten* had landed, had the added attraction of having an ethnic German population.

The sudden appearance of the *Prominenten* on that cold, wet morning caused excitement among the waking inhabitants of Niederdorf, the nearby village. Among the first to be recognised was Kurt Schuschnigg, not surprisingly given he was dressed in traditional Tyrolean attire and would have been well known as the former Chancellor of an Austria to which most of the German-speaking population still felt allegiance. Most would have known that he was a native of the region, having been born near Lake Garda in the nearby Trento province. He even spoke the local German dialect.[6]

The German military prisoners, accompanied by Payne Best, decided to walk to the village, brushing aside only token objection from the remaining SS guards. As they were passing the Post Office in the village which served as a *Wehrmacht* communication post, General Georg Thomas's name was called out. It happened that the officer in charge of the small local garrison was an old friend and was astonished to see Thomas in this remote location. This chance meeting was to have significant consequences, as it opened up the prospect of the *Prominenten* securing *Wehrmacht* protection against the designs of the SS.

Sante Garibaldi and Davide Ferrero didn't head for the village initially. Instead, they wandered off in the direction of a nearby railway crossing. At a gatekeeper's cabin they got into conversation with the occupant who, on learning who they were, disclosed the fact that he was an NCO in an Italian partisan group. A meeting was quickly arranged with the local leadership. The partisans populated the forests overlooking the town and had, most likely, been observing events, curious to know who these new arrivals were.

These partisans were part of the Garibaldi Brigade, a largely communist partisan movement named in honour of Sante's grandfather, Giuseppe Garibaldi, the hero of the *Risorgimento*, the nineteenth-century struggle for Italian liberation and unity. They were overjoyed to meet the scion of their hero and promptly appointed him their leader. A meeting was arranged in the small railway gatekeeper's house and Harry Day, Jack Churchill and Peter Churchill were invited to attend. When they arrived they found, much to their delight, a table containing the ample remains of a feast of roast lamb to be washed down with wine. Garibaldi, still in his concentration camp attire, chaired the meeting involving the British officers and the local partisan leadership wearing their red bandanas. Peter Churchill, who was fluent in Italian, acted as translator.[7] The partisans offered to attack the SS and free the hostages that very day. Three days previously, on 25 April – this date is now commemorated as Liberation Day in Italy – an insurrection, timed to coincide with an Allied offensive, had been declared against the Germans and their Italian fascist allies. Already, Milan had been liberated and the local partisan group were no doubt anxious to make their contribution to the looming victory. Jack Churchill was enthusiastic about joining in the attack, but Day advised caution. He feared that if the SS were attacked they would turn their guns on the defenceless women and children among the *Sippenhaft*. It was decided, therefore, to defer the attack until their safety could be assured. It is noteworthy that there were no representatives of the local village community present at the meeting involving the partisans. The inhabitants of Niederdorf were predominantly *Tedeschi* – Germans – who were suspect in Italian eyes.

Meanwhile, most of the German and Austrian contingent among the *Prominenten* had walked into Niederdorf and made themselves known to the villagers. Anton Ducia, a railway engineer, was sent for. He had been appointed logistics officer by the German authorities and one of his tasks was to secure lodgings for visiting army, SS or other Nazi dignitaries. However, he was also secretly a member of a South Tyrol resistance group, recently formed from within the German-speaking community.[8] Schuschnigg, accompanied by Payne Best and some of the German officers, met with Ducia, who informed them of his role in the opposition and assured them he would do what he could to ensure their safety and eventual liberation.[9] With the active support of the local Parish Priest, Joseph Brugger, he then set about making arrangements for the feeding and housing of all the members of the group.

These separate Italian and South Tyrolean resistance contacts were to lead to some indecision, and division, about to whom the hostages should ally themselves. Although most of the *Prominenten* knew little of it at the time, there were complex tensions then existing, both within and between the Italian- and German-speaking communities and the choice of protector could feed into these frictions. To understand the cause of these conflicts, it is necessary to know something of the early twentieth-century history of the province.

The South Tyrol or, to give it its Italian name, Alto Adige, is a place of great natural beauty. Snow-capped Alpine peaks tower over fertile valleys and rustic settlements. In late April 1945, though, the weather remained wintery and the mood too was far from tranquil. The population of the province was divided by language, politics and nationality. It had been part of the Austrian Tyrol until the end of the First World War, after which it was transferred to Italy as a reward for its participation in that war against the Axis powers. For the Italians, their claim to the territory had military and political significance. The Brenner Pass was the most important Alpine pass linking Italy and Austria who had fought in two wars within living memory. Politically, the Italian government needed to justify their participation in the First World War by way of territorial gains. The majority German-speaking population of the province, not surprisingly, resented being incorporated into Italy against their will.

Mussolini implemented a policy of forced Italianisation on the population. German was systematically abolished as a mode of instruction in schools, although, under pressure from the Vatican, an exception was made for religious instruction. German teachers were transferred south while Italians took their place. Families were required to use the Italian versions for their names. Only Italian could be used in state institutions, including the courts. German newspapers were suppressed, place names were changed, local mayors were replaced by Rome appointed *podestá* and the *Deutscher Verband*, an organisation representing the German-speaking population, was outlawed. New industrial jobs in the capital Bozen, renamed Bolzano, and other towns were largely filled by migrants from Southern Italy. The result was hatred of Italians and Fascism among the German-speaking community and a growing support for pan-German nationalism and Nazism. Underground Nazi-inspired youth organisations sprang up and, following Hitler's rise to power in Germany, a Nazi party, the *Völkischer Kampfring Südtirols* (VKS) was founded, aimed at converting the people of the South Tyrol to National Socialism.[10] At this time, in the mid-1930s, relations between Germany and Italy were strained and there were street fights between VKS Nazis and Italian Fascist squads. After one such confrontation, Mussolini praised his *Squadrismo* for their role in affirming Italian rule 'in a region where Germans were to be treated as abusive guests'.[11]

Hopes that Germany would come to the aid of the German-speaking population were to be dashed. Hitler, even before his rise to power, desired an alliance with Mussolini, and to achieve this he was prepared to renounce any claim to the South Tyrol.[12] The two dictators reached a formal agreement in June 1939 on the future of the province that put an end to hopes of absorption into a greater Germany. Under an agreement concluded between the two countries, the German-speaking population were to be given an unenviable choice: be relocated to a new homeland in the Reich, or remain and accept Italianisation and possible relocation within Italy. The VKS, ever obedient to Hitler, was forced into a U-turn; rather than demanding that the territory be absorbed into the Reich, the people were now to be encouraged to transport themselves to an undetermined territory inside of it. Instead of '*Blut und Boden*' ('blood and soil'), the call now was '*Blud oder Boden*' ('blood or soil').[13]

The issue was hugely divisive. To opt to stay was depicted as a betrayal of German identity, a rejection of Hitler and Nazism. This was far from a democratic plebiscite. Individuals were required to state whether they personally planned to stay or leave by submitting a form with their name on it.[14] The process lasted months and immense pressure was put on individuals and families to opt to leave. True to type, friendly persuasion was not the favoured approach of the home-grown Nazis or their now Italian Fascist allies. Those opposed to leaving were harassed and terrorised. The leadership of the opposition came mainly from parish clergy, although not from their bishop:

Johannes Geisler, Bishop of Bressanone (Brixon), was a German nationalist sympathetic to National Socialism.[15]

Eighty-six per cent of the German-language population – 185,000 people – opted to leave. Although the war prevented the scheme being fully put into effect, a tearful exodus of 75,000 did take place. The process, combined with the terror tactics used by the Nazis – some of the opposition ended up in Dachau – left deep divisions within the German-speaking community. It was a civil conflict; although caused by the machinations of Mussolini and Hitler, the agents of persecution were local. Like all such intra-communal conflicts, enmities persisted: 'Families were torn apart, best friends parted for good, children turned against parents, siblings against each other.'[16]

Events led to the South Tyrol being ruled by a Nazi administration from 1943. Following the dismissal and arrest of Mussolini by his own Fascist Council, and a subsequent armistice between the Allies and the new Italian regime led by Marshal Pietro Badoglio, the German army occupied Northern Italy. The South Tyrol was declared to be part of a German military zone; *Operationszone Alpenvoreland* ('operational zone of the Alpine Foreland').[17] Italian administrators were dismissed and German language and customs were restored. Franz Hoffer, a leading Austrian Nazi, was made *Gauleiter* of a unified North (Austrian) and South Tyrol. Most welcomed the German military occupation, for it promised to free them from the oppression of the Italian regime. German and Italian community tensions increased as old scores were settled.[18]

Though communal tensions remained, German military rule became unpopular within both communities. Conscription into the German forces began for South Tyrolean racially acceptable males of military age. Many deserted or hid. According to one study, 276 South Tyrolean *Volksdeutsche* ('people of German race') were sentenced to death for desertion.[19] To the occupying German forces the remaining German population were suspect, composed as they were of those who had not resettled within the Reich. The Italian population were also considered traitorous because of their government's desertion of Germany in 1943. Arrests of suspected anti-Nazis from both communities took place and the small Jewish population were rounded up and sent to a concentration camp in Bozen/Balzano and onward for extermination in Auschwitz.

By the time the *Prominenten* entered the South Tyrol, it was, in effect, annexed to the Reich, though this was *de facto* only, as it was still officially part of Italy. This was a fig leaf for Mussolini's diminished authority. (The Germans had rescued him from imprisonment and installed him as head of their puppet regime, the Social Republic at Saló.) There were now two Italian regimes and three fighting forces: Mussolini's not unsubstantial fascist militias; the reconstituted Royal Italian army, now in alliance with the Allies; and the disparate bands of partisans, tenuously united under a Committee for National Liberation (CLN). The largest partisan group was the Garibaldini whose red bandanas signified their claimed past links to Giuseppe Garibaldi's nineteenth-century 'Red Shirts' and to their current Communist orientation. Other partisan groups represented different political philosophies.

As the Germans retreated into the Alpine foothills, the partisans focused most of their attention on Mussolini's fascist troops. They set up remote road blocks and, after relieving the Germans of their arms, generally let them pass. Not so with the Italian Fascists. It was at such a road block near Lake Como on 27 April, the day before the *Prominenten* reached Niederdorf, that Mussolini was discovered in a German army truck near Lake Como. He was executed the next day and his body was later left hanging upside down in Milan along with that of his mistress Clara Petacci and eighteen other Fascist notables. The macabre display was revenge for similar exhibitions of the bodies of executed partisans by the Fascists at that spot.[20]

It was becoming obvious that the German army and their Italian allies were in full retreat and that the war was almost over. Consequently, the thoughts of the warring factions were becoming focused on their post-war future. The German-speaking Tyrolean resistance, represented by Anton Ducia in Niederdorf, hoped for a post-war settlement that would result in their reintegration into Austria. Their resistance activities, even if belated, could add credibility to this aspiration. They judged that the unexpected arrival of the *Prominenten* could work to their advantage. They saw that there were among them persons of stature who might influence the content of a post-war settlement. The generosity of the people of the Pustertal Valley might well be repaid. That such thoughts are likely to have occurred to their leaders does not imply that the hospitality of the ordinary people shown to the prisoners was self-serving; those who opened their homes, hotels and larders were, by and large, oblivious to power politics.

The Italian partisans had different interests. They had scores to settle with the fascists as well as the occupying German forces. The uneasy CLN partisan alliance was unlikely to survive the peace. For the communist leadership there was a class struggle to be won. But on one thing the various Italian forces were agreed; there would be no surrender of Italian territory. Their sacrifices – about 63,000 Italians died in the struggle – would not permit it.[21] The partisans, too, would also help to feed and protect the *Prominenten*, and its leadership may have also expected some benefit to accrue. But their attitude to the hostages was ambiguous at best. Some of the Germans among them had been enthusiastic supporters of the Nazis before falling into disfavour; the businessmen and aristocrats were never likely to be sympathetic to their cause; two of the Italians among them had been detested police chiefs in the Saló Republic before their arrest and some, at least, of the Soviet contingent were renegades and deserters from the Red Army, considered vile by the Italian communists. This contributed to the partisans' relationship with the *Prominenten* becoming fraught at times.

The SS guards also had reason to consider their best survival strategy. Should they submit themselves to the judgement of the victors, continue to fight, or take flight? As we have previously observed, Stiller was clearly examining his options. Accusations of crimes committed in Dachau, might, he hoped, be set against his protection of the lives of these important prisoners assigned to his care. They might even testify on his behalf. For Bader, and his contingent of SS guards, surrender was not an option. Their past as *Einsatzgruppen*, responsible for the murder of Slavic intellectuals, Jews, and others, allowed for no defence. Their only hope was to disappear, to merge into obscurity among the multitudes now on the move. Witnesses who knew of their past and could identify them, such as their present charges, were best eliminated. Their presence did not auger well for the *Prominenten's* survival prospects. Nor did their present location. The Nazis preferred to carry out mass killings outside of the Reich, in stateless territories with no recognised system of civil governance.[22] The South Tyrol was not part of the Reich, nor was it functionally part of the Salo Republic; it was a German military zone with no civil authority other than that of a handpicked and fanatical *Gauleiter*. No atrocity that the SS might perpetrate would, from a Nazi standpoint, breach any laws.

The *Prominenten* had to find a way to avoid such an eventually. For this they needed allies, but it was not clear whom – a beleaguered German army, the Tyrolean resistance or Italian partisans – would offer the best protection. Alternatively, they could attempt to make their own way to Allied lines. Such judgements could determine whether the hostages would survive or die under the shadow of the Dolomites.

CHAPTER FOURTEEN

NIEDERDORF

Niederdorf, or Villabassa, to give it its Italian name, is a pretty alpine village nestled in the Pustertal Valley located in the east of the South Tyrol close to the Austrian border. The village is flanked by forested hills with snow-capped peaks visible beyond. The domed church of St Stephan overlooks the village from an elevated position. The town hall in the central plaza is a handsome three-storey building. Hotel Bachmann, where many of the VIP prisoners resided, is situated near the north-eastern corner of the plaza.

28 April 1945

The village must have seemed initially to the arriving hostages to be untouched by the war, that is until they reached the railway station on the northern perimeter where they found evidence to the contrary. There, a little over a month before, a train loaded with ammunition was targeted in an Allied bombing raid. Twenty-two military personnel and five civilians were killed.[1] Most of the soldiers were young men from the locality drafted into the South Tyrolean Security Service established by the Nazi *Gauleiter*, Franz Hofer, in 1943.

Despite this tragedy, the townspeople proved to be generous hosts to all, including the British airmen. Some kin families were taken into the homes of villagers who provided them with a change of clothes and washing facilities. The parish priest, Josef Brugger, played host to the clerics and some others in his large parochial house. He and Tony Ducia arranged for all to be fed in stages in the village. The real VIPs dined in the Hotel Bachmann. This group included the Blums and Schuschniggs, the Greeks and Hungarians and some of the

German officers along with Payne Best and John McGrath. Peter Churchill dined with General Halder and his wife, Fabian von Schlabrendorff and Wilhelm von Flügge and others in the Goldener Stern. It was the first time in years that they had been served food in a restaurant. To enhance the pleasure, wine supplemented the meal. Bertram James described the meal as 'like manna from heaven'.[2] Somehow the villagers managed to feed over 180 people, prisoners and guards, a feat that would have used up much of their communal winter food reserves. A festive atmosphere prevailed, although there were cautious glances towards the SS guards, some of whom were getting progressively drunk. The parish priest encouraged the villagers to ply them with drink. 'Go ahead, go ahead, get them drunk,' he told the landlords.[3] He assumed that a comatose SS man could do no harm, but Martin Niemöller, who had more experience of the SS from his seven years in captivity, was not convinced. He warned that bouts of drinking often preceded executions. He told Stevens that he sensed 'a build up to a killing'.[4]

Payne Best approached Thyssen and Schacht with a proposal. He suggested that they attempt to bribe Stiller. He felt that the SS lieutenant was looking for a way out of his dilemma. The war was lost and he had to be concerned about his future prospects. It was known that he had orders not to allow the hostages to be rescued by the Allies, but mass murder was likely to result in his own subsequent execution. Payne Best proposed to the two wealthy Germans that they come up with the money for the bribe. He judged that 100,000 Swiss francs would be needed in exchange for the safe delivery of all the hostages to the Swiss frontier. The amount of money didn't seem to concern Thyssen or Schacht, but neither was prepared to put the proposal to Stiller, even when Payne Best offered to accompany them. The bribe was never proffered.[5]

General Thomas arrived late for his meal at the Hotel Bachmann, having been detained by his *Wehrmacht* acquaintance at the post office. He had conveyed to his army friend his fears that the SS guards intended to kill some or all of the group and the officer offered to help in any way he could. Thomas recounted this conversation to his table companions that included most of the German officers along with Payne Best. They discussed how they might take up the offer of assistance. The Englishman suggested that General Vietinghoff, the Commander of German forces in Italy, should be informed of their presence and asked to vouch for their safety. Colonel von Bonin disclosed the fact that

that he knew General Röttinger, second in command, and indicated that, if allowed the use of army communications, he would seek his protection.[6] Von Bonin presumably had made Röttinger's acquaintance when he served as Chief of the Operational Branch of the Army General Staff. Von Bonin, as an 'honour' prisoner, had been allowed to continue to wear his uniform, rank insignia and honours, including his swastika-embossed gold cross awarded for bravery in combat. His ambiguous prisoner status created uncertainty among the SS guards about how they should treat him. After their meal von Bonin and Thomas set off for the post office. The call was put through without difficulty. General Röttinger was not available to take the call, but his adjutant promised to pass on the request. What the two German officers in the post office in Niederdorf did not know was that Röttinger was at that time involved in a dramatic meeting in Bozen, in the office of the *Gauleiter*, Franz Hofer; a meeting that would determine the future of the war in Italy.

The talks involving General Karl Wolff and Allen Dulles of the OSS about a possible surrender of German forces in Italy had been resumed. Wolff had returned to Bozen following a meeting with Dulles in Berne and called all the senior staff to a meeting to brief them on developments. The meeting was attended by, among others, Vietinghoff; Röttinger; Rudolf Rahn, the German ambassador to Mussolini's Social Republic; and Hofer. Wolff reported that a surrender had been agreed and that two emissaries were being flown to Allied headquarters in Caserta, near Naples, to sign the necessary documents. The ceasefire was to come into effect on 3 May. General Vietinghoff knew that this was in the offing, but had asked for honourable ceremonial conditions to accompany to the handover of power. Wolff told him that the allies would agree to nothing other than unconditional surrender. Hofer, though, remained obstinately opposed. The *Gauleiter* refused to countenance any surrender terms that did not contain a commitment that the South Tyrol would be reunited with Austria. When told by Wolff that this was not possible, Hofer demanded that he be given the final say on all matters, military and political, in respect of South Tyrol. The generals knew that this was unobtainable and the meeting ended inconclusively.[7]

Hofer felt entitled to claim jurisdiction in regard to South Tyrol matters. Two weeks earlier, Hitler had appointed him Reich Defence Commissioner of the *Alpenfestung*. However, as he had no direct means to enforce his claim,

Hofer decided to appeal to Field Marshal Kesselring, the commander of the Western Front who was shortly to have the Italian theatre added to his command. The Field Marshal had commanded the Italian front until a few weeks previous and knew of Wolff's contacts with the Americans, but was told nothing about an unconditional surrender. Vietinghoff and Röttinger were summoned to Innsbruck by Kesselring and threatened with court martial. Kesselring had no authority over Wolff, but the SS General had faced a similar threat from Himmler ten days earlier.

Himmler, growing ever more concerned about Wolff's liaisons with the Americans, and badgered on the subject by Kaltenbrunner, had summoned Wolff to his headquarters in Hohenlychen, north of Berlin. There a confrontation took place, with Kaltenbrunner accusing Wolff of being treasonably involved in surrender negotiations. Himmler, however, avoided taking sides. Wolff was nevertheless worried, for he would have been aware that Kaltenbrunner had the ear of Hitler's influential secretary, Martin Bormann. In desperation, Wolff gambled: he proposed the three of them meet with Hitler in the Reich chancellery. Himmler declined to travel, but his two generals were driven in the same car to Berlin that night.

According to Wolff's account, when they both entered the conference room in the bunker, Hitler demanded to know why Wolff had disregarded his orders and begun talks with the enemy. Wolff was prepared for the challenge and referred the Führer to a conversation they had had in early February when he suggested that they seek contact with the Allies. Wolff explained that he left that meeting with the understanding that he had been given a clear hand to do this. Consequently, he was now happy to report that he had made contact with representatives of the US and Britain and awaited the Führer's instruction on how to proceed. Wolff's audaciousness seems to have shocked Kaltenbrunner into silence. Hitler mellowed, but left a decision until after he rested. After a tense few hours he approached Wolff and told him that he expected Western allies to fall out with Stalin shortly and that he would wait until that occurred and play one off against the other. Wolff was off the hook. In truth, the dark, broody, scar-faced Kaltenbrunner was always at a disadvantage against the blond, blue eyed and eloquent Wolff.[8]

In the Niederdorf post office, von Bonin and Thomas, who knew nothing of these events, were still discussing their own predicament when Stiller entered with one of his men. The SS transport leader had somehow learned of the plan to make contact with Röttinger and was not pleased about it. 'Don't you realise you are a prisoner?' he said, addressing von Bonin. 'Whatever your rank and honours, you cannot do as you like when you are in the hands of the SS.'[9] Von Bonin, in a tone that didn't hide his disdain, told Stiller that he was a fool if he didn't comprehend his altered position and promptly ordered him out of the building. Stiller glanced at the four *Wehrmacht* soldiers present, members of the small communications contingent, whose demeanour made it obvious that they sided with the colonel. After a momentary hesitation, the SS Transport Leader turned about and walked out with his attendant in tow.

Meanwhile, in the Hotel Bachmann, Payne Best and McGrath, having consumed the wine left over from dinner, decided to see if they could procure some more. Learning that there was wine to be had in the kitchen, they went downstairs to find two SS men well advanced in their mission to consume the hotel's entire stock of schnapps. Payne Best asked if they could join them. He was hoping to take advantage of the guard's inebriated state to see if he could extract information from them about Stiller and Bader's intentions. One of the two SS men present was the motor cycling, master sergeant known to the hostages only as Fritz. His companion, believed to have been one of Bader's men, was very drunk. Fritz began talking forlornly about his wife and children before becoming truculent, declaring that the war was all the fault of the Jews and that he would never be taken alive by the enemy. McGrath soon departed the company. He didn't have enough German to understand everything that was being said, but would have known enough to feel uncomfortable.

Payne Best persevered, telling Fritz what a good fellow he was and the compliment was returned. The two drank *Brüderschaft*, a ritual token of brotherhood requiring each to drink from the other's glass while crossing arms. Payne Best assured Fritz that he would put in a good word for him with the Allies. This provoked another angry outburst from Fritz who boasted about how many of the enemy he would kill if they tried to arrest him. When he calmed down he said, 'Yes, I know you are my friend and would help me if you were alive.' He then pulled a document from his pocket which, he indicated, contained orders for the execution of Payne Best and other members of the *Prominenten*. Payne Best tried to appeal to the man's better half, 'We have just drunk *Brüderschaft*; surely you don't intend to take part in killing me.' Fritz sadly assured him that he had to follow orders but, knowing from experience that this could be a messy business, as a friend, he was prepared to make sure Payne Best had a clean and instant end. To ensure this, he promised that he would personally shoot him in the back of the head. Fritz was referring to the infamous *Nackenschuss* for which he seemed proud of being an expert. Perhaps sensing that Payne Best was not entirely convinced of the generosity of his offer, Fritz decided on a demonstration. Clumsily removing his pistol from its holster, he asked his English friend to turn around. Payne Best declined, no doubt hoping Fritz would not be too upset at his unwillingness to rehearse his demise. Not apparently offended, Fritz turned and roused his by now near unconscious companion and asked him to help show the Englishman how the *Nackenschuss* is performed. The woken SS man looked around glassy eyed and muttered, 'Shoot them all down – bum-bum-bum,' while he swung his arm in a drunken imitation of firing a submachine gun, while sweeping bottles and glasses to the floor.[10]

Payne Best decided to follow McGrath's example and left to seek more convivial company. Later that night, Payne Best having joined some of the German officers and Isa Vermehren and Vera Schuschnigg in a guest room in the Bachmann Hotel, encountered Fritz again. Now completely drunk, the SS man entered the room swaying unsteadily and waving his gun in the air. His face was contorted with rage as he ordered those present to go to bed. It was a tense moment: in his drunken rage he was liable to shoot somebody. Von Bonin, who was present, reached into his pocket to grasp a pistol he had secretly acquired. But rather than producing it, he spoke, as Vermehren later recalled, in a voice, 'so full of rebuke and disgust, that the senseless rage of the drunken SS-man was extinguished faster than a straw fire and he was filled with cold fear and the doubt that the reality in which he used to live didn't exist anymore'.[11]

In the Town Hall, a different type of dispute, although also drink-related, arose when some of the Hungarian contingent, who had wined and dined well and late, found themselves without a bed for the night. They proceeded upstairs to the only room in the building that contained beds, ones that had been allocated to some of the German family hostages. The Hungarians ordered the Germans to vacate the room. The Germans were not prepared to move and an angry stand-off resulted. Harry Day was told of the row and asked to intervene. For reasons of diplomacy, he first sought out Baron Peter Schell, a minister of the Interior in the ousted Hungarian government, with whom he had formed an acquaintance, and they both went upstairs. Seeing the upset caused to the children, Day's tone was one of anger and disgust. He told the Hungarians: 'Get out at once, or I will personally see that you and your luggage are chucked into the street.' Schell, wasn't along just to translate – he was equally annoyed with his countrymen who sullenly retreated to the banqueting room below to join the majority of men who were preparing to sleep on the floor.[12]

Colonel Jack Churchill decided to abandon the group. As far as the commando officer was concerned, they were still at war with the Germans and he wanted to return to the fray.[13] After getting Day's approval, he prepared for a trek into the mountains, intending to try to reach Allied lines. Day helped him gather warm clothing and provisions and walked with him to the edge of the village and watched as his friend disappeared into a nearby forest. Payne Best, on learning of Colonel Churchill's departure, considered it 'a cowardly action', claiming that it could put everyone else at risk. He repeated this accusation long afterwards in his account of these days.[14] It was a malicious attack on the reputation of a brave man. Whatever level of danger they faced from the SS was unlikely to be influenced by Jack Churchill's decision to return to active service, an ambition that never appears to have troubled Payne Best during his five and a half years of captivity.

Bader must have been alerted to Jack Churchill's absence, for soon afterwards he arrived at the Town Hall with a number of his SS men and pointedly asked Peter Churchill, 'Where is your cousin?'. Churchill told him he didn't know where he was. 'Perhaps he's already upstairs asleep,' he ventured. No attempt was made by Bader to locate the colonel. Instead, Bader said, as if by way of explanation, 'Well, we have a special room for you British officers.' Day, who was listening, said to Churchill, 'Tell him we don't want any special rooms, we'll doss down with Colonel Churchill and all the others.'[15] Peter Churchill translated and, after some hesitation, the SS men departed. The offer of accommodation was seen as a deadly ruse: an attempt to gather them together to execute them. They had reason to fear this. Apart from the overheard SS conversations on the bus, it was rumoured that a letter had been extracted from the pocket of a drunken SS man, perhaps the aforementioned Fritz, that contained an order to liquidate scores of the hostages, including the British servicemen.

The joviality of that memorable day had subsided by nightfall as it became clear that the SS were intent on restoring the control they had lost earlier, perhaps with deadly intent. In the banqueting room of the town hall, forty-five of the male hostages began to bed down on a thin layer of straw that covered the floor. As they did so, they observed that SS guards had entered and assumed a crouched position at two corners of the room, their submachine gun strewn across their knees. Some of the hostages decided to stay awake in order to sound an alert if there was any attempt to murder them. Unarmed, they would not have been able to do much if the SS did decide to shoot them, but at least, they decided, it would be preferable to being murdered in their sleep. In the hotel where the VIPs were housed, SS sentries were less in evidence, but outside in the plaza they stood guard at their lorry which contained their armoury, including the crates of hand grenades. Other guards patrolled the village. They seemed nervous; perhaps they, too, were also expecting to be attacked.

At 2 a.m., a message was received by the *Wehrmacht* contingent in the post office in response to the earlier appeal for protection. General Röttinger reacted positively, stating that he was willing to provide protection and was sending troops to Niederdorf, who were due to arrive later that day. Röttinger would no doubt have consulted Wolff about the matter of the *Prominenten*, given it was an SS operation. (Fearing he would be arrested, Röttinger had not journeyed to Innsbruck in response to Kesselring's summons, after Hofer's accusation of treachery following the surrender arrangement.) General Thomas, who received the message from the post office unit, woke Payne Best to tell him the good news. The Englishman slept soundly thereafter, but not his roommate, General Falkenhausen, who was kept awake by Payne Best's loud snoring.[16]

Most of the hostages awoke that Sunday morning knowing nothing of these dramatic events. However, it soon became apparent that the attitude of the SS towards them had changed. A normally foul-mouthed SS NCO entered the Bachmann Hotel and, cap in hand, called out, 'I wish the arrested gentlemen a good morning.' The astonished silence was broken by von Falkenhausen declaring 'Now, Hitler *has* lost the war.'[17] In the Town Hall the less pampered members of the group awoke to find that there were no longer any SS guards present. Cushing sat up and announced gleefully 'Everybody up. The SS bastards have gone. We've got our own parade this morning.'[18]

The good cheer of the previous afternoon resurfaced. There had been no killing. It seemed like the SS had reconsidered their intention to eliminate them. Or maybe that was never their intention, at least not then. Their night-time vigilance may have been for the purpose of protecting themselves. They almost certainly feared an Italian partisan attack during the night, and they probably had good grounds for believing that some of the hostages, particularly the British military personnel, intended to join in that attack. Could it be that they knew everything about the meeting with Garibaldi and the partisans? This would explain why they were concerned about Jack Churchill's disappearance and why they wished to corral the rest of the British in one place. Stiller appeared to have known of their every move. He had shown up at the post office shortly after Thomas made the call to Army headquarters in Bozen. Bader seemed to know about Jack Churchill's absence soon after he had departed. Niederdorf was a small enough village to have allowed the SS guards to keep an eye on the movements of the hostages, but the extent of their knowledge suggests that they had an informer, or informers, within the group. But who?

As already noted in Chapter 4, Spence was suspected of being a stool pigeon in Sachsenhausen, although there is no evidence he acted as an informer at this stage. The two trustees, – Visintainer, and Paul Wauer – might have been expected to inform on any potential escape attempt. Both had been subjected to cruel treatment before being trusted enough to be assigned to the prison bunker in Dachau. Neither could ever feel secure in their current roles and would have feared having to endure again their previous experiences, a fear the SS would have encouraged to guarantee their continued submission. Yet there is no evidence to suggest that either were informing on the *Prominenten*; on the contrary, there is ample testimony of their kindness and commitment to help the special prisoners and that they had their trust.[19]

So, if it wasn't any of these, who was the spy in the camp?

CHAPTER FIFTEEN

CUCKOOS IN THE NEST

There were a number of strange and incongruous individuals within the hostage group. One was Friedrich Engelke, a shadowy and illusive figure among the *Prominenten*. He kept a low profile and is not mentioned in individual memoirs. The others may have viewed him as an unlikely, if uninteresting, member of the group. In records of the group, he has been described as Dr Friedrich Engelke, an official of the Reich Ministry of Economics, arrested in October 1944 due to 'a denunciation'.[1] Elsewhere he has also been described as a *Großkaufmann* ('merchant'), which doesn't appear to correspond to his declared civil service role.[2] However, that occupation would link him to an SS colonel, Friedrich Engelke, who worked procuring materials for the SS in Paris from 1942–4. This man was involved in a massive fraudulent, black-racketeering racket in occupied France, one in which vast amounts of money changed hands, much of it invested in properties on the Cote d'Azur or smuggled to Argentina. Bizarrely, the fraud involved a partnership that linked the SS man with an undercover Russian Jewish businessman. The detail of this extraordinary story need not detain us here, but is recounted in Addendum IV of 'Supplementary Tales' in the final section of this book.

Engelke, though clearly in disguise, was an unlikely informer. He had nothing to gain. He was almost certainly posing as a minor civilian apparatchik in order to conceal his SS past. He may well have been placed among the *Prominenten* by a powerful figure within the SS, perhaps even Himmler himself, as Engelke is believed to have acted as personal assistant to the SS Reichsführer for a time. He had been promoted by the Reichsführer to the rank of colonel shortly before his arrest in Paris and subsequent appearance among the hostage group in Dachau. It is possible he was being hidden within the *Prominenten* because he knew the location of a cash pile that he had squirrelled away. Whatever the truth, Engelke's best strategy was to keep a low profile, while maintaining the identity he had assumed; one of a mere functionary within the Ministry of Economics, a victim of a malicious complaint. He would have nothing to gain by acting as informer for Stiller, a lowly SS lieutenant.

The two Italians, Tullio Tamburini and Eugenio Appollonio, were, as previously noted, also strange inclusions in the hostage group. Tamburini had a background as a small-time hoodlum who had made a reputation for himself as a brutish Fascist in Florence.[3] Mussolini, wishing to control the more violent of his *squadristi*, dispatched him to Africa in 1925, where he was free to indulge in his sadistic tendencies on unfortunate Libyans.[4] However, he was later back in favour and, from 1936–41, he served as prefect of a number of cities, including Trieste. After the creation of the Social Republic, Mussolini promoted Tamburini to chief of police, but he and his deputy Appollonio were dismissed in 1944 for illicit enrichment. Subsequently, when the Germans suspected they were attempting to make contact with the Allies, they were both arrested and sent to Dachau in early April 1945. Within a week or two, for reasons that can only be speculated on, they were allowed to join up with the *Prominenten* on a journey back to Italy. It may have been to save them from *Wolkenbrand* – the planned annihilation of Dachau – or, perhaps, it was thought that their familiarity with the Italian scene might aid the SS. If it was to act as informers within the hostage group, it would have been ill-conceived; their background was known among the group, and they were distrusted. Even if they were willing informers, they would not have been privy to the details of the meeting involving Harry Day, Jack Churchill and the local partisans. There was, however, another Italian who would have been in a position to know everything: Colonel Davide Ferrero.

Ferrero had greatly impressed the British officers. Harry Day described him as a 'tall, vigorous, soldier-of-fortune type, fresh-complexioned, built like an athlete'.[5] Peter Churchill, a fluent Italian speaker, and a former diplomat and intelligence officer who would have prided himself as being a good judge of character, was likewise impressed. He stated that:

amidst all this galaxy of historical figures I was drawn most [to] the outstanding personality of Colonel Ferraro [*sic*] of the Italian Partisans.

A tall, powerfully-built man with a ruddy complexion and curly brown hair, he smoked his pipe placidly amidst the hubbub and *looked* for all the world like a champion golfer waiting patiently in a crowded club-house for his turn to tee off.[5]

Bertram James also acclaimed the Italian.[6] They all knew him as a much-decorated veteran of the French Foreign Legion – he claimed to be a recipient of a Croix de Guerre and two palms for three outstanding actions – who later became leader of an Italian partisan group. In Dachau, he had attached himself to the venerable General Sante Garibaldi, and, following Sante's elevation to leadership of the local partisans in Niederdorf, Ferrero acted as his adjutant.

One not impressed was Fey von Hassell, the daughter of the former German ambassador to Italy. On meeting with her Italian compatriots in Innsbruck – having lived in Italy most of her adult life, she considered herself Italian – she viewed the 'partisans who had been captured by the Germans' as an embarrassment. She disdainfully observed that: 'The Partisans strutted around like peacocks, as if they, and only, they, could save Italy. They claimed, quite illogically, that they would break out of prison, go to France, and from there reconquer Italy.'[7] Garibaldi and Ferrero were the only two possible partisans present within the group, although Garibaldi never claimed to have been an Italian partisan prior to his arrest for suspected French resistant activities. Von Hassell's observation related to the time when she and the others were gathered in Innsbruck, when Garibaldi was attired in prison garb, so he could hardly have then been accused of strutting about like a peacock. It seems, therefore, that she had the more militarily attired Ferrero in mind. With her aristocratic upbringing, von Hassell would have had a keen nose for an *arriviste* ('upstart') and, while her dislike may have been due to snobbishness, she was right to suspect him. However, even she could not have imagined the full truth. Colonel Davide Ferrero was indeed an imposter; but no ordinary one.[8]

Ferrero was never in the Foreign Legion, or in any French regiment. His only military experience was as a corporal in the Italian army. He did, however, as a young man, make the short journey from his home in Savona across the frontier to Nice and lived there for a time before moving to Morocco. We know this because Roberto Gremmo, author of a recently published Italian book

detailing his exploits, discovered that he was before French courts three times
– twice in the Nice district and once in Marrakesh. He was a petty thief and
confidence trickster who conjured up hair-brained schemes that led to his
imprisonment. He was in prison when, in the chaos that enveloped Italy
following the dismissal of Mussolini and the German takeover in September
1943, he was able to walk free. As the Italian civil and military administration
collapsed, prisoners walked out of their jails and Ferrero joined the thousands
of others on the move. The country was in turmoil; food and other basic
necessities were scarce and there was widespread disorder and looting.[9] In the
pandemonium, Ferrero decided to form a patriotic partisan group in the
commune of Canelli, in the Provence of Asti in Piedmont.[10] He had given
himself the title of Captain Davide presumably to burnish his prestige among
potential recruits. His story about being an officer in the French Foreign Legion
was probably conceived of at that time, a tale made credible by his knowledge
of French and Arabic. Ferrero recruited a large number of young men into his
patriot group but soon, for reasons that are recounted in Addendum IV, he
allied himself with the Germans. He was eventually arrested when the Germans
suspected him of planning to switch sides again.

None of the other prisoner hostages ever learned of Ferrero's duplicity or
suspected him of being a spy for Stiller. But he almost certainly was. It would
have been an inexcusable oversight for the SS not to have planted an informer
within the group. The SS concentration camp system, for which Dachau was the
prototype, was heavily dependent on a network of informants to report to the
SS any infraction of the rules or escape plans by individual prisoners.[11] Stiller, as
transport leader, would have had the flexibility to add to the convoy persons he
could rely on to keep him informed of escape attempts or conspiracies. Ferrero,
because of his closeness to Sante Garibaldi, was the ideal choice, especially as the
old General clearly knew nothing about his adjutant's true identity.

How Ferrero, like some others portrayed in this book, came to be integrated
into the *Prominenten* in the first place is unknown. Gremmo thinks he bluffed the
SS into believing that, when captured, he was an officer in the Allied forces. It's
just possible that there may have been some confusion about his identity when
Ferrero entered Dachau, and it's conceivable that he could have employed his
undoubted charm and ability with languages to convince his captors he was part
of the Allied forces and deserved special treatment. But even if the SS in Dachau

didn't know his background, surely Tamburini, the former Social Republic police chief who now accompanied him within the *Prominenten*, would have recalled the name. He was police chief until March, 1944 after Ferrero made his alliance with the Germans, an event that that was the subject of much agitation within the fascist administration.[12] Although allied to the Germans, Ferrero remained a bitter enemy of the fascists and his 'Patriots' were a thorn in their side. It's highly unlikely that the police chief would not have had knowledge of this and have recalled the name of the leader of the 'Patriots Battalion'.

Assuming he did know who Ferrero was, why would Tamburini not mention it to Stiller or to the prisoners within the *Prominenten*? The only conceivable reason he would have remained silent about Ferrero was that the SS had required him to. Ferrero was almost certainly included in the *Prominenten* to keep Stiller informed of any escape attempts or planned resistance. This would explain the Italian's eagerness for Day and Dowse to abandon their attempt to hide in Dachau to await the Americans. It would also explain why it was that he knew in advance that the group were to be taken to Italy. Ferrero had already demonstrated his willingness to work with the SS and although, like everyone else, he knew the way the wind was blowing, there is every reason to assume that he would have wanted to keep all his options open. Ferrero was probably Stiller's most important informant in Niederdorf. As Garibaldi's adjutant, he was now part of the local partisan leadership. Stiller needed to know what the Partisans were intending, especially of any plan to attack, and Ferrero was in a position to tell him. He had attended the meeting where the decision was taken to attack the SS. Although, subsequently, this was deferred, this may not have been made clear as the SS were clearly still expecting an attack that night in Niederdorf. To protect his informant, Stiller would have wanted to ensure that his past remained a secret. And that secret would have allowed Stiller to use a threat of its disclosure to keep Ferrero on side.

By a combination of good fortune and double dealing, Ferrero had so far avoided disaster. He was now in Italy and, in the eyes of most, on the winning side. But he still wasn't in the clear. At any moment an arriving partisan, fascist or German soldier might recognise him and give the game away. If his new friends among the partisans found out he had been in an alliance with the SS, his life would be forfeit, for the Garibaldi brigaders didn't hesitate to shoot collaborators, past or present.

CHAPTER SIXTEEN

HIGH NOON

29 April 1945

Sunday was set to be a defining day for the hostage group. It began with a Mass by Bishop Piguet and his fellow hostage, Canon Neuhäusler, in the village church which was attended by most of the hostage group. The clergymen gave thanks for the group's overnight survival and the Almighty was beseeched to continue to protect them that day.[1] It seemed that their prayers were answered when a group of *Wehrmacht* soldiers appeared in response to von Bonin's appeal for protection. Was this, they wondered, the prelude to their deliverance? The troops were led by Captain Wichard von Alvensleben, an amiable Prussian, whose aristocratic family was known to some of the kin hostages. His brother was the notorious Ludolf von Alvensleben, Himmler's adjutant, who led an ethnic German militia in occupied Poland where they murdered thousands of Polish and Jewish civilians.[2] Fey von Hassell, who knew of him, approached the Captain and asked about his brother. He responded: 'Let's not talk about him. As you can imagine, he's the black sheep of the family! He has always been a Nazi, and I only hope for his sake that he doesn't make it through the end of the war.'[3]

Although friendly and sympathetic to the plight of the hostages, Alvensleben and his small detachment proved to be a disappointment. Payne Best found him to be charming, but weak-willed.[4] The *Wehrmacht* captain was understandably reluctant to enter into any conflict with his fellow countrymen; his orders were to protect the group from their SS guards, not to arrest them. In any event, the SS greatly outnumbered his unit so he decided to radio for reinforcements. In the interim, he stationed his soldiers outside the town hall facing the SS vehicles parked on the square opposite, which was serving as their makeshift headquarters. But there was no display of hostility; rifles remained shouldered and the two machine guns in their possession were not set up.

Payne Best discussed the situation over breakfast with Colonel von Bonin and Franz Liedig, who was a former German naval officer and *Abwehr* agent. They decided to test Stiller's resolve, hoping the presence of the *Wehrmacht* patrol and the promise of reinforcements would unnerve him. As Stiller was walking alone near the Hotel Bachmann, Payne Best and his two German friends approached him and invited him into the hotel for a consultation. Inside, von Bonin questioned him aggressively, making sure Stiller saw the pistol he had acquired. Roles were reversed: it was the SS officer who was now being interrogated. The three inquisitors challenged Stiller on reports that an execution list had been discovered and put it to him that rather than protect them as he had promised, that he intended to have them murdered. Stiller denied that this was the case, but fingered Bader, his fellow SS officer, as their potential executioner. He claimed that he himself had been threatened by Bader when he told him he would not allow any of the hostages to be shot. He pleaded, 'You can count on me to do anything I can to help, but I can't do anything with Bader.'[5] Taking advantage of the fact that Stiller was admitting that he was unable to protect them, Payne Best suggested that he himself take over command of the group. This was an extraordinary proposal, effectively he was demanding that the SS lieutenant relinquish his role and disobey his orders to keep the hostages in custody and not allow them to fall into enemy hands. Stiller, however, seemingly agreed to the suggestion, while warning that he couldn't vouch for Bader. He described his fellow SS officer as a dangerous man. It was decided that a formal handover of leadership would be announced at a gathering of all the hostages at midday.

As they were leaving the hotel following their encounter with Stiller, Payne Best, von Bonin and Liedig, bumped into Harry Day and John McGrath. They exchanged information on their respective plans. Day and McGrath were told of Payne Best's plan to take command of the hostage group while awaiting the protection of the *Wehrmacht*. Day objected, informing the others of the planned partisan attack on the SS scheduled for that night. The two Germans accompanying Payne Best must have been alarmed; they feared the partisans more than the SS. Payne Best himself was appalled to learn of Day's collaboration with the Italians and of the fact that he and other British officers intended to assist them. He had little regard for Garibaldi's partisans. He viewed them as nothing more than 'a lot of village youths who had tied red scarves round their neck', believing that 'just a little while back they had probably cried Viva Mussolini! or Heil Hitler!'.[6] There were, no doubt, some opportunists among recent partisan recruits, but they were led by brave men and women who had fought the Germans and the Fascists for nearly two years while suffering great deprivations in the mountains, knowing that torture and certain death faced them if they were caught. Their sacrifice contrasted with that of Payne Best who, at that time, was 'leading the well-fed life of a prize poodle' as he was to describe his own existence after 1943 in Sachsenhausen.[7]

Payne Best was reluctant to place himself in outright opposition to his fellow officers. Day outranked him, as did McGrath. He also had to consider the Wing Commander's popularity among the British contingent, especially his fellow airmen. If any of the British were to assume command of the hostage group, the obvious choice would have been Day. But Payne Best was popular with the other nationalities, the Germans in particular. His ability to speak fluent German, Dutch and French, and his outgoing personality gave him an advantage over Day who was less fluent in German and an altogether more reserved person. Conscious of his advantages in this regard, Payne Best suggested that the choice of tactics be left to a meeting of the full hostage group which was being convened for noon that day.

In advance of that meeting, Payne Best and his two German colleagues sought out Garibaldi, hoping to convince him to call off the planned attack. Garibaldi had established his headquarters on the top floor of the town hall and, having discarded his prison attire, he was resplendent in a partisan officer uniform. With Ferrero alongside him, Garibaldi warmly greeted the three arrivals. He listened to their concerns that an attack on the SS would endanger the lives of the hostages. Payne Best cunningly played on Garibaldi's patriotic instincts, suggesting that the future of the South Tyrol as part of Italy could be jeopardised if prominent persons such as Blum or Schuschnigg were killed as a consequence of partisan action.[8] He announced that an 'International Committee' was to be established from amongst the hostage group and that the issue would be considered by this committee who would recommend a course of action to the assembled group. Garibaldi seemed happy with this, but Ferrero raised furious objections. He wanted the attack plan, as agreed with Day and

Jack Churchill, to proceed and didn't want decisions devolved to a civilian committee. Ferrero had earlier visited Kurt von Schuschnigg in his lodgings and tried to persuade him to place himself and his wife and child under the protection of the partisans. Ferrero told the former Austrian Chancellor of a plan to have the hostages moved to Cortina where the partisans had their regional headquarters.[9] Schuschnigg was wary of the offer. He would have feared that the Communists who dominated the Garibaldi Partisans would be hostile to him, perhaps recalling that he had executed and imprisoned communist and socialists while in power in Austria. He felt safer with *Wehrmacht* protection, but deflected Ferrero's proposal with a reminder that the hostage group had committed themselves to acting collectively.

Ferrero had good reasons for wanting the action to proceed. As Garibaldi's adjutant, he had become a conduit for communication with the regional leadership of the Garibaldi brigade in Cortina and he would also have been anxious to enhance his reputation within the organisation. To have the plans of the Niederdorf partisans altered by an external group, especially one that included Germans, was never going to be approved of by the partisan leadership. Moreover, he probably had orders to have Schuschnigg placed under partisan custody. News of the former Austrian Chancellor's arrival in the Pusteral had circulated widely and he was being treated as a dignitary, almost like a head of state. Soldiers in the local ethnic German militia, stood to attention as he passed. His presence encouraged the German-speaking population to believe that their dream of the South Tyrol being returned to Austria would be realised.[10] Although there is no evidence that the partisan leadership planned to harm Schuschnigg, placing him in protective custody would have helped to dampen such expectations. Ferrero would have had more personal concerns. If, as speculated, Stiller knew of Ferrero's past as a German collaborator, he had good reason to have the SS lieutenant permanently silenced.

Garibaldi eventually dismissed Ferrero's objections and agreed that the matter be left to the newly constituted 'international committee'. Payne Best then set about selecting the committee which he confidently expected would prefer *Wehrmacht* to partisan protection pending the arrival of the Allies. Day, McGrath, Falconer and Stevens, as well as Garibaldi and Ferrero were included in the committee, but Payne Best made sure that they would be outnumbered by nominating his two companions – von Bonin and Liedig – as well as the

Greek General Papagos, Canon Neuhäusler, a Slovakian, Major Stanek, and General Privalov from the Russian contingent.

The committee met soon after with Tony Ducia and Captain von Alvensleben also in attendance. Payne Best's proposal that they rely on German army protection was opposed by all the other British officers with the exception of Hugh Falconer. The matter rankled with Payne Best; long after he complained about 'the opposition of my colleagues'.[11] However, as he anticipated, he had the support of Germans and others who feared the Italian partisans more than the German military.

Before the planned meeting of all the *Prominenten* which would finally decide on the issue, Stiller was observed apparently having difficulty explaining his decision to retire as transport leader to his SS comrades. A heated discussion was seen to be taking place among the guards as they gathered around their munitions truck in the village square. It seemed they couldn't agree among themselves about what should happen to the hostages. To the onlooking hostages it must have seemed that Stiller was about to lose control to Bader and his bloodthirsty henchmen. The SS guards collectively were on edge. The partisans had begun infesting the village, possibly still expecting the planned action and unaware of Garibaldi's wish to defer it. Tension was mounting, but Alvensleben was still reluctant to act. He didn't feel he had the authority to disarm the SS. Colonel von Bonin, fearing an outbreak of shooting was imminent, decided to take action himself. He told Alvensleben that the SS must be disarmed and that he would personally take command and be responsible for the consequences. The captain was relieved to have von Bonin, who he regarded as a senior officer, assume responsibility. Von Bonin gave orders that the two machine guns be set up with barrels pointing across the square.

Then, in a moment of high drama, von Bonin strode boldly towards the body of SS men. He ordered them to throw down their weapons, warning them that, if there was any sign of resistance on their part, the machine gunners would open fire. For a tense moment the SS men hesitated, then let their guns fall to the ground. Almost as soon as the weapons were discarded, red-scarved partisans appeared and carried them away. Even Bader seemed pacified and meekly asked von Bonin to help him secure petrol so that his men could escape, a request von Bonin refused.[12] The SS lorry was searched and it was found to contain scores of purloined Red Cross parcels among the crates of hand grenades. Later in the day, Bader did manage to procure some petrol and he drove off accompanied by most of the SS guards. However, eleven of Stiller's men stayed put, trusting that their presence among the hostage group would protect them from the partisans. Stiller himself was unsure about what to do, but later he decided to attempt to make his own way over the Brenner Pass back home to Austria.

At noon, all the hostages gathered in the dining room of Hotel Bachmann for their meeting. They listened in silence while Stiller, standing on a chair, formally declared that the leadership of the group now rested with Captain Payne Best. Captain von Alvensleben assured them that his men were there only for their protection, and Tony Ducia, speaking on behalf of the Tyrolean district government, told them to 'consider yourselves our guests'.[13] They had ceased to be prisoners; it was by then a statement of the obvious, but it was nonetheless exhilarating to hear it confirmed. Something they had hardly dared to dream of had finally become a reality; they were free!

But not yet out of danger. Von Bonin, the hero of the hour, stood up on a table alongside Payne Best and they both addressed the assembly; von Bonin in German and Payne Best translating into English and French. They announced that although they were no longer prisoners, the situation remained hazardous. The war was not yet over and fighting between the retreating German troops and partisans continued. They were also told that tension between ethnic Germans and Italians could create a parallel conflict. Tony Ducia, who had finally managed to extract the German military residents from the hotel high up in the mountains, told the assembled group that they would be moving to this more remote accommodation where they could be more secure under the protection of Alvensleben's men until Allied troops arrived. There was no dissent. Day and his colleagues were no doubt still unhappy with having themselves placed under the protection of the Germans, but, with the capitulation of the SS guards, plans for joint British, partisan action were superfluous. Characteristically, Payne Best later portrayed the SS's capitulation to be the result of his and von Bonin's bold initiative. But even if Stiller was intimidated by his three interrogators he could easily have reneged as he still had military supremacy at that stage. The evidence points to him being relieved that responsibility for the hostages was taken from him. He, like everyone else, knew the war was in its final days. There was little doubt that he had orders not to allow the *Prominenten* to be rescued, but, with the war lost, it was no longer in his interest to murder them. The more hardened Nazis among Bader's unit may have wanted to take revenge on some or all of the hostages, but there was no longer the prospect of doing this covertly.

Evidence that the war was in its final days was everywhere. Truckloads of German soldiers, some carrying plundered loot, had begun passing through the village, some calling out, exuberantly, if prematurely, that the war was over.[14] Some stopped long enough to pass on a rumour that the British and Americans were about to join the fight against the Soviets, a bit of make-believe that offered solace to a defeated army.[15] The sight of fleeing German soldiers emboldened the partisans who set up road blocks and began to disarm them.

The rumour about the war being over, may have been just that, but it wasn't without substance, as some of them may have known. Later that very day, in the Royal Palace at Caserta near Naples, emissaries of Generals Vietinghoff and Wolff put their signature to the unconditional surrender of the one million German troops still in Italy.[16] The capitulation was only to come into effect three days later, allowing both sides time to inform all their units. It was the first German front to entirely surrender. It was unauthorised and, as indicated, Kesselring had attempted to forestall it by having Vietinghoff and Röttiger court-martialled and shot. Vietinghoff and Wolff finally had the courage to defy him and Hitler.

Alvensleben telephoned General Röttiger, to inform him that the SS had been disarmed and to seek further instructions. Röttiger reacted with alarm: 'How could you do this? It's your head or mine.' General Wolff must have been beside him for he came on the line and calmly told Alvensleben to send the SS to his command headquarters in Bozen.[17] Röttiger's reaction was probably due to the strain he was under at this time. As a result of his involvement with Wolff and General Vietinghoff in surrender talks involving Allen Dulles, he was, like his colleagues, under threat of court martial and execution. Wolff, the instigator of the surrender process, was more sanguine. He rightly judged that Kesselring and Kaltenbrunner no longer had the means to carry out the threat.

Vehicles were found to ferry the hostages to the hotel in Lago di Braies, high up in the mountains. A heavy snowfall prevented them from navigating a steep track, so most occupants had to disembark and trudge for over an hour through deep snow to the hotel.[18] Thomas Cushing didn't join them at that stage. He had settled into a tavern where he was pleased 'to find that my long incarceration had not impaired my appreciation of strong liquor'.[19] After his alcohol refuelling, he walked twelve kilometres through the snow to the hotel, presumably immune to the cold.

PART IV

FREEDOM

The streets buzzed with a succession of rumours: we all had to leave, a gunfight had taken place somewhere, in a few hours the partisans would be there, Niederdorf would become a theatre of war. But all those reports were merely the cries of seagulls around a ship moving tranquilly on its way. The river of freedom, once it had burst its banks, surged out in all its diversity, unstoppable, into our manifold ways and doings and it was no longer possible to return it to the old, narrow bed of cautious obedience.

–Isa Vermehren

Reise durch en letzen Akt

CHAPTER SEVENTEEN

A DEATH IN SHANGRI-LA

L ake Braies – Lago di Braies – is a magical location. Its turquoise waters rest in the Braies Valley in the Dolomites 1,500 metres above sea level. It is surrounded on two sides by near vertical cliffs of dappled brown and grey stone that reach down to the lake and are reflected on its still surface. A large five-storey hotel, Pragser Wildsee, is situated on the more gently sloped western shoreline, surrounded by pines, with terracing reaching to the edge of the lake. Opened in 1899, it was once a fashionable summer retreat for Austrian high society, including members of the Imperial household. Archduke Franz Ferdinand, the crown prince, was a guest in 1910, four years before his assassination in Sarajevo led to the First World War.[1] Largely untouched by the twentieth century and its horrors, the hotel seems frozen in time; a secluded remnant of *La Belle Époque*.

30 April 1945

Most of the *Prominenten* were in no position to appreciate the beauty of their surroundings when they arrived at the hotel. The temperature was sub-zero and everything was covered by a deep blanket of snow. Those who had to walk most of the way were tired and cold. Frau Emma Heiss-Hellenstainer, the attractive young proprietress, had been contacted earlier and generously agreed to put the hotel at their disposal. She had little, though, beyond accommodation to offer them. The hotel was not just frozen in time, it was literally frozen. It had not been in operation as a hotel during the war, although German officers had recently occupied some rooms. An inspection of the boiler house revealed burst pipes, with little prospect of repair. Preparatory arrangements, including room allocation, had been made by the International Committee. The kin families with children were allocated the more spacious and least cold first-floor rooms, as were elderly couples, including the Blums, Halders and Thyssens. Both Blums were ill for most of the duration of their stay in the hotel and consequently were to play little part in subsequent events. Other prominent civilians and senior officers, including Day, Payne Best, McGrath and Stevens, were placed in second-floor rooms and others were assigned the smaller and coldest third floor and attic rooms. It was the first time since captivity that most of them had a real bed to sleep in. Nevertheless, there were complaints about room allocation. Some of those in the upper floors argued that the Germans, as representatives of the soon to be vanquished, should endure the worst conditions. Again Harry Day was required to arbitrate and again, to his credit, he refused to alter the arrangements.[2] Further discord occurred later when it was discovered that blankets went missing from rooms on the higher floors and were discovered in the room of one of the Greek generals.[3]

Calm was restored when a communal meal was served in the spacious dining room. A husband-and-wife team, Käthe and Josef Mohr, took responsibility for the cooking. They were among the relatives of Jakob Keiser, a Catholic trade union leader and member of the German resistance, who had gone into hiding, contributing to the arrest of his relatives. The Mohr's were assisted by the two Dachau trustees, Paul Wauer and Wilhelm Visintainer. A sack of semolina had been procured and semolina soup was made. It was far from a banquet, but at least there was enough for everyone. Frau Heiss donated wine and Kurt Schuschnigg made a punch with the aid of some spices. Everyone was in celebrity mood when the proprietor generously invited anyone who wished to imbibe some more to join her in the hotel's wine cellar. The invitation was not spurned by many, although one or more persons abused her hospitality by liberating nearly all of the cellar's remaining stock of wine. This was only the first in a series of incidents where members of the group were found to have squirrelled away food, liquor and tobacco. The compulsion to hoard would have been acquired during years of concentration camp existence.[4]

1 May 1945

The news of Hitler's death caused great excitement and rejoicing among most of the group now resident in the hotel; the German soldiers present didn't celebrate, but showed no reaction, just shrugged their shoulders, apparently now indifferent to the fate of their Führer.[5] The news had been heard on an old radio set that Hugh Falconer, a trained signals officer, had managed to restore to working order. One of the SS guards who had opted to stay with the group, came across a number of people listening to the BBC and protested that that was illegal. He was sternly reminded of his altered status within the hotel. It was also May Day and General Privalov decided to celebrate both occasions. Josef Müller and John McGrath were among the few non-Russians invited.[6]

A co-operative form of organisation took hold in the hotel. Daily noon assemblies took place. Members of the group were assigned responsibility for particular functions and chores. Conventional gender and status roles were revived. The women took responsibility for washing and food preparation. The Irish orderlies were required to keep the halls and corridors clean. Those SS guards who had opted to remain with the group were put to peeling potatoes. The quality of food improved as meat and vegetables were gifted or purchased locally by the group. A library, pharmacy and a laundry operation were established and a system of rationing involving the issuing of coupons was introduced.[7] Payne Best took on the role of hotel manager. Elizabeth Keizer acted as the secretary of the committee, and Franz Liedig and John McGrath assisted with management tasks. The latter had some experience in this, not just from his theatrical management past, but also from his role as adjutant to the officer in charge of a military hospital in Lancashire after the First World War. McGrath had somehow acquired military-style clothes and a 'red-topped artillery forage cap' and attempted to introduce some military discipline to proceedings which Payne Best found tiresome.[8] It was most likely an attempt by the Irishman to control the activities of his countrymen, causing Walsh, who had taken on the role of batman to Payne Best, to complain about McGrath's officiousness. Payne Best conceded that McGrath was extremely active, but claimed he was never sure what his functions were.[9] This might have had something to do with the fact that the Englishman was by then consuming, by his own account, 'the best part of a bottle of brandy a day'.[10] The liquor was a gift from General von Vietinghoff who had donated sixty bottles of Italian brandy and a case of Asti Spumante. This was in compensation for his recall of Wichard von Alvensleben and his men, although he promised that they would soon be replaced. The Italian Partisans provided protection for a period until a replacement unit of German soldiers arrived, led by another Alvensleben, Gebhard, a cousin of the departed Wichard.

Despite individual indiscretions, discomforts and tensions, living conditions in the hotel became tolerable and, as the weather improved, there were the opportunities to stroll outside and admire the scenery. Although warned not to wander much beyond the vicinity of the hotel, the younger contingent ignored this restriction and walked to nearby settlements where they were often generously provided with food and wine by the local population. The more energetic took to mountain tracks and wandered the valleys. Bertram James and Sydney Dowse enjoyed the company of Isa Vermehren and her cousin, Countess Gisela von Plettenberg. Fey von Hassell and Alexander von Stauffenberg strolled together and during their wanderings the handsome couple were frequently invited into peasant homesteads and plied with wine and food.[11]

A subject of more salacious gossip was the relationship between Ray van Wymeersch, the French RAF man, and Heidi, the mysterious German 'blonde bombshell'. They took off in an acquired motor car for what others cynically called 'a mountain honeymoon'.[12] Whether because of his involvement with the despised Heidi or out of jealousy, Wymeersch was not liked by some of his fellow aviators, so when he eventually returned with a broken arm after crashing the car, he received little sympathy.[13]

Garibaldi and Ferrero had remained in Niederdorf, with the former as leader of the local partisans now nominally in control of the village and surrounding areas. Although the war was almost at an end, the situation remained tense. Retreating German soldiers were being disarmed resulting in the partisans acquiring a substantial haul of weapons. One group of Germans, possibly SS, were not prepared to be disarmed and a fire fight resulted. Ferrero was said to have shot a number of them. The rest were taken captive and Ferrero ordered twelve of them to be executed. Garibaldi, when he discovered this, overruled his adjutant, refusing to allow his men to adopt the tactics of the SS.[14] One can only wonder if Ferrero's decision to execute the Germans was the result of heightened passions or his fear that he might be recognised as a collaborator. Notwithstanding Garibaldi's leadership position, his control over events was weakening. Tensions between the German and Italian communities had heightened. New, exuberant units of partisans had entered the village and began indulging in some 'coat trailing'; driving around and waving the Italian tricolour while firing their weapons into the air and entering and searching houses.[15] There were also tensions between the different politically aligned partisan groups.

Ducia, no doubt concerned for the safety of his Germanic community, decided that an appeal be made to the Allies to despatch troops to the area. He reasoned, no doubt correctly, that the Allies would want to rein in the communist-led partisans as the war came to an end. However, a call to assist a small remote German community was unlikely to be awarded priority, while a plea to rescue beleaguered VIP hostages was much more likely to attract a response. Ducia decided to attempt to cross the German lines himself to request help and Harry Day eagerly volunteered to accompany him on the journey.[16] Day was determined to make one final escape attempt, even though the war was virtually over. One can assume he remained uncomfortable with Payne Best's reliance on *Wehrmacht* protection and on his close alliance with von Bonin, Liedig and the German generals. There had been a tangible cooling off in the relationship between the RAF contingent and the German officers, one of whom noted a 'subtle change in the relationship' between the British and the Germans around this time, 'with some of the former strong feelings of comradeship fading'.[17]

2 May 1945

Hugh Falconer also decided to leave, for he was anxious to return to service. He commandeered a small car he found in the hotel garage and, after making it operational, drove to Niederdorf accompanied by Peter Churchill. Their first port of call was Garibaldi's headquarters in the Town Hall. The building was now bedecked with Italian tricolours and thronged with heavily armed partisans. Falconer conferred with Ferrero, his supposed former French Foreign Legion colleague, about the military situation. They must have talked at some stage about their time in the Legion, and assuming they did, the Englishman may have harboured some suspicions about his 'comrade's' story. He and Churchill moved on to another village about fifteen kilometres distant – most likely Toblach / Dobbiaco – where they found an American army unit in situ. They approached the officer in charge and told him of the location of the hostage group, but the American was disinterested. He and his men were exhausted. They were miles in advance of their base and 'worn out' by the continuous joyous attention of partisans en route.[18]

3 May 1945

In the morning, a plane flew over the valley dropping leaflets containing a message from Field Marshal Alexander – the British Commander of Allied Forces in Italy. It informed readers that General von Vietinghoff had surrendered and ordered all troops under his command to cease hostilities.[19] The surrender had come into effect and the Allies were broadcasting the good news. When the content of the leaflet became known to the hotel inhabitants there was further jubilation. But not among the Russians; they knew it was likely to mean their repatriation to a dismal fate in the Soviet Union. Bessonov decided to depart, announcing that he wasn't going to wait around and have the Allies return him to Russia to be shot. He disappeared into the mountains with a gun and some ammunition that he had acquired.[20]

Little Vassily Kokorin also had a decision to make. He approached Bertram James, who spoke some Russian, and asked him what the Allies would do with him when they arrived. James told him that 'if you want to go home they will send you back to the Soviet Union'.[21] He perhaps thought that this reply would give the young Russian the assurance he was seeking. He seemed happy with it, but whether this was because James had implied that he would be allowed to go home, or because he had indicated that repatriation wouldn't be mandatory, is not clear. His mind would soon be made up for him.

That afternoon, a vehicle arrived at the hotel carrying three heavily armed partisans and a French officer. The partisans were not part of the group now installed in Niederdorf, but were from headquarters in Cortina. One of them had the title of Commissioner for Partisan Security. The French officer was introduced as Captain Lussac.[22] They demanded to see both Kokorin and Léon Blum, stating they had orders to offer them special protection. Lussac went to meet Blum, who was delighted and overcome to meet a uniformed French officer. In his memoir, he doesn't mention any offer to be taken away. In any event, his sciatica would have made a journey through the mountains a painful ordeal. Also, he would have been wary of an offer of Communist Party protection. Apart from the brief period of co-operation that led to his Popular Front government, the Communists had shown themselves to be bitter opponents and at times their anti-Blum vitriol rivalled that of the extreme right of French politics. Kokorin was of more interest to the partisan security officer.

Payne Best, acting as spokesperson for the group, told the partisans that while he had no objection to them conversing with any member of the group, he would not permit the removal of anyone from the hotel. Recognising the weakness of his negotiating position, he donned the mantle of an Allied officer, claiming, falsely, that he had already been in contact with the Allies and that all must remain until such time as they arrived.[23] It became clear, however, that the partisans were intent, come what may, on removing Kokorin. The British contingent tried to persuade him not to leave. They had grown immensely fond of the young Russian and were concerned for his safety. His boyish face always betrayed his emotional highs and lows; his small stature made him seem child-like, an impression accentuated by his complete failure to grasp the rudiments of German grammar. They assured him that it would be better for him to remain securely within the group. However, some of his Russians colleagues, for whatever reason, encouraged him to leave. The following partisan report recounts what happened:

a Russian officer insisted that the partisans take away Wassilij Wasiljewitsch Kokorin and accompany him to the Soviet diplomatic representation in Italy as soon as possible: he was the alleged grandson [*sic*] of the Russian Foreign Minister Molotov and a young Red Army Air Force second lieutenant. Having ended up a Nazi prisoner on a mission in 1942, he had been held captive with Stalin's son, whose death he had, in fact, witnessed. Kokorin appeared nervous: probably his secrets would go beyond what is stated, perhaps fearing to become in any way a new hostage of the Americans. To comfort him, Sala [Vittorio Sala, one of the partisans] lent him his gun and the partisan 'commando' decided to kidnap him on the spot. The three partisans and Molotov's grandson – who left a written statement on his voluntary departure with Gebhard von Alvensleben – rushed towards the Balilla [their car] which was parked along the road, by the meadow, jumped in and ran away, without the Germans noticing.[24]

The partisan report is confusing. Why would 'Sala' hand his weapon to Kokorin to comfort or calm him, unless, of course, Kokorin felt threatened? In any event, it seems clear that the partisan commando group intended to take Kokorin with them, with or without his permission. And how did they learn about the presence of Molotov's relative and of his association with Stalin's son? Could it be that they learned about it from Ferrero? They appear to have known in advance of Kokorin's story and it's possible they wanted to interrogate him about the circumstances of Yakov Dzhugashvili's death. It's also possible they were acting as agents for Soviet intelligence. It's even possible that the order emanated from Molotov, or even from Stalin himself.

Through persuasion or intimidation, Kokorin left with his inquisitors, ignoring the pleas of his British friends. He signed the note prepared for him, stating he was leaving voluntarily. The daily noon meeting was just about to begin when Payne Best was told that Kokorin was leaving. He rushed out and tried to stop him. Kokorin seemed frightened, he said: 'I don't want to be slaughtered,' and ran from the hotel in the company of the partisans.[25]

Soon after Kokorin's departure, Payne Best and McGrath made their way down to Niederdorf to try to enlist General Garibaldi's support to locate the Russian.[26] The General, who was also fond of Vassily, was supportive, but it soon became evident that he had little influence over the partisan regional headquarter staff in Cortina. At some point before or after Kokorin's departure, Josef Müller was approached by Ferrero and Garibaldi with a proposal to have him escorted to Rome, but he, like Schuschnigg earlier, distrusted the partisans and declined the offer on the basis that all the hostages should all stay together.

The British officers were right to be concerned for the young man's safety. Kokorin was taken by the partisans to a refuge high in the mountains where he died some days later. Gangrene was reported as the cause of death, with his previously frostbitten feet said to have been a contributory factor.[27] But this raises more questions. Why, four years after having been frostbitten, did this suddenly become critical? Why the need to take him into an icy alpine climate when the war in Italy was over? Why not take him to Cortina, which the partisans controlled, as a prelude to taking him to the Soviet diplomatic mission in Rome as suggested by his fellow Russians? The truth of what happened to Kokorin may never be known. If the purpose was to interrogate him about his friend Yakov's death in order to prepare a report for the Soviet leader, it seems that they weren't successful for, as we have discovered, Stalin was still making enquiries about his son six years later. The other possibility was that the Commissioner for Partisan Security was acting at the behest of the NKVD to deal with an awkward problem for Molotov. The international press was likely to broadcast news of Kokorin's existence within the hostage group and questions were likely to be put to him about his time with Stalin's son. This would be embarrassing for the Soviet Foreign Minister and for the Soviet leader. A tragic death in an isolated location, from wounds earlier inflicted by the Germans, would solve the problem.

CHAPTER EIGHTEEN

RESCUE

Three days before the Italian surrender came into effect, Harry Day left with Tony Ducia in the latter's beaten-up Volkswagen in an attempt to cross German lines and reach the Allies. Day had borrowed a homburg hat from Prince Phillip of Hesse and a civilian overcoat from Payne Best, which he wore over what remained of his uniform. While inside German lines, Ducia portrayed himself as acting in his official capacity as a regional billeting officer, with Day posing as his assistant. After spending the first night in Ducia's flat in Bozen, they took off hoping to reach Trento. At one check-point, a German NCO attempted to commandeer their car, probably as a potential get-away vehicle, however, following a closer look at its condition, he changed his mind. The German's judgement was borne out, when, a few kilometres later, the car engine expired. They walked the remaining distance into Trento, which was then in the process of being captured by the partisans. Realising that their persona as German officials was now likely to get them shot, Day dispensed with his borrowed attire and presented himself for what he was, an escaping POW, while Ducia assumed the identity of Peter Churchill. They approached the first group of partisans they met and conveyed that they had very important information to deliver to the Americans. A car was quickly found and they continued on their journey, now accompanied by eight heavily armed partisans, all crammed into a small Dacia Beetle. They only got a short distance before it too died under the strain. Another car was requisitioned, but it didn't last much longer as its rear axle broke. A third, larger car was acquired and, with only three partisans now on board, it chugged on for about an hour before the clutch burned out while attempting to climb a high track into the mountains. They had taken to primitive mountain roads in order to avoid the tarred roads which German armoured vehicles still patrolled.

There was nothing for it but to take off on foot. The three partisans and Ducia were younger and fitter than Day and he found it difficult to keep up with them as they clambered over the rough mountainous terrain. After six hours, they reached a small village and, tired and thirsty, they entered a bar. The proprietor was friendly and served them grappa and a meal as well as providing them with a bed for the night. They encountered similar displays of hospitality in other remote mountain hamlets as they attempted to reach Allied lines. Eventually, guided by local partisans, Ducia and Day, who was now sporting a red partisan armband, reached the German defensive lines. From a high vantage point, they could see Americans in the distance. Skirting German gun entrenchments, they descended towards their allies. To reach them, they had to cross open ground within range of German fire. They gambled that the Germans would not target them, thereby risking retaliatory American fire for the sake of a few partisans, knowing the war was virtually over. This proved to be the case, and as they crept along, they suddenly encountered an American soldier camouflaged under a bush. 'I'm a British officer, can we come over?' called out Day. 'Sure, come on over, all of you,' was the reply.[1] Soon he and Ducia were in Padua, and later Bologna and Florence, in each location reciting to perplexed American officers the story of the *Prominenten* still marooned high in the Dolomites.

4 May 1945

Janot Blum awoke from a feverish sleep to the sound of vehicles in the courtyard of the hotel. Looking out the window, she called excitedly to her husband, 'Come, come quickly.' When Léon Blum went to join her at the window, he first noticed the partisans with their red bandanas surrounding the vehicles, but then he saw others alighting from armoured cars and, with delight, recognised their unmistakable American helmets.[2] Day's appeals to have the group rescued had finally produced a response and this American unit had been roused from their sleep and ordered to proceed through the night to rescue what they were told were important prisoners still held by the Germans.

Elsewhere in the hotel, Andy Walsh, acting as Payne Best's batman, ran into the latter's room excitedly announcing that 'Ities' were entering the rooms of the ladies and threatening them with their guns.[3] Payne Best didn't need much convincing of the partisans' dastardly behaviour and he rushed downstairs where he found General Garibaldi in conversation with an American officer. Garibaldi had come with his men to show the Americans the way to the hotel, and to assist in case the German troops offered any resistance. Payne Best assured them that they were perfectly safe and prevailed on the senior American officer present, Captain John Attwell of the 339th Infantry regiment, to have the partisans removed from the hotel as they were frightening the women and children and he feared for the safety of the many German civilians and military personnel present. The American officer acquiesced and asked that the partisans depart, which they did, doubtlessly sullen and annoyed at the attitude of those whom they were prepared to risk their lives in rescuing less than a week earlier. They had been searching the hotel merely to disarm the remaining German soldiers, a task the American's took over.[4]

Other residents were at breakfast when they saw, through the ground-floor dining-room windows, the arrival of the Americans. Peter Churchill noticed with surprise that the actual moment of rescue proved to be something of an anti-climax. A few didn't even bother to interrupt their breakfast for the occasion. What had become a relatively peaceful and pleasant interlude was about to end and thoughts now turned to uncertain futures. When would they be able to go home? Did they still have a home to go to? Were their loved ones still alive and, if so, what would be their reaction to their return? The four remaining Soviet servicemen had little to look forward to. They knew that Article 58 of the Soviet Criminal Code made surrender treasonous and the best they could hope for was lengthy imprisonment as an alternative to being shot. The French knew that their country was already liberated, but for other nationalities the future was far from clear. The Greeks would have known that their homeland was on the brink of a civil war between forces on the left and right. The Hungarians were aware that the Red Army was now in control in Budapest, and as members of a government that had joined the attack on Russia, a return home for them was not a prospect they would relish. The German kin prisoners could only hope that their homes and estates were not destroyed or occupied by the Russians. Fey von Hassell would have had a feeling of nervous anticipation about the prospect of being reunited with her two young sons. Alexander von Stauffenberg had to accept, sadly, that Fey would return to her husband. The other German officers couldn't be sure that their oppositional activities would be believed, or that their stories would mean anything to the Allied soldiers. Badoglio and the two former police chiefs of the Salo Republic were already in their homeland, but would have feared retribution for their role in the Fascist administration.

Most of the British officers could expect to return to something like normality, but the four Irish squaddies could only be apprehensive about how their superiors would judge their earlier association with the *Abwehr*. Spence had most to fear, but Cushing too would have sensed that many of the officers still suspected him and might make accusations against him. Walsh on the other hand was popular and his association with Payne Best was likely to protect him. Peter Churchill, too, was not without concerns. He could only hope that his beloved Odette was still alive. He hoped to be able to start a new life with her, although the fact that she was already married presented an obstacle.

A generous distribution of cigarettes, chocolate, blankets and food by the Americans rekindled spirits. The tired and bewildered Americans were invited in for breakfast. It's likely they had no idea who these supposedly important people were – they probably had never heard of Blum, Schuschnigg or Kállay – but the presence among them of some pretty women would have attracted their attention. Isa Vermehren, for her part, found the easy-going mannerism of the gum-chewing, cigarette-drooling Yankees fascinating.[5]

5–9 May 1945

Arrangements for the evacuation of the former hostages, and the German army and SS men, all now prisoners of war, took some days to organise. Everyone awaited departure with varying degrees of anticipation and trepidation. The evacuation was to take place in stages and John McGrath was in charge of allocating individuals to particular vehicles. The day before the first set of evacuations was due, a posse of international reporters and photographers arrived at the hotel. The story of the *Prominenten* was, briefly, to become an international news story: prominent personalities, politicians, clergymen, aristocrats, military officers from many European countries, all former prisoners of the SS, whose whereabouts had been unknown until then, had suddenly been discovered in a remote mountain resort in Italy. A photograph of the group, with smiling faces, clustered around the pipe-smoking Niemöller, who held little Sissi Schuschnigg in his arms, was published in many newspapers around the world. Reporters sought out Blum, Schuschnigg, Kállay, Niemöller and Payne Best for interview. Schuschnigg was asked about his plans for the future. He replied, 'We have not yet thought about plans. Of course we want to go home as soon as possible.'[6] He didn't know it then, but the one place he would not be allowed to travel to was home.

The evacuation began on 8 May when Europe was celebrating the end of the war. The group were taken by the Americans to Verona in convoys of cars and buses before being flown to Naples. There, they were met by more photographers before the Germans and those from the former Axis nations were separated from the rest to be questioned about their activities during, and before, the war. For Isa Vermehren the separation dashed her vision of a harmonious post-war world. She had been luxuriating in the beauty of the countryside, and the kindness of her American hosts, when the atmosphere changed:

When we arrived in Naples, we were met first by the innumerable lenses of the countless press photographers, and then by the girls of the American Red Cross. They pounced on us with overwhelming kindness, treated us to coffee and the children to lemonade and cocoa, little pancakes, they gave us bags full of useful things; a piece of soap, a toothbrush, a face cloth, a pack of cigarettes, etc. They pressed newspapers in our hands, beamed at us as if we were their dearest children, and kept coming up with new ideas for the part they played in 'Our Peace'.

Suddenly, the dream was shattered: a sentry stepped in our way, with orders to separate the members of the Axis powers from those of the Allies, and to forbid any further contact between them. As swiftly as night follows day at the equator, the light made way for the engulfing darkness; being German became a bad fate that cast a sudden shadow over us. With a rather forced smile we waved adieu to our new friends, and had to battle for a long time against a painful feeling of nausea. The American girls, undaunted, maintained their natural warmth, and in their unrivalled sympathy there appeared genuine maternal feelings that did not alter for national differences, but that was feeble consolation in this profound sadness over the fact that 'being a human being among other human beings' only ever happens in dreams of perfect world.[7]

Vermehren faced only cursory questioning before being released. Other Germans were subjected to more intensive interrogation. Generals von Falkenhausen, Thomas and Halder, along with Colonel von Bonin, Hjalmar Schacht and Fritz Thyssen were detained for questioning about their past association with the Nazis. The Hungarians were also subjected to continued detention and interrogation.

Most were taken to Capri where the German civilian group remained separated from the rest. It was far from a disagreeable detention; all were housed in hotels where they could enjoy delightful views of the azure blue sea while awaiting their imminent departure to their various homelands or places of exile. Following a Homeric-like odyssey of over a thousand miles, having seen the unparalleled evil of Nazism, they would soon have the opportunity to attempt to recover, physically and mentally, from their ordeal. They had emerged from *Nacht und Nebel* ('Night and Fog') to the warm spring sunshine of the beautiful island of Capri where they could contemplate, with varying degrees of optimism, a return to normality.

CHAPTER NINETEEN

SEQUELS

For many of those who were able to make it home, feelings of exhilaration and expectancy gave way to disappointment and, for some, a sense of loss. The routine of domestic life could not but appear dull in contrast with the adrenalin-fuelled last few weeks of captivity. Years of communal living, however trying and stifling, had created strong interpersonal bonds, affections and dependencies that were suddenly sundered. Those re-entering their marital homesteads faced the difficulty of re-establishing relationships with spouses, and sometimes children who did not know them. They had suffered varying levels of ill-treatment in the camps and had witnessed dreadful scenes that might affect their future mental and physical health. What follows is a summary of the afterlife of most of those featured in the proceeding chapters. The altered lives of John McGrath, Ferrero and others are described in the relevant addendums.

Harry Day and Sydney Dowse

For Harry Day, depression and disillusionment was his lot for a time. Immediately on his return to England, he telephoned home. His friend and biographer describes what happened:

> It was brief just as he had expected. He knew he had no home but he had hoped to talk to one of the children. Instead [his wife] Doris came on. Their greetings were cold and brief and held no future promise. She had other bad news for him too. His mother had died peacefully at Salisbury in November 1944. Wings hung up as a great wave of desolation engulfed him.[1]

He later remarried, but that ended in even greater humiliation and bitterness. In an unforgivable act of betrayal, Sydney Dowse, the man who was probably closest to him in captivity, ran off with his new wife.[2] A book, *Wings Day*, celebrating Day's career and escape adventures, was published in 1968. It was written by his friend and fellow RAF prisoner of war, Sydney Smith. This should have been a consolation, but even here problems arose. In the original manuscript it was implied that the four Irish soldiers who were imprisoned with him in Sachsenhausen were traitors. One of them, most likely Cushing – who had his own book, *Soldier for Hire*, published a few years previously – learned of this and threatened to sue. Although, initially assuring his publisher that he had proof, Day was eventually forced into an embarrassing climb-down.[3] He sought solace in drink and went through a tough period. But there were good days, too. The DSO and OBE awarded to him were just recognition for his bravery and perseverance in organising multiple escape attempts. He died in Malta in 1977.

Sydney Dowse became a rich playboy and a serial womaniser after the war. He married three times, including Day's ex-wife, and had several mistresses. While not universally popular, he was well connected in high society and was made an equerry at Buckingham Palace. He suffered from Alzheimer's disease in his final years, but at least he had the good fortune to have one of his lovers look after him. A rich married lady, she bought a house for him near her and her husband's country mansion so that she could care for him. He died in 2008.

Bertram James

James was awarded the Military Cross in 1946 in recognition of his multiple escape attempts. He married 'a beautiful Irish nurse', Madge Tughan, whom he met in Berlin that year.[4] They had one son, Patrick, but, sadly, he died young. James had used his time in captivity to some advantage, having learned to speak French, German and Russian. He continued to serve in the RAF until 1958. As a civilian, he was appointed General Secretary of the Great Britain–USSR Association and subsequently had a career in the British diplomatic service.

Although a modest man, he became a regular contributor to TV documentaries and radio programmes talking about his experiences, especially following the success of the film *The Great Escape* in 1963. This seems to have irritated Dowse, who accused James of cashing in on the subject. But then, James was never well-off like most of his former RAF campmates. His book *Moonless Night*, the last of the memoirs, was published in 1983. He died in 2008, a few months before Dowse. When Dowse heard the news he burst into tears. His caring lover, surprised at this reaction, reminded him that he hated 'Jimmy', he nodded, sobbing 'but I loved him too'.[5]

Sigismund Payne Best and Richard Stevens

The return home of the two MI6 operatives was not something to be celebrated in 54 Broadway, the then secret London headquarters of the Intelligence Service. Stewart Menzies, the service's chief, and his assistant, Claude Dansey, were never likely to welcome reminders of their most embarrassing wartime failure, for which both shared responsibility. Payne Best, more wily than Stevens, decided to use the chief's discomfort about the Venlo incident to his advantage. Dissatisfied about his pension, he threatened to disclose embarrassing facts unless his payments were enhanced.[6] This presumably related to Payne Best's intention to write a book about his adventures. *The Venlo Incident* was duly published in 1950, with Menzies's approval. The book sold well and provided its author with a good income for a number of years, although he was later declared bankrupt.

Payne Best initially returned to his home in The Hague to live with his second wife Maria van Bess ('May'). However, they separated in 1953 and he moved back to England where he married for a third time. Stevens, with the exception of a BBC radio interview in 1947, said little publicly about his kidnapping and subsequent captivity. Payne Best, however, took exception to the content of what Stevens said during that broadcast. The cause of his ire was Stevens's bleak portrayal of the conditions he endured while in the prison bunkers of Sachsenhausen and Dachau. Payne Best wrote to Stevens rebuking him for exaggerating about his treatment. He contrasted what he had said on the radio with what Stevens had told him and went on to quote McGrath's note to Payne Best in which the Irishman said that Stevens 'had everything a man could wish for'.[7]

Payne Best for some reason harboured a strong sense of resentment against Stevens. Although he was correct in claiming that his former intelligence partner exaggerated about his prison camp conditions, his resentment went further. He implied that Stevens was the more culpable in relation to their capture and in the information disclosed to the Germans. Also evident is a pitiful, 'I suffered more than you did' refrain. But Payne Best also had a contemporary motive. He concluded his letter by saying: '[W]e should one and all do everything in our power to eradicate the feelings of hatred engendered by the war. Untrue stories of ill-treatment suffered as a prisoner in Germany are to my mind, at the present juncture, nothing less than criminal and I shall always do everything in my power to unmask them.'[8] These sentiments could be considered laudable, except 'the present juncture' he referred to was a time when the full horrors of the Holocaust had become known. Payne Best was opposed to all war crime trials, so it seems he was prepared to excuse even mass murderers.

Payne Best died in 1978 aged ninety-three. Stevens, who had worked as an interpreter with NATO, predeceased him, having died eleven years earlier, aged seventy-three.

The Four Irish 'Traitors': Cushing, Walsh, O'Brien and Spence

The return to Britain at the end of the war of Cushing, Walsh, O'Brien and Spence was bound to involve some investigation into suspicions that they had collaborated with the enemy. The officers who soldiered with the Irishmen in the concentration camps, were, as part of their debriefing, asked to identify suspected traitors. A number of them mentioned all four in this context, although they generally left open the question of their guilt. For example, Day, in his written report, said that O'Brien and Walsh 'had agreed to do sabotage and espionage work for the Germans in order, they maintained, to escape'. A similar allegation was made about Cushing. In respect of Spence he recorded that he 'agreed to broadcast for the Germans in the hope of getting an opportunity to escape'.[9] Peter Churchill submitted a report on Spence that, it seems, left no doubt about his belief that he was a traitor. MI5 also had evidence from the interrogation report of an SS Officer that Cushing was a stool pigeon for the Friesack camp commander and this report also confirmed that Spence had worked for the German Broadcasting Service to Ireland.[10] It fell to Cecil

Liddell, the head of MI5's Irish section, to decide if court-martial proceedings were called for. His decision to recommend no action was influenced by the evidence of Father Thomas O'Shaughnessy, the chaplain assigned for six months to the Irish camp.

After extracting himself from Friesack in January 1942, the priest confirmed during his interview with a British Secret Service agent that John McGrath worked to sabotage the German project. He went on to identify a small number of individuals who he believed were active collaborators, but he tended to excuse the actions of Cushing, O'Brien and Walsh, expressing the view that they had no intention of working for the Germans. O'Shaughnessy had a particularly favourable opinion of Walsh who he described as 'one of the most reliable men in Friesack ... completely trusted by McGrath'.[11] This assertion was confirmed by McGrath in his post-war deposition.[12] The priest felt that O'Brien, although a rough character like Cushing, had no traitorous intentions. He even speculated that they may have been selected by McGrath to keep an eye on Cushing. Another factor in the men's favour was that they had been detained in the military prison in Oranienburg after their arrest by the Gestapo. For all these reasons, Liddell, while noting McGrath's poor opinion of Cushing, doubted that they were guilty of treason.[13] The guilt or otherwise of Spence, was another matter entirely but, if there are files about his investigation, they remain closed. It seems clear that no action was taken against him, for Peter Churchill later stated that 'for some unaccountable reason there was an amnesty towards a certain class of individual like him [Spence] and my affidavit was never used'.[14] The fortunate Spence will, however, reappear shortly in this postscript.

Patrick O'Brien died a few years after the war. Thomas Cushing took leave to go home to his native Tipperary, before returning to the ranks and seeing more action in Korea. He later married and settled down in County Cork. Andy Walsh, the most popular of the four, found himself in trouble shortly after returning to England. Imprisoned in Wellington Barracks in London in July 1945, he contacted Sydney Dowse to seek his help. Dowse, in collaboration with Harry Day, secured his release.[15] The reason for his imprisonment is not stated, but in a UK National Archive file there is reference in a 1951 memo of him being 'at the Old Bailey not so long ago in connection with an attempt to steal gold from an airliner'.[16]

Walsh was again arrested in 1962, this time in connection with an armed payroll robbery at Heathrow Airport. This was a well-planned and sophisticated robbery of £62,000, the equivalent of about £2 million today. It was carried out by a London gang, some of whom took part in the more notorious Great Train Robbery the following year. Walsh, although probably not directly involved in the robbery, was charged with being part of the conspiracy. Again, some of his POW officer comrades came to his aid. Peter Churchill, Harry Day and Johnnie Dodge arranged for him to be defended by a solicitor and barrister and they were each prepared to give character evidence of Walsh's 'fundamental honesty and loyalty'.[17] Walsh escaped conviction. It is to the immense credit of Churchill, Dodge and Day, that they put their formidable reputations on the line for the Irishman.

Walsh had retired from the army by this time and was not in good health. He had had a kidney removed and blamed this on being kicked and beaten by the Gestapo after his arrest in 1942. He married after his return to England and lived in Hayes End, West London, a few miles north of Heathrow Airport. With a meagre pension he found it difficult to make ends meet and this may have tempted him to earn a little 'easy money'. He died in 1969, a few weeks short of his sixtieth birthday. A few days before he passed away, a letter arrived requesting that he provide evidence to an investigation by the Munich Public Prosecutor into the death in Sachsenhausen of Stalin's son.[18]

Peter Churchill and Hugh Falconer

While others were shipped home, the two SOE men were flown back to London on 12 May 1945. To Churchill's great delight, he found that Odette was waiting for him in the SOE offices in Oxford Square. Until then he was not certain if she had survived. She nearly didn't; she had been tortured and sentenced to death while in Ravensbrück and only survived when the Camp Commandant, Fritz Suhren, judged, wrongly, that it would redeem him in the eyes of the victors if he personally handed her over to the advancing Americans.[19] Peter and Odette married in 1947 and both were the recipients of honours. He was awarded the DSO and, from the French government, the *Croix de Guerre*; she received the George Cross personally from King George VI. A book about her wartime role was published and made into a film, *Odette*, in which she was played by Anna Neagle and Churchill by Trevor Howard.[20] Perhaps their love burned too brightly, for the real-life couple divorced in 1955 after Churchill left her for a former model. He went to live on the Cote d'Azur, where he worked as an estate agent. He died in 1972.

Hugh Falconer, after being reunited with his wife, returned to Germany to serve in the British sector of the Allied Control Commission that governed the country prior to the establishment of the German Federal Republic.

Johnnie Dodge

As we learned in Chapter 5, Dodge accepted a German proposition to be flown home on a 'peace mission'. It's unlikely that Dodge ever got to pass on a message to his cousin Winston Churchill. The war was virtually over by then and he probably had no real inclination to do so anyway, notwithstanding his strong anti-Soviet leanings. He resolved, however, to return to politics. He had been selected to stand for the Conservative Party before the war and, with the post-war general election set for 5 July 1945, he returned to the hustings. He failed to get elected: he lost out narrowly to his Labour rival in an election won nationally by Labour in a landslide, in large measure due to the support of those still in uniform. Dodge decided to give up electoral politics and returned to work in his stockbroker firm. Unfortunately, for his reputation, he later became a strong supporter of apartheid in South Africa. He died in November 1960, aged sixty-six.

Jack Churchill

After departing Niederdorf alone, Jack Churchill made his way to Verona, where he met up with American troops. By this time the surrender had taken place, so the commando officer, ever eager to return to battle, got himself shipped out to Burma. By the time he reached India en route, the Japanese had surrendered after the atomic bombs had been dropped on Hiroshima and Nagasaki. Resentful at being deprived of a final tilt at the enemy, he is reported have said, 'if it wasn't for those damn Yanks, we could've kept the war going another ten years'.[21] Churchill was no doubt playing up to his reputation as an eccentric warrior, although such remarks tended to somewhat unfairly earn

him a Colonel Blimpish image. He did later see some action in Palestine. He
retired from the army in 1959 and died in 1996, aged eighty-nine.

The Sachsenhausen Compensation Controversy

In February 1968, an acrimonious debate took place in the House of Commons
concerning the conditions experienced by the British military prisoners in
Sonderlager 'A' in Sachsenhausen. The context was the payment of one million
pounds by the Federal Government of Germany, to compensate British victims
of Nazi concentration camps. The Foreign Office decided to share this amount
among British survivors of these camps, but excluded those detained in
Sonderlager 'A', or in the prison section of Sachsenhausen, on the basis that they
weren't in the main camp. Their exclusion was bound to be controversial, for
Day, Dowse, Dodge and James were national heroes following the screening of
The Great Escape a few years earlier.

Their cause was taken up by Airey Neave, a Conservative MP and former
POW renowned for his successful escape from Colditz Castle. (He was later to
be murdered by the INLA.) The Foreign Secretary of the Labour government
in power at the time, George Brown, although initially well-disposed to having
the group included in the compensatory pay out, felt obliged to defend his
officials. The case made by the department was that these special prisoners did
not have to endure the same conditions as the prisoners in the main part of the
camp. Extracts from books written by Peter Churchill and Payne Best were
quoted as evidence of this. Churchill, in *The Spirit in the Cage*, described his
initial impressions of the *Sonderlager* as a 'haven' and a 'playground'.[22] Payne
Best in the *Venlo Incident* referred to his cell in the prison in Sachsenhausen as
a 'haven of peace'.[23] These were relative comparisons and were taken out of
context. Most had spent periods in the camp prison where they were kept in
isolation and manacled hand and foot for a time. However, it was true that
conditions in *Sonderlager* 'A' were more in keeping with POW status than
concentration camp life and this influenced the Foreign Office civil servants
against the special prisoners.

Another factor contributing to the original decision to exclude the group,
was that it would have included those Irishmen who were suspected of
conspiratorial acts of 'anti-British subversion'.[24] As indicated earlier, this

characterisation is probably unfair, except perhaps in the case of John Spence. Strangely though, Spence alone among them had an advocate in the House of Commons during the debate. Sir David Renton, MP for Huntingdonshire, told the House of his meeting with the Irishman:

> My connection with the subject of the debate started on a lovely afternoon during the General Election of 1964. I was going along a country road, and spoke to a party of road-menders. One of them, with a broad Irish accent, drew attention to the Anglo-German compensation agreement of which he had seen mention in the newspaper. He asked me whether I could do something about it. He saw me after the election, and told me his story.

> The man was Gunner J. Spence ... He was an Irishman who, fairly early in the war, volunteered—he did not have to, for he was living in Ireland—to serve in the British Army. He joined the Gunners and was captured. The Germans apparently tried to persuade him, as they tried to persuade many Irishmen, but Gunner Spence, like the others, remained loyal. This annoyed the Germans very much and he was put into Sachsenhausen. Mr. Spence tells me, incidentally, that although it is not mentioned in Appendix A [of the Parliamentary Commissioner's Report], he was put into the cell block for some months.

> In Sachsenhausen his health suffered badly. He has been able to do only very light work recently. When I said that I would take up his claim, he told me that he was not looking for a lot of money and did not expect it but that it would be nice to have some compensation to give him some of the comforts in life that he lacks. I put his case fairly early in 1965, when I wrote to the then Minister of State rather than to the Foreign Secretary. The Minister of State saw me. I spent a lot of time with him. Shedding tears he said, in effect, that my constituent had not got his facts right about himself—which I took a bit hard—and, secondly, that if he had got them right he was not qualified because he had not really been in the concentration camp.[25]

The decision not to exclude the Sachsenhausen prisoners was overturned and they received compensation of £917; that is, except Spence, who, it seems, was deemed to have missed the deadline for application.[26]

Political Leaders

Léon Blum and his wife received an enthusiastic welcome when they returned to France on 24 May But their joy soon turned to dismay when they learned that his brother, René, had died in Auschwitz and that her son, Georges Torrès, had been killed in action. Blum was a key witness in the trial of Marshal Pétain. It was, in a sense, a reverse of Blum's own trial three years earlier, with the Marshal taking his place in the dock. Blum appeared fragile in the witness stand, when he spoke about the abuse of moral trust committed by Pétain, which he said amounted to treason.[27] Although sentenced to death, the former Vichy leader had his sentence commuted to life imprisonment by de Gaulle. Pierre Laval was not as fortunate. After being sentenced to death, he wrote to Blum urging him to intervene to help save him. At the urging of Janot, who credited Laval with arranging for her to join Blum in captivity, he wrote to de Gaulle suggesting a new trial, on the basis that the original trial was hurried, while emphasising that he was not seeking a pardon for Laval. Blum knew from past experience how manipulative Laval was, but felt compelled to act. De Gaulle paid no heed and Laval was executed.[28]

Blum was elected to the National Assembly in 1946 and briefly served again as French Prime Minister in 1948 in an attempt by him to forestall the Communists and Gaullists. He died in 1950. Janot lived until 1982.

Alexandros Papagos, who had been commander in chief of the Greek army before the German invasion, also returned home to a hero's welcome. In 1949, he was reinstated as head of the army, which he led in battle against communist-led forces during the Greek Civil War. In 1951, he resigned from the army to form a political party which won a landslide victory the following year, leading to him becoming Prime Minister. He died in office in 1955.

Kurt Schuschnigg was not allowed by the Allies to return to Austria or Germany. He and his wife Vera and daughter Sissi remained in a displaced persons camp in Capri until he managed to secure an academic position in St Louis University in the United States where they settled. Tragically, Vera died in 1959. After his retirement, Schuschnigg was permitted to retire to Austria and died there in 1977.

Miklós Kállay, the former Hungarian Prime Minister, and his Hungarian colleagues had no desire to be repatriated to their native land which was now occupied by the Red Army. Kállay, like Schuschnigg, settled in the US.

The German Generals

Franz Halder was fortunate in avoiding death during the war, and escaping relatively unscathed after it. After about two years of internment, he was freed and in the 1950s worked as an historical advisor for the US Army. **Alexander von Falkenhausen** wasn't as fortunate. He was put on trial in Belgium for the deportation of Jews during his period as military commander of that country. Despite evidence from some former Jewish concentration camp inmates that he was instrumental in saving lives, he was sentenced to twelve years hard labour. After serving about a third of the sentence, he was released and returned to West Germany where he was pardoned by Chancellor Adenauer. **Goerg Thomas** died while still in American captivity in December 1946.

SS

Edger Stiller made it back to Austria, but was later arrested and sentenced to five years in prison in connection with his role in Dachau. After his release in 1950, he was again rearrested and charged with being an accessory to the murder of Georg Elser. Payne Best, hearing of this, offered to testify in his defence and appealed to other members of the *Prominenten* to do the same during legal proceedings in 1951. He praised Stiller for helping to save the lives of the hostages in Niederdorf, and stated, 'Even if Stiller knew of Georg Elser's end and even if he gave orders for his execution and was present when these were carried out, it was not he who committed murder but the man who signed the order and whose liberty is concealed by "illegibility".' (The signature on the written order was illegible.) This was a classic 'acting under orders' defence that would fail to impress most judges. However, in spite, or because of, Payne Best's contribution, Stiller was acquitted.

Ernst Bader and his coterie of SS guards were believed to have been killed by partisans soon after fleeing Niederdorf.[29] However, there are no known first-hand accounts of this.

Karl Wolff was imprisoned with Göring and other leading Nazis in Nuremberg, although he didn't face trial there. He was later sentenced to four years by a German court, but, as he had already spent that time in confinement, he was released. He was rearrested in 1962 and charged with contributing to the Holocaust. After a trial in 1964 he was sentenced to fifteen years' imprisonment. Throughout his interrogations and trials, he referred to his role in liberating the *Prominenten,* along with ending the war in Italy, as examples of his 'good deeds'.[30]

The Russians

Nikolay Russchenko, a junior officer among the Russian prisoners managed to somehow avoid being repatriated to Moscow. Peter Churchill offered to provide him with lodgings in England, but his efforts to secure him entry into Britain were unsuccessful. Nevertheless, Russchenko managed by his own ingenuity to remain in the West under an alias.[31] He visited Churchill in London a few years later and told him that he had returned briefly to the South Tyrol where he found **Ivan Bessonov** milking a cow while working for a local farmer.[32] The story is a complete invention; Bessonov's attempts to avoid repatriation to the Soviet Union were unsuccessful. He was arrested when he arrived in Moscow and was kept in prison for nearly five years before being sentenced to death for treason in April 1952. He was shot immediately after his conviction.[33] It is likely that Lieutenant Colonel **Victor Brodnikov** suffered the same fate. **Major General Pyotr Privalov** was kept in jail under interrogation for nearly six years before his trial for treason went all the way to the USSR Supreme Court. His appeal was unsuccessful and he was executed on 30 December 1951. His case was reviewed in 1968 and he was posthumously rehabilitated.[34]

Selected Others

Hjalmar Schacht was tried and acquitted at Nuremberg for 'crimes against peace'. He was, however, convicted in 1947 of being a 'major offender' under the de-Nazification process.[35] He was sentenced to eight years' detention and virtually all of his considerable fortune was confiscated. However, by 1958, he had established a bank and was a sought-after economic advisor in developing countries.

Isa Vermehren studied to become a teacher after the war and later entered a convent. As a nun she became widely known in post-war Germany as the host of a popular religious TV show *The Word for Sunday* and was the recipient of many awards. She wrote her account of her captivity *Reise durch den letzten Akt* ('Journey through the final Act') in 1946, although it wasn't published until 2005.

Sante Garibaldi founded a new political party, the Garibaldian Antifascist Partisan Movement of Italy, in August 1945. The party, based on democratic, republican and federalist principles, didn't prosper and he died the following year.

The Appeal on Behalf of the South Tyrol

In April 1946, most members of the *Prominenten* were sent a document printed in English, French and German. It began:

> A year ago, you have seen the day of liberation in the South Tyrolese Dolomites. The South Tyrolese who from the earliest times have been a free people of the mountains, proved to you they are willing at any time to support the just cause against oppression.

> Your South Tyrolese friends from the days of May 1945 are now fighting for the freedom of their native country. The South Tyrolese population ask you, wherever you may be, to speak an open, friendly word in favour of the just struggle of the South Tyrol. The South

Tyrolese demand the right of self determination. They wish to return to Austria, to which they belonged for centuries.[36]

The appeal, signed by Professor Reut-Nicolussi, a South Tyrolean leader, was sent to 121 of those present in Hotel Pragser Wildsee. All of the recipients must have provided home addresses which are listed in the document, with the exception of the Italian contingent, who, for obvious reasons, would not have been canvassed. The only omission from the list of Germans is Friedrich Engelke. It is reasonable to assume that the reclusive merchant did not wish to leave a forwarding address. (See Addendum IV, 'The Strange Tale of Friedrich Engelke'.)

It's not known if any of those in receipt of the appeal made any representations. In any event, although there was sympathy for the South Tyrolean case, cold war politics dictated that the region remain within Italy. This led to civil unrest and a low-intensity guerrilla war, until the granting of significant regional autonomy in 1972.

SUPPLEMENTARY TALES

COLONEL JOHN MCGRATH: TRUTH AND INVENTION[1]

John McGrath was the catalyst for the research that led to this book. Finding information about his background, however, proved challenging as there are many misleading 'facts' about him. To begin with, his name wasn't John. He was christened Michael Joseph McGrath when he was born on 20 January 1894 in Elphin in County Roscommon. His father, whose name was John, farmed over forty acres in the district. His mother was Mary Jane O'Hara from Coothall in the same county. He attended a secondary school in Carrick-on-Shannon where he resided with his uncle Michael McGrath, who later became a Fianna Fáil County Councillor. When he was seventeen he moved to Lancashire where he enrolled in an Officer Training Corps. In his application he named himself as Joseph McGrath – it is believed that he wished to avoid being labelled a 'Mick'[2] – and he only later switched to John. He added two years to his age and made the unlikely claim of having attended Trinity College Dublin. Officer Training Corps catered for students in public schools and universities, so, to gain entry, it was essential to list a college. Telling a few harmless untruths was worth the risk to gain a commission in the British Army; it was, conceivably, his only point of entry into polite society. McGrath also invented for himself a middle-class pedigree: he listed his father's profession as Judge on his application form. One can only wonder what it was that prompted such precocious reinvention.

The young man gained his commission and, during the First World War, saw action in Gallipoli and France. He must have distinguished himself for he won a promotion to captain. He was wounded twice, with the second injury resulting in him being shipped back to England and a lengthy period of hospitalisation. He spent the last year of the first war in a military infirmary in Blackpool. He made efforts to remain in the army but was decommissioned in 1929.[3] He returned to Ireland in the early 1930s and secured work as a cinema manager. The Elliman family owned a number of cinemas and theatres and, having built new modern cinemas in Dublin, Cork and Limerick, appointed McGrath to manage each one in turn. However, the family's most ambitious investment was in the newly rebuilt Theatre Royal in Dublin, reputed during its opening in 1936 to be the largest theatre in Europe. McGrath was its first manager. On the opening night he was warmly applauded by an audience of 4,000 citizens, among them a host of civic and state dignitaries. He had just presented, on behalf of the proprietor, a donation to the Lord Mayor, Alfie Byrne's charity. Responding, the Mayor told the audience that 'it gave him the greatest pleasure to reintroduce to them Mr John McGrath, whom they formally knew at the Savoy, and who had now come back to Dublin to manage that wonderful new theatre'.[4]

Although he prospered in civilian life – he was a director of a number of companies in addition to his theatrical work – he remained an army reservist and was recalled in 1939. Living in Dublin, he could easily have ignored the summons. From the little we know of his personality, he seems to have been an avuncular man, liked and generous, but with few, if any, close friends. He never married, although an entry in the Elphin parish register indicates he contemplated it in the 1920s.[5] He never stayed for long in the same location and doesn't appear to have ever owned a property. The impression gained is of a restless individual, for whom a return to the army promised new adventures. We cannot, however, discount more noble reasons for him wanting to join the fight. If he was close to anyone in 1939, it was Louis Elliman and through him he would have become acquainted with many in the Jewish community in Dublin, so it's probable he was appalled by the Nazis' persecution of Jews.

His active service in the Second World War wasn't to last long, for he was among those who didn't make it across the channel from Dunkirk. Nevertheless, he must have again distinguished himself in action with the British Expeditionary Force, for he won a field promotion to major. After being wounded and captured at Rouen, he joined thousands of others in a horrendous

350-mile trek from Normandy to Trier in Germany. He claimed to have escaped at one point together with a group of soldiers, some of whom were shot. This incident was recounted during his post-war debriefing, but, as he couldn't recall any names or other details, we are left with the impression that his interrogator was unconvinced about the veracity of this.

The circumstances of his transfer to the Irish Camp at Friesack, north of Berlin, is recounted in Chapter 2. As recounted, the *Abwehr* were seeking an officer with an Irish nationalist background. Apart from his uncle's involvement in Fianna Fáil, he had cousins on his mother's side, O'Haras, who had been in the IRA during the War of Independence so he had credibility in respect of this.[6] His move to Friesack was prompted by a superior officer in his first POW camp. The officer concerned, Brigadier Nicholson, died in captivity, which meant McGrath could not have this verified post-war, but, fortunately for McGrath, the document he had smuggled out of Friesack confirmed his subversive activities in that camp.

John McGrath returned to Dublin in mid-June 1945 shortly after his army debriefing and was reinstated in his managerial position in the Theatre Royal. His return attracted the attention of Irish newspapers. However, the focus of interviews, was not about conditions in Dachau or Sachsenhausen which the world was learning about in gruesome detail, but about the 'Attempt to Enlist Irishmen as Agents'[7] in the Irish camp in Friesack. He managed to re-establish contact with Father Thomas O'Shaughnessy, who had acted as chaplain for a time in that Camp. They met in Dublin where Louis Elliman laid on a banquet for them, 'which lasted for four hours'.[8]

McGrath wasn't in fact a lieutenant colonel as he claimed. As he stated in the document he had smuggled out of Friesack, something he repeated during his debriefing, he self-promoted himself for tactical reasons. He might have had a reasonable expectation that the rank would be retrospectively approved, given the risk he had taken, but the War Office wasn't at all impressed. Far from granting the promotion, they wanted to reduce him to the rank of captain for pension purposes, on the basis that his acting field promotion to major was of such short duration, given his early capture after Dunkirk. His treatment seems at variance to his compatriots. His adversary Stevens had been promoted to lieutenant colonel while in captivity and most of the others appeared in the honours list.

McGrath didn't have much opportunity to enjoy his homecoming. His incarceration seems to have had an effect on his mental and physical health. He had to resign from his restored management role in the Theatre Royal due to a 'nervous disorder'.[9] He also suffered from intestinal problems and he died just seventeen months after his return home. Father O'Shaughnessy administered the last rites to him in his rooms in Merrion Square, Dublin.

He is buried in his native Elphin in County Roscommon alongside his father and mother. The tombstone records that Colonel John McGrath, OBE, died on 27 November 1946. But there is no record of him ever having been awarded an OBE, or a CBE, as he is credited with having in some newspaper obituaries. The claim to have been honoured, which can only have emanated from him, is puzzling. It could be viewed as an attempt at self-aggrandisement, but there may be a kinder, if sadder, interpretation. While McGrath was never a mainstream concentration camp prisoner, his treatment during his time in Sachsenhausen was severe and he is likely to have witnessed the torture and death of others. On his return home he learned that his mother had died and that his brother, his only sibling, was in a mental institution. All this, combined with the disgraceful post-war treatment of him by the army authorities, may well have pushed him over the edge. If so, he may have taken the mental leap, from reality, to what should be. The British Army was vitally important to him; it made him, and in the end, it may have broken him. After all he'd sacrificed and experienced, perhaps he *had* to believe that right prevailed.

MÜLLER, BONHOEFFER AND NIEMÖLLER

The Catholic and Protestant churches did little to impede the Nazis' rise to power and, in some respects, they assisted it. In the crucial early years of Hitler's chancellorship, the Catholic Centre Party, led by a priest with close links to the Vatican, voted for the Enabling Law that allowed Hitler to rule by decree before dissolving itself. A majority of Lutheran pastors aligned themselves to the German Christian Church with its Nazi symbols and anti-Semitic doctrines. While most religious were cowed or passive, there were some brave clerics who actively opposed the regime. A number of them became part of the *Prominenten* group. The most prominent was Pastor Martin Niemöller whose arrest in 1937, and his continued detention after his sentence had expired, caused international outrage. Dietrich Bonhoeffer, a renowned theologian and cleric, an ally of Niemöller before his incarceration, also opposed Hitler. During the war he entered into a conspiracy with Josef Müller a Catholic lawyer who had been a leading member of a Catholic party in Bavaria in the Weimar Republic. Müller and Bonhoeffer were both arrested in April 1943.

Müller was of peasant origin and was known as 'Joey Ox' (*Ochsensepp*), due, it is said, to his childhood role of caring for his father's oxen on their farm in Franconia, although it was possibly also an allusion to his physical strength as a young man. He was a veteran of the First World War and had been awarded the Iron Cross. His veteran status allowed him to gain free post-war entry to Munich University where he studied sociology and economics under Max Weber before taking a law degree. He prospered in civilian life, becoming a businessman and politician in pre-war Munich while simultaneously managing a busy legal practice. He was a devout, but not austere, Catholic – he maintained a Bavarian fondness for beer – and became active in the Bavarian People's Party (PVP), which was allied to the Centre Party, until their joint dissolution in 1933. He had been a friend and advisor to the last PVP Prime Minister of Bavaria, Heinrich Held, and had helped him escape to Switzerland when the Nazis seized power.[1] Müller was also close to Cardinal Faulhaber, the Archbishop of Munich, and he also got to know the future Pope Pius XII when, as Eugenio Pacelli, he served as Papal Nuncio to Bavaria. Pacelli later, as Vatican Secretary of State, arranged for Müller and his bride to be married in St Peter's Basilica in 1934.[2]

With the Nazis in power, Müller began to represent the Church in legal cases concerning breaches of the 1933 Concordat. This treaty had been the product of negotiations between Pacelli and the then German Vice Chancellor, Franz von Papen, and was intended by the Vatican to protect the practice of the Catholic religion in Germany. However, the Concordat neutered Catholic opposition to the Nazi regime as, under its terms, the hierarchy were obliged to swear an oath of loyalty to the Reich and the clergy were required to desist from all political activities. This contributed to the dissolution of Catholic lay organisations and bolstered Hitler's prestige. Many practising Catholics, previously prevented from joining the Nazi party under penalty of being denied the sacraments, were now free to do so. The result was that the Church was made to appear, at best, benignly neutral towards the regime. Despite the benefit accruing to the Nazi Party, the provisions designed to protect the Church were routinely ignored.

Working with Cardinal Faulhaber's close aide and cathedral cannon, Johann Neuhäusler, who was also to become a fellow *Prominenten*, Müller took responsibility for preparing reports of violations for the Vatican. These included suppression of Catholic publications, the expropriation of church properties and the arrest of priests who dared to criticise the regime. Müller owned a small aeroplane which he flew to Rome on his regular visits. There he dealt with the former leader of the Centre Party, Monsignor Kaas, who was now permanently resident in Rome. He also liaised with a Bavarian Jesuit, Robert Leiber, who acted as Pope Pius XII's personal secretary.

Müller's regular visits to Rome not surprisingly came to the attention of the *Abwehr*. Fortunately for him, the organisation was peppered at the top level with oppositionists, who included Hans Oster, the deputy head of the organisation. He recruited Müller into the conspiracy and arranged for him to become a special *Abwehr* agent. Under this cover, Müller was able to travel to Rome more frequently – he claimed to have made 150 journeys from 1940 until his arrest in 1943[3] – briefing the Vatican and carrying messages from the opposition within the *Wehrmacht*. Oster was the prime mover within the military opposition which also included General Ludwig Beck the former Army Chief of Staff, who had resigned from the *Wehrmacht* in 1938 after disagreements with Hitler. Beck's successor, General Franz Halder, took over his role in the oppositional intrigues. The anti-Hitler plotters wanted to obtain some assurances from the British that peace terms would be on offer in the event of Hitler's overthrow. Müller conveyed a commitment from the generals that, following a successful coup, Poland and Czechoslovakia would have their independence, although Austria was to remain part of Germany. Surprisingly, the usually cautious Pontiff entered into this conspiracy and put his weight behind an appeal to the British to treat with the German opposition.

The title of John Cornwell's controversial book on Pius XII, *Hitler's Pope*, is a misnomer in so far as it infers that the Pontiff was an admirer of, or colluded with, the dictator. As the author himself concedes, Pacelli disliked Hitler and abhorred Nazi racial theories.[4] The fact that the Pontiff entered into an anti-Hitler conspiracy, one that endangered him personally, as well as the institutions of the Church in Germany and Italy, makes a nonsense of him being 'Hitler's Pope'. Cornwell was on surer ground when he observed:

> for all Pacelli's distaste for the explicit racism of National Socialism, his fears were overshadowed by the known aggression and goals of Communism. The Holy See's attitude towards Hitler was ambiguous: if it came to comparisons, the Nazis had not vowed to destroy Christianity, in fact they had made soothing gestures towards the Catholic Church. From the Secretariat of State's view of the Church in the world, the threat of Communism was an altogether different matter.[5]

This more clearly explains the Pope's actions in 1940 and early 1941 when he facilitated Müller's representations. At that time Hitler and Stalin were effectively allies and this was Pius's worst nightmare come true. The Nazis' only saving grace, their role as a bulwark against Bolshevikism, seemed to have been foregone, and the evil empires were united. This changed everything: entering into a conspiracy to have Hitler supplanted by an anti-Bolshevik administration would have been worth almost any risk.

Müller, informed by his contacts in the *Abwehr*, even went so far as to convey information to the Vatican about the impending German attack on France and the Low Countries. The Pope arranged for this information to be passed on to the Belgium and Dutch governments and personally told the British Ambassador to the Holy See of the threat to France in the sure knowledge that it would be passed on to Paris.[6] However, the Germans intercepted a message from the Belgium Ambassador to his government, in which the date of the planned attack was revealed, thus alerting them to the existence of a spy operating at a senior level within the regime.[7] Hitler ordered Reinhardt Heydrich, head of the SS's Foreign Intelligence, and Admiral Canaris head of the *Abwehr*, to jointly investigate the matter. Canaris was, at the very least, a passive supporter of the opposition and for this reason, and because he and Heydrich were rivals, little co-operation ensued and the investigation went nowhere.[8] Its failure was guaranteed when Josef Müller, the chief culprit, was appointed by Canaris to conduct the Rome aspect of the investigation on behalf of the *Abwehr*.[9]

Notwithstanding the Pope's urging, the British were reluctant to offer any firm assurances to the plotters concerning their intended putsch. The fiasco at Venlo had made them suspicious of any such representations. Moreover, the senior Foreign Office civil servant, Alexander Cadegan, had his doubts about Kaas, perhaps recalling his role in the dissolution of his own Centre Party, the last democratic obstacle to the Nazis' power grab.[10] Nevertheless, Halifax, the Foreign Secretary, was still anxious for peace and some messages were exchanged. A one-page summary, typed on Vatican notepaper, containing a list of what the British would require of a new German regime was eventually produced, although probably without the knowledge of the British, and circulated among sympathetic military leaders.[11] However, the generals failed to move and, with the success of the German blitzkrieg in France, Hitler's popularity in Germany soared and the plotters became dispirited.

Müller had been joined by Pastor Dietrich Bonhoeffer in his efforts to persuade the British to treat with the plotting generals. In contrast to the

Bavarian's modest background, the pastor's family could lay claim to generations of distinguished ancestors. The younger man – at thirty-nine, Bonhoeffer was eight years younger than Müller – had bravely fought against pre-war Nazification of German Protestantism, and with Martin Niemöller, had formed the Confessing Church in opposition to the regime supporting German Christian Church. Bonhoeffer was particularly appalled by the racist and anti-Semitic laws which affected his family directly: his brother in law was a Jew who had converted to Protestantism. Contrary to the mores of his time, Bonhoeffer wasn't in the least racist. While studying in the United States in the early 1930s, he chose to worship with and, for a time live within, a black community.[12] In this respect, he differed from his colleague Niemöller who, pre-war, displayed anti-Semitic tendencies.

Bonhoeffer's concept of God was, like many pious Protestants of his era, individualised and internalised, and, for a time, he awaited a signal that God would approve of his participation in a plot to overthrow Hitler. It was his non-believing brother Klaus and his wife Emmi, both active in the resistance, who pushed him towards involvement. Emmi admonished him: 'You Christians are glad when someone else does what you know must be done, but it seems that somehow you are unwilling to get your own hands dirty and do it.'[13] He agreed to be recruited into the *Abwehr* conspiracy; his entry was facilitated by another in-law, his sister Christel's husband, Hans von Dohnányi, who worked under Hans Oster, and who was himself a courageous and committed opponent of the Nazis. Bonhoeffer was tasked with a similar mission to Müller, in his case using international Protestant channels in attempts to secure an undertaking from the British government concerning a planned coup.

In their joint endeavours, Bonhoeffer and Müller became close allies. In order to hide him from the worrying attention of the Gestapo, Müller arranged for him to reside for a winter in a Benedictine monastery at Ettal in the Bavarian Alps. The pastor was a committed Lutheran, but he was far from being sectarian. He attended mass and discussed theological issues with the Abbot, with whom he was on friendly terms.[14] During 1942, Bonhoeffer accompanied Müller on a visit to Rome, where he was taken to the Vatican and introduced to Fathers Kaas and Leiber. Kaas took Bonhoeffer into the crypt of St Peter's Basilica to show him the excavations he was supervising in the hope of discovering the remains of St Peter. The monsignor may well have secretly hoped that sight of the supposed relic would somehow convert the schismatic.

In May 1942, Bonhoeffer travelled to Stockholm to meet George Bell, Bishop of Chichester, with whom he had become acquainted during his time in London ministering to the Lutheran community there in the mid-1930s. Bell agreed to make representations to the British Government, seeking the same type of assurances as sought by Müller in Rome. The Bishop lobbied Anthony Eden, who had by then become Foreign Secretary in the Churchill administration, but the initiative was vetoed by the Prime Minister who was opposed to any unilateral dialogue. By then the Germans had attacked Russia and the Prime Minister didn't wish to endanger relations with Stalin. After the Casablanca Declaration in January 1943, that made unconditional surrender the only terms available to end the war, all hopes of a negotiated peace faded.

Müller and Bonhoeffer, nevertheless, continued to conspire against the Nazi regime until they were both arrested on 5 April 1943. An *Abwehr* agent who had participated in some of the visits to Rome came under suspicion of currency violations and, under interrogation, he divulged the fact that Müller, Bonhoeffer and his brother-in-law Dohnanyi, had been seeking peace terms from the British. The three men were arrested and held in the Tegel military prison in Berlin. While the first few days of confinement were difficult, conditions improved due to the fact that Bonhoeffer's uncle, General Paul von Hase, also a secret oppositionist, was the military commander in Berlin. Müller and Bonhoeffer were subjected to questioning about different matters. Müller was questioned about the purpose of his visits to Rome and his contacts in the Vatican. He adopted the strategy of refusing to provide any information on the basis that he was in Rome on official *Abwehr* business and that only Canaris, the head of the *Abwehr*, could oblige him to answer.[15] Canaris, although under a cloud at the time, still remained in charge of military intelligence and, for reasons that remain unclear, he was then being shielded by Himmler.[16] Bonhoeffer seemed to have been suspected only of non-treasonable charges at this stage. He was being accused of evading the army draft and of assisting others in his Confessional Church to do the same. He was also being accused of money laundering:[17] This related to his use of *Abwehr* money to help smuggle Jews to Switzerland.[18] At that stage the Gestapo knew nothing of a plot to kill Hitler.

Müller was eventually brought to trial and accused of using his role as a reserve *Abwehr* agent to conspire with the enemy. The military court found him not guilty, but he was immediately rearrested and sent back to the military prison.[19] There he and Bonhoeffer remained confined until July 1944. They knew from information smuggled to them that another plan to kill Hitler was being hatched. Bonhoeffer's uncle, General Hase, was deeply involved in the plot now being led by Clause von Stauffenberg. Hase visited Bonhoeffer in his cell on 30 June 1944: an event that caused much kowtowing by the prison staff. He brought with him four bottles of champagne – the pastor, like his Catholic collaborator, was not abstemious – and stayed for more than five hours. Although there was no mention of the plot, Bonhoeffer felt sure that the visit was confirmation that the coup was imminent and that they were toasting a hoped-for liberation.[20] His future prospects and that of his brother-in-law Dohnanyi as well as Müller were dependent on Stauffenberg, succeeding in blowing up Hitler.

After the failure of Stauffenberg's bomb to kill Hitler, General von Hase was among the first batch of plotters to be executed. Canaris and Oster were arrested and Canaris's diary and other incriminating documents were discovered by the SS, in which both Müller and Bonhoeffer's names appeared. On 8 October 1944, they were taken to Gestapo Headquarters in Berlin. Canaris, Oster, Dohnanyi and Fabian von Schlabrendorff – a cousin of Bonhoeffer's fiancée, who had himself almost succeeded in killing Hitler – were among those being interrogated there at the same time. They were held in isolation in tiny underground cells. Müller was handcuffed and had his legs shackled. He was beaten with rubber truncheons during interrogations and he became emaciated due to inadequate food rations.[21] Four months later, Payne Best and his group from Sachsenhausen came to be housed for a short time in the same building and Müller and Bonhoeffer were taken with them to Buchenwald Concentration Camp.

As recounted in Chapter 6, Bonhoeffer was executed in Flossenbürg along with other *Abwehr* conspirators. Müller, although taken to be executed, survived and was taken to Dachau with other members of the *Prominenten*. There he met Martin Niemöller, who had been imprisoned on Hitler's orders in 1937. Three Catholic priests were housed with Niemöller in Dachau. They had been placed in close proximity to the pastor for a particular reason. It had been discovered that the Lutheran pastor was considering converting to Catholicism and the SS wished to encourage this because a conversion would discredit him in international Protestant circles.[22] In the end, Niemöller decided to stick with Luther. Perhaps, realising the Nazis' scheme, the priests, the most prominent of whom was Canon Neuhäusler, didn't try too hard to convert him.

Martin Niemöller survived the war and for a time was hailed as a brave victim of Nazism but the revelation that, pre-war, he had been anti-Semitic tarnished his reputation. Nevertheless, having returned to ministry post-war, he was elected president of the World Council of Churches in 1961.

Josef Müller, as we have learned, joined Niemöller and the rest of the *Prominenten* on their journey into the Alps. During his post-war interrogation in Capri, he requested of his American inquisitor that he be taken to Rome so that he could demonstrate his claimed links to the Pope. The Americans agreed and he was flown there accompanied by his assigned US intelligence officer. In the Vatican, the Pope greeted him warmly and granted him a lengthy private audience.[23] On his return to Munich, Müller became a founder member and the first chairman of the Christian Social Union, the Bavarian sister partner party allied to the German Christian Democrats.

ALEXANDER VON STAUFFENBERG AND FEY VON HASSELL: A LOVE STORY

Sippenhaft – kinfolk being liable for their relatives' crimes – was applied from the earliest days of the Third Reich. 'Blood purity' was a fundamental tenet of Nazi ideology and preventing the 'pollution of German blood'[1] was a justification for the Nuremberg race laws. Thoughts or actions designed to undermine the Nazi state demonstrated bad blood lines and the remedy was not merely to eliminate the individual but the blood line as well. From 1933 to 1935 *Sippenhaft* was used extensively to terrorise and intimidate the opponents of Nazism, principally communists and social democrats. Relatives were taken into 'protective custody', and sometimes murdered in retribution for the actions of a family member. It was also applied against the relatives of those who fled the country in order to deter others from leaving and to constrain those living abroad from saying or doing anything hostile to the interests of the regime. Loss of citizenship, property and employment was part of the punishment for a relatives' crime. Yet, for most of the period of Nazi rule, there were no specific laws, or even guidelines, to regulate the practice. It was a system of arbitrary terror, used by different agencies of the regime; the Nazi party, the Gestapo and the SS. Sometimes the practice was ordered at central level, more often, especially in the early stages, the initiative was taken by local Nazi functionaries.[2] As overt opposition to the regime declined due to these and other terror tactics, the use of *Sippenhaft* became less frequent, only to resurface again in wartime, when it was directed against the families of soldiers who deserted or joined the enemy. The practice reached its apogee after the attempt on Hitler's life on 20 July 1944 when about 5,000 people were arrested, for no other reason than their being related to one of the suspects.[3]

When Colonel Claus Schenk Graf von Stauffenberg placed a briefcase containing a bomb under a table near Hitler in the Wolf's Lair, he knew the risk he was taking, not just for himself, but for his family. He knew they would suffer if his plan to kill the Führer and execute a *coup d'etat* failed. Stauffenberg was summarily shot the next morning. Scores of his co-conspirators suffered a more agonising death. After being tortured and interrogated, they were brought before a People's Court where they were harangued and condemned by the hanging Judge, Roland Friesler. They were then immediately executed, effectively by strangulation, having been, on Hitler's orders, 'hung up like meat carcasses'.[4] Stauffenberg's brother, Berthold, a co-conspirator, was among the victims. Himmler told a meeting of Gauleiter that the family of Graf Stauffenberg 'will be wiped out down to its last member'.[5]

Himmler assigned Ernst Kaltenbrunner head of a special investigation unit to identify those implicated in the 20 July plot. To his surprise, the conspiracy was found to involve a not insignificant proportion of the senior officer cadre within the *Wehrmacht*. Those involved were mainly from the landed gentry and *Sippenhaft* arrests disproportionally encompassed this class. The relatives of Claus and Berthold Stauffenberg were among the first to be arrested. Eleven of them were sent to an isolated hotel, the Hindenburg Baude, located in forested Silesian hills near the present-day Czech–Polish border. Among them were siblings, uncles, aunts and cousins of the two brothers, including children. Also present were members of Claus's wife's family, the von Lerchenfeld's. His wife, Nina, who was pregnant at the time of her arrest, was kept in solitary confinement while under interrogation in Berlin. She was later transferred to Ravensbrück concentration camp where she gave birth to her fifth child. All her children were taken from her and placed in an orphanage with the intention of having them adapted by Nazi families. Berthold Stauffenberg's widow, Mika, was among the other Stauffenberg family members held in the Hindenburg Baude, as was Alexander, the twin of Berthold and only surviving, brother of Claus.

Count Alexander von Stauffenberg was an academic; a professor of ancient history in Würzburg University in Bavaria, before the war. Being also a *Wehrmacht* reserve officer, he was assigned to the Russian front where he was twice wounded before being transferred to an administrative post in Athens. Although sharing his brother's dislike for the Nazis, they did not involve him in their conspiracy, in part because they regarded him as somewhat indiscrete,[6] but mainly to protect him. In any event, as a junior officer stationed far from Berlin there was little he could contribute. Nevertheless, when he heard about his brother's involvement, he knew he was sure to be arrested. He made no attempt to flee, knowing the likely repercussions for his wife, Melitta. She was part-Jewish by family background – a *Mischling* (mixed race) under the racist Nuremberg Laws – and for this reason she was especially at risk.

Melitta von Stauffenberg was deemed to only partly belong to the German race and nation and, although still entitled to Reich citizenship, she would have been regarded as suspect. Despite this impediment, she had become a highly accomplished aeronautic engineer and a decorated Luftwaffe test pilot holding the rank of captain, accomplishments that allowed her to officially obtain 'equal to Aryan' status.[7] She was arrested, as Alexander feared, but was released within two months because she was seen as indispensable to the war effort. She was involved in designing and testing night flying equipment and in test piloting prototype aircraft, including the Messerschmitt 262 turbo jet fighter, the first jet-powered fighter aircraft.[8] The only condition placed on her release was that she no longer use the Stauffenberg name. Alexander, however, faced indefinite imprisonment. He was arrested on 26 July and brought back to Berlin. Although the SS eventually accepted that he knew nothing of his sibling's activities, there was no prospect of a brother of Claus von Stauffenberg being released, and he was detained along with other members of his extended family in the Hindenburg Baude.

There was another large family group detained along with the Stauffenbergs. They were relatives of Dr Carl Goerdeler, a former conservative Mayor of Leipzig and a leader of the civilian opposition who had been destined to be Chancellor had the coup succeeded. At first, he too had supported Hitler, believing, like so many other conservatives, that his radicalism would be tempered by advice from the likes of himself. Goerdeler managed to hide after the coup failed, but he was later captured and executed. His wife and their daughters, his brother and daughter-in-law and grandchildren – thirteen Goerdeler relatives in all – were arrested. The two extended families must have been relieved to find their assigned place of detention to be a hotel rather than a concentration camp and to discover that they were to be treated like guests. There was no shortage of food and they were served meals daily by the hotel staff. They were even allowed to roam the nearby forest tracks without undue monitoring by the few SS guards present.

A lone and distraught woman joined the Stauffenbergs and Goerdelers in October 1944. Fey von Hassell was the daughter of Ulrich von Hassell, a former career diplomat and a leading member of the underground opposition. Fey had led a privileged life until her father's arrest. The von Hassell's were of noble Hanoverian lineage and Ulrich von Hassell had been appointed ambassador to Italy by the Weimar administration in 1932. Fey's adolescence had been spent in Rome, living in her father's ambassadorial residence. She married, aged twenty-two, an aristocratic Italian, Detalmo Pirzio-Biroli. (His family had claim to the title 'Count di Brazzà' and Brazzaville, the capital of the Congo-Brazzaville, is named after Detalmo's grand-uncle.) Fey had resided in the family's splendid villa 'Brazzà', near Udine with her two children while her husband served in the Italian army. Although concerned about her father and her brothers who were in the *Wehrmacht*, as well as her husband, she otherwise led an idyllic existence on her estate in a locality untouched by the war. That all changed in September 1943, when the German military occupied Italy, following the overthrow of Mussolini. Detalmo went into hiding to avoid being imprisoned by the Germans and joined a partisan group. Meanwhile, Fey had to accommodate a unit of the German army who were billeted in her house.

In the early morning of 9 September 1944, Fey was awoken by the officer in charge who bluntly informed her that father had been executed. Later that day, she herself was arrested and held in a prison cell in Udine. After ten days, she was released and allowed to return home under house arrest. This was only a temporary reprieve, for a week later, she and her two sons, aged two and three, were taken to Gestapo headquarters in Innsbruck where, to her unspeakable anguish, her children, the eldest screaming for his mother, were forcibly taken from her.[9] After three difficult weeks in prison in Innsbruck, on 22 October, which happened to be her birthday, she was escorted on a long series of train journeys to the Hindenburg Baude.[10]

In the hotel, Fey met another woman who, like her, had had her children taken from her. She was Ilse-Lotte von Hofacker whose husband, Caesar von Hofacker, a Luftwaffe colonel, had been a leading member of the opposition while stationed in Paris. The two women comforted each other and became close friends. Fey also became friendly with members of the Stauffenberg family who took her into their fold. She was particularly taken with Alexander. He was charming, friendly and erudite, and he and Fey became close.

One day she found him attempting to read Dante's *Inferno* in Italian using his knowledge of Latin. She offered to teach him Italian and they would take walks together, both sharing confidences and consoling each other.[11] Alexander was, at thirty-nine, a good deal older than Fey. He was a tall, handsome man with a head of tousled black hair. Although at times understandably melancholic, he could be good company and had a mischievous sense of humour, often mimicking and ridiculing their SS minders. The fair-haired Fey was an attractive woman and the couple were compatible by upbringing, both displaying the confidence and bearing of their privileged family backgrounds. They were both well-travelled, knowledgeable and appreciative of European high culture as well as being conversant in French and English. They shared a love of poetry, Goethe in particular, which they liked to recite, and found consolation and solace in each other's company.

The kin hostage group's pampered existence in the Hindenburg Baude ended in late November 1944, when the twenty-two residents were told to prepare for an immediate move. They were transported to a railway station to begin a long and arduous three-month odyssey during a harsh north German winter. Their first stop was a concentration camp, Stutthof, near Danzig (later Gdansk), where they arrived on 2 December. On entry, the group were addressed by the camp commander, Paul-Werner Hoppe, who told them:

> You are the so-called prisoners of kin. You all have relations who were involved in the attempted assassination of the Führer. Until your fate is decided, this barrack is at your disposal. You are permitted to walk around the outside of the barrack until nine o'clock in the evening. If you go out later, the guards have orders to shoot. You are not allowed to speak to the guards, nor are you permitted to say your surnames aloud.[12]

Originally housing Polish prisoners after the German invasion, Stutthof was converted into a concentration camp in 1942. The camp, surrounded by thick forests and swamps, was, used to house Soviet POWs, who were made to work for ethnic Germans farmers.[13] By the time of the kin group's arrival, the camp had become vastly overcrowded, as Jewish prisoners from camps further east were being relocated there due to the advance of the Red Army. The SS dealt with the resulting overcrowding by systematic murder. In early October, a month before the kin prisoners arrived, a series of 'selections' took place. These involved an SS medical officer walking along rows of assembled prisoners, selecting those judged too weak or too sick for work detail to be dispatched to the camp gas chamber.[14]

The kin prisoners were not immediately aware of these horrors. They were housed in a hut situated at the perimeter of the camp complex and initially had little contact with the main camp prisoners. They were not required to work, other than to keep their accommodation clean and tidy and to chop timber for their stove. Nevertheless, their conditions were in stark contrast to what they enjoyed in the Hindenburg Baude. They were perpetually hungry, fed only with watery soup during the day and a small portion of bread and weak ersatz coffee in the evening. They also suffered from the cold; the winter of 1944 was extreme and the stove they were provided was totally inadequate to heat their barrack hut. They had to huddle close to it to feel any warmth. Chopping wood would generate body heat, but Alexander, probably unused to the task, almost chopped off his toes in the process. He was bandaged and sent to bed, but had the consolation of being tended to by Fey.[15]

A typhoid epidemic raged in the camp and hundreds were dying daily. Despite their relative isolation from the main camp, the kin prisoners were not immune. Three of them became infected, including Fey von Hassell. Others suffered from scarlet fever and dysentery. The camp commander had orders to keep these prisoners alive, at least for now, and he provided some medicines and an isolation sick room. The group were also fortunate in having a physician amongst them, Dr Bogislav Goerdeler, a brother of the former mayor of Leipzig, who tended to the sick at great risk to his own health. Few dared visit the sick room. Alexander was one of them, having volunteered to keep the stove burning. Knowing Fey was too weak, he didn't try to talk to her, but one day, when she was showing signs of recovery, he placed a piece of paper in her hand. It contained a poem he'd written for her. The following translation of the final lines are taken from Fey's autobiographical account:

Like sweet smelling blossoms
Flouting under trees, I greet you.
With longing wonderful and sweet I greet you,
But only in dreams,
So let me dream.

Console me now as we wander,
Pathless, starless,
I cannot reach or touch you,
But through the wall I hear your laboured breaths,
So near, so near, through twelve sad nights of Christmas.[16]

The poem was composed by Alexander in the days following Christmas and, as Fey explained, the final line refers to German folklore that predicts that whatever you dream during the twelve nights after Christmas will come true. It is a poem of romantic longing, symbolically, but cautiously expressed as a dream.

The typhoid patients slowly recovered although they remained weak. The rest of the group weren't much stronger. Due to their inadequate diet and the extreme cold, they found it difficult to do any work and the Camp Commander, still concerned about the consequences for him should any of them perish, assigned two Russian women from the main camp to assist. Mika von Stauffenberg spoke Russian and learned from them about the horrors of the main camp and its gas chamber.[17]

As the kin prisoners huddled in their barrack hut in mid-January 1945, they began to hear the sound of artillery in the east. By the end of the month, Uncle Moppel, an elderly member of the Stauffenberg clan, drawing on his First World War experience, calculated that the front was only seven kilometres away. Shortly thereafter, as if by way of confirmation, the camp commander entered their hut to announce their imminent departure. In a blizzard, they clambered into vans which took them to a railway station. There, they were herded into an unheated train carriage with most of its windows broken. As a howling gale drove snow flurries into the carriage, they huddled together for warmth. It was a dreadful journey with many halts due to snow drifts on the line, at which the able-bodied men would be ordered out to help clear the snow. Meanwhile, the ordinary prisoners in Stutthof faced a nightmarish ordeal of incomparable magnitude: 5,000 of them were marched to the Baltic coast, where they were forced into the icy water and machine-gunned by their SS guards.[18]

The next stop for the kin prisoners was Matzkau, a punishment camp for offenders from within the SS. The conditions there were a little better than at Stutthof as they were fed on SS rations. It was here, though, that they lost one of their number: Anni von Lerchenfeld, the mother-in-law of Claus von Stauffenberg, died after contracting pneumonia. The camp was near an estate owned by Alexander's wife's family, and in his anger and grief, he demanded that the SS arrange for Anni to be buried there. To the group's astonishment they agreed.[19] That SS officers, who very likely had been involved in the callous murder of prisoners, should show such consideration, demonstrates, at the very least, an ambivalence on their part about the practice of *Sippenhaft*. It may also signal the persistence of class as well as racial bias. German prisoners in the concentration camp system, even the criminal and anti-social categories, were treated better than other nationalities and, within the German contingent, the upper-middle-class prisoners were the least harshly treated.

The group were moved to Danzig, and, after a sojourn there, to Berlin and onwards from there to Buchenwald Concentration Camp. A separate carriage of their train contained a mysterious group of non-German prisoners with whom the kin prisoners were not allowed to have contact. Fey, however, managed to furtively meet with them to discover that they were Hungarians; members of the government ousted by Hitler and included the Regent's son, Miklós Horthy. The Hungarians were in constant fear of being overtaken by Russians who they feared more than their captors. It was a close call at times, for as Fey von Hassell recalled, often 'we would leave a town just before it was occupied or a station just before it was blown up' in a bombing raid.[20] At stations, men and women with children in a pitiful condition begged to be allowed board the train, but were refused. Count Clemens von Stauffenberg, another elderly relative of Alexander, fell gravely ill on the approach to Berlin, and he, accompanied by his wife, was taken to the nearby Sachsenhausen camp hospital.

In Buchenwald, the group were housed in a barrack building, isolated from the main camp. The building already housed other kin prisoners, some of them relatives of the new arrivals. Fey met a friend of her mother's, who spoke of her father's defiant courage during his trial and subsequent execution. Fey, who had secretly hoped that she had been lied to about his death, was grief stricken: her hopes that her much-loved father might still be alive were dashed.

Ten days into their stay in Buchenwald, a small aircraft circled the camp before landing nearby. Soon after Alexander was summoned; the pilot was his wife Melitta who been searching for the group since they left Stutthof and had landed at Buchenwald on the off-chance that they might be there.[21] She had also been looking for, and eventually succeeded in locating, the whereabouts of her and Alexander's nieces and nephews,[22] the children of Claus and Berthold, who like Fey's children, had been sent to a Nazi-controlled orphanage. Melitta, in visiting her husband, was taking advantage of her role as an illustrious test pilot to conduct her searches, although she was risking court martial. It seems that she was aided by a sympathetic Gestapo major, who, in exchange for covering for her, sought an assurance that she would vouch for him after the war.[23]

Melitta visited Buchenwald again, this time bringing Elizabeth and Clemens von Stauffenberg with her. Hearing that they were in Sachsenhausen, she decided to rescue them before the Russians reached that camp. The SS had agreed to release the still very ill Clemens and Melitta was allowed to take him to his home, providing she first dropped his wife Elizabeth off in Buchenwald as she was required to re-join the kin prisoners.[24] As American forces approached Buchenwald, the kin prisoners were evacuated in the company of some of the *Prominenten*. This didn't prevent the brave and resourceful Melitta continuing to track their journey, flying to their new location to deliver food and other essentials. To be able to land in fields she had to fly a light reconnaissance plane. This was doubly risky for, apart from risking arrest, she was in danger of being shot down in her slow light aircraft. On 8 April, while she was on her way to visit Alexander, at his then place of detention in Schönberg, her plane was attacked by an American fighter. Although she managed to crash land, she died soon after from her wounds.[25]

It is unlikely that Melitta knew anything about her husband's growing attachment to Fey von Hassell. In any event, he was not likely to have been unfaithful to her in a physical sense. His relationship with Fey, up to this point at least, probably constituted little more than a growing emotional dependence. After Melitta's death, the grief-stricken Alexander was now, more than ever, in need of Fey's consoling presence.[26] He had lost his two brothers, and now his loving and brave wife. He clung to Fey like a shipwreck survivor clutching a buoy.

The group were quickly on the move again. They arrived at the gates of Dachau on 17 April where they faced the same lengthy delay experienced by other *Prominenten* arrivals. When they were eventually allowed to disembark from their bus, the men and women were ordered into separate lines. The men were told that they were being drafted into the *Volkssturm*, Himmler's home army type militia. Panic ensued as it seemed that husbands and wives, brothers and sisters, Fey and Alexander, were to be separated. Eventually, the Camp Commandant, the obsequious Weiter, appeared and apologised. He claimed it had all been an unfortunate misunderstanding and that they would remain together.[27]

Fey and Alexander shared the tensions and vicissitudes of the *Prominenten* journey into the Alps until they reached the Hotel Pragser Wildsee. There they were able to resume the walks they had begun in the Hindenburg Baude. During their wanderings the handsome couple were frequently invited into peasant homesteads and plied with wine and food.[28] It would be prurient to speculate on the nature of the intimacies they may have shared during this bitter-sweet interlude. What is certain is that they were in love. But for Fey there could be no future for the relationship. Her priority was to find her two boys and return with them to the security of her marriage. Alexander had nothing to return to. The people most dear to him were dead. With the prospect of imminent rescue now virtually certain, they had to contemplate their inevitable separation.

Shortly before their final departure from the Pragser Wildsee, Alexander suggested they visit a small, ornate chapel adjoining the Hotel. He was a talented musician, and as she later recalled:

> As he sat playing the little organ inside, tears rose up in my eyes. I felt profoundly touched by the beauty of the sacred music, the silence of the mountains, and the mystical atmosphere of the chapel. I realised that we two would soon be parting going back to families, friends, and

relationships that would have to be strengthened anew. The thought of leaving Alex, who was in many ways so helpless and who had lost so much, made me immensely sad.[29]

Their final sojourn before separation was in Capri where they were taken after their rescue by the Americans. There they were housed in the Hotel Paradiso Eden where for a few days they could wander and enjoy the beauty of that island. Fey managed to have a telegram sent to her husband, Detalmo, telling him of her whereabouts. Two days later he landed on Capri. It was a joyous reunion, tempered by Detalmo's disappointment on discovering that their two sons were not with her. That night, Fey's last on the island, her husband hosted dinner in a restaurant for all the kin family group. Speeches and toasts were made, but Alexander remained subdued. His predicament may be best described by Goethe's 'The Farewell':

Let mine eye the farewell say,
That my lips can utter ne'er;
Fain I'd be a man to-day,
Yet 'tis hard, oh, hard to bear!

The next morning, as Fey and her husband were about to leave the island, Alexander pressed a piece of paper into her hand, just as he had done when she lay seriously ill in Stutthof Concentration Camp. As before, it contained a heartfelt poem he had composed. The last lines read:

You are mine, I shout it to the winds,
The sea as in blue foam, it overwhelms the rocks
You must hear my call this cruel summer night.
I now dream of a dark time
When unreal happiness possessed my heart,
When a nymph, in a Dolomite forest, with magic wand
Did touch me and give me hope.

As the boat sailed away, Fey, comforted by her perplexed husband, began to cry uncontrollably.[30]

It was six months before Fey and her husband were reunited with their two boys. Fey's mother, after much searching, had located them in a former Nazi orphanage located in the then Soviet zone of occupation in Austria. With courage and determination, she had managed to extricate them and bring them back to her home in Germany. However, it initially proved impossible for Fey or Detalmo to get a permit to enter Germany to pick up their children. However, he was by then working as an aide to the Italian Prime Minister, Ferruccio Parri, the man that SS General Karl Wolff was obliged to have released in order to begin talks with Allen Dulles in Switzerland. Detalmo's position allowed him to meet with General Clark, the most senior US general in Italy, and the necessary pass was secured and they were joyously reunited with their two young boys.

Alexander returned to academia and was appointed professor of ancient history in the University of Munich after the war. He remarried in 1949, but before and after that he continued to correspond with Fey and they met occasionally when he visited Rome.[31]

THE STRANGE TALE OF FRIEDRICH ENGELKE

Friedrich Engelke was a shadowy and illusive figure among the *Prominenten*. He kept a low profile and is rarely mentioned in hostage memoirs, probably being generally perceived as not very interesting. The others may have viewed him as an unlikely, if uninteresting member of the group. He made no claim to prominence or notoriety. As noted in Chapter Fifteen, he has been described as a *Großkaufmann* ('merchant').[1] At other times, he is listed as 'Dr Friedrich Engelke', an official of the Reich Ministry of Economics, who was arrested as in October 1944 due to 'a denunciation'.[2] The merchant designation would link him to a Friedrich Engelke who worked for the SS in Paris from 1942 to August 1944, a man who led an extraordinary, self-enriching existence during that time.

SS Colonel Friedrich Engelke worked as a merchant trader before becoming an SS officer. After the occupation of France, he was put in charge of purchasing for the SS in Paris, a function that could, if one wished to obfuscate, be passed off as coming under the umbrella of the Ministry of Economics. At the end of the war, SS Colonel Engelke was detained in a civilian internment centre[3] indicating that he had been posing as a civilian and that his SS status was, at the time of his detention, unknown. The SS colonel had good reason to assume a new identity, for he had been involved in an exceptional level of corruption and was likely to be a wanted man at war's end. For all these reasons, it seems certain that the two are one and the same person. What follows, is an outline of Engelke's extraordinary existence in occupied France.

Engelke was born in Hanover in 1900 and joined the SS sometime in the 1930s where he was assigned to its central economic administrative service. Around June 1942, he was transferred to Paris to manage the organisations purchasing office there. He was well qualified to fill this role, having previously worked as a textile trader. Paris had a corrupting effect on its German occupiers. The availability of goods scarce in Germany, which, due to the artificially low exchange rate imposed by the conquerors, were cheap if paid for in French francs, encouraged cross-frontier black-market buying and selling. This was small beer for most, but not for some. It contributed to what one economic historian describes as 'economic delinquency on a level unknown in Germany'.[4]

Following the occupation, the Germans set about pillaging French financial and material resources. German imposed indemnities varied from 300 to 500 million francs per day.[5] Various military and bureaucratic organs of the Reich set up purchasing outlets in Paris that employed a middleman to procure for them products and materials that were in short supply. When it became clear that conventional channels could not provide the volume or type of materials needed, more and more, the black market was resorted to. The German purchasing bureaus – at one stage there were about 200 of them[6] – competed with one another, driving up prices and encouraging ever more black-market activity. The Germans were not initially concerned by the resulting price inflation because of the artificially low exchange rate and, because, most of the money to purchase the goods came directly, or indirectly, from the French treasury.

To facilitate his trading activities, Engelke struck up a close working and personal relationship with one of the most successful war-time black-marketeers and smugglers in France, Michel (originally Mendel) Szkolnikoff. The use of third-party purchasers, not identifiably connected to the German military, suited French business owners who, in many cases, wished to avoid being known as suppliers to the occupying forces. The relationship between Engelke and Szkolnikoff was to become a lucrative, if improbable, partnership, all the more so given that Szkolnikoff was a Russian-born Jew. Born in 1895, in what is now Belorussia, he also had a background as a merchant, specialising in textiles, having once been involved in a business supplying cloth to the Tsarist army. When he arrived in Paris in 1933, he again set himself up in business as a textile merchant. Clever and ambitious, he was prepared to take risks and was in frequent trouble with the French authorities. When the Germans invaded France in June 1940, he set out to make himself indispensable to the occupying forces. The Russian began as a supplier of textiles to the *Kriegsmarine* using his knowledge of the industry to procure what was needed, sometimes legitimately, more often through the black-market. This again got him into trouble with the Vichy police, but the Germans now intervened on his behalf. It was a strange interdependence; although he used nominated 'Aryans' to front up his companies, it is likely that at least some of the Germans with whom he did business would have at least suspected his Jewish background, but were prepared to ignore this inconvenient detail as long as he could produce the goods.[7]

By the time Friedrich Engelke arrived in Paris in the summer of 1942, Szkolnikoff was well established as a merchant provider for the Germans. And he had become extremely rich in the process, owning properties in Paris and the Cote d'Azur. He lived in a villa in Chatou, an affluent suburb of western Paris, and his country residence was on an estate of 17 hectares in Adé, Saône-et-Loire.[8] Engelke became a regular visitor to both of Szkolnikoff's residences and was an honoured guest at dinner parties hosted by his friend. These were usually attended by assorted senior German officials, French collaborators, gangsters, actors and singers, including, according to one account, Maurice Chevalier and Édith Piaf.[9] Engelke and Szkolnikoff were not simply friends. The German was a valuable ally, protecting the Russian from the French police and German security institutions, who were suspicious of his background and his shady business dealings. On a number of occasions, in 1943 and 1944, Szkolnikoff was arrested and Engelke intervened to have him freed.[10] The German was taking risks in shielding his friend, although his protection was unlikely to be freely provided. The two men were clearly business partners at this stage.

To illustrate this, in March 1942 Engelke was the prime mover in the sequestration of a Jewish-owned textile business in Paris under the anti-Jewish laws and he arranged for the large stock of printed fabric to be sent to Szkolnikoff's warehouse.[11] The American ambassador to Vichy France, William D. Leahy, believed that they were jointly involved in the purchase of a number of hotels on the Cote d'Azur.[12] The choice of location was significant. From November 1942 to September 1943, the eastern French Riviera was occupied by the Italians who resisted German and Vichy French pressure to deport foreign Jews and, much to the annoyance of their German allies, exempted the territory from Vichy anti-Semitic ordinances.[13] There was also a suspicion that Engelke, aided by Szkolnikoff, may have been acting for high-level Nazis in exporting large sums of monies to Latin America to facilitate their escape at war's end.[14] If that was the case, Engelke was likely to have been part of a conspiracy involving leading Nazis, perhaps including Himmler, for whom he was believed to have acted as private secretary for a time.[15]

Things began to go wrong for the pair in the spring of 1943. Göring, having earlier decided that the best way to counter the French black market was to 'exhaust it', reversed direction as price inflation and rampant exploitation of the black market threatened to entirely sink the French economy. Göring had illegal trading outlawed and most of the purchasing offices were closed, although not Engelke's, and 'the gaudy years of official blackmarketeering came to an end'.[16] Szkolnikoff, whose business was now in decline, and no doubt taking stock of a likely German defeat, began to make preparations to move to Spain and from there onward to Argentina. He had himself appointed vice-consul at the Argentine Embassy in Madrid, a new position that may have been created for him in consequence of his transfer of large sums to Argentina.

In May 1944, as he was in the process of moving cash to Spain, he was arrested by the Spanish police for money smuggling. Again Engelke went to his aid, but his influence in Spain was limited and, while he managed to have Szkolnikoff's lover freed, he didn't succeed in liberating his business partner before returning to Paris.[17] By then, the Normandy invasion was underway and, of even more concern for him, he was himself coming under increased surveillance within the SS. He had previously been arrested following an investigation by a commissioner of the criminal police from Hamburg, but was later released. (The timelines aren't clear, but that seems to have occurred in January or February 1944, well before his trip to Spain, so it must be assumed he was released on that occasion.[18]) It may in fact have been his friendship with another Russian Jew that caused his later incarceration.

Walter Kleinknecht, was a businessman and German informer. He, too, was a Russian Jew, but he kept this well hidden. He had assumed a new persona that allowed him to assimilate into the German community in wartime Paris. His wife Laure, a former French showgirl, hosted soirees in their elegant townhouse that were attended by Nazis officers and leading figures within the Vichy administration, including Pierre Laval. Colonel Friedrich Engelke was a frequent guest in the luxurious Kleinknecht apartment in Neuilly.[19] Laure

Kleinknecht, the hostess, doubled as a Gestapo spy, frequently bedding her guests to obtain information through 'pillow talk'. After the failed attempt on Hitler's life in July 1944, she journeyed to Berlin where, it appears, she had meetings with both Himmler and Hitler.[20] She allegedly disclosed information to them that implicated a number of Paris-based army officers in the plot to kill Hitler.

The military commander of German-occupied France, General von Stülpnagel was deeply implicated in the plot to assassinate Hitler.[21] As a result, he and many of his subordinate officers were arrested. So, too, were the Kleinknechts, possibly because they didn't provide information about the plotters soon enough. The husband, Walter, was shot, but Laure survived and prospered for a time in liberated Paris enjoying the status of a 'victim of National Socialism' based on her brief imprisonment and her husband's execution.[22] Engelke, because of his connections with her and her husband, may have come under suspicion. It's highly unlikely he had any truck with the opposition, although he may have had a financial link with one or more of them. It is possible that the investigation pursuant to 20 July events in Paris exposed his corrupt activities and his association with Szkolnikoff. Whatever the case, he would have had to have been removed to Germany before the liberation of Paris in August 1944. Why he ended up in Dachau, among the *Prominenten* can only be a matter for speculation. If, as rumoured, he was personally acquainted with Himmler, and had been helping him to acquire a nest egg, it's possible he was made a special prisoner, with ensuing privileges, on the Reichsführer's orders. In Dachau, he was placed in a cell beside the soon-to-be executed General Delestraint.[23] We know that Delestraint arrived in Dachau in the summer of 1944, so Engelke must have been placed in Dachau no earlier than then, which would be consistent with his being the same SS Colonel Engelke removed from Paris in early autumn of that year.[24] In Dachau, he wished to be known only as a minor functionary within the German Ministry of Economics, an innocent victim of a malicious complaint.

Colonel Engelke doesn't appear to have been recognised as an SS fugitive after the war as he was detained in a civilian detention camp. When he was freed from there, he returned to his native Hanover. However, in June 1951, a military tribunal in Paris tried him in absentia and found him guilty of stealing and looting and sentenced him to ten years in prison. A demand was made to the British authorities for his extradition from the then British sector of occupation in Germany. In response, the British asked for sight of the file on the case, but it seems to have been lost or, perhaps, stolen. As a result, Engelke was never extradited or prosecuted.[25]

It's not certain if Engelke's former partner, Szkolnikoff, survived. A body, partially burned, and officially identified as his, was found in El Molar near Madrid in June 1945. A grave in the local cemetery is said to be his, but doubts remain as to the true identity of the victim, and it's possible the real Szkolnikoff made it to Argentina.[26]

COLONEL DAVIDE FERRERO AND HIS PATRIOT BATTALION

Davide Ferrero's real name was Enrico Ferrero and he was born in 1910 in Savona, an Italian Riviera town. Ferrero was in his mid-twenties when he returned to his native town after his exploits in France and Morocco, having been fortunate to escape a jail sentence for fraud in both locations. He secured employments as a trustee (*fiduciario*) of a local branch of the Bricklayers and Allied Trades Union. Under Mussolini, only fascist unions were permitted and even these were incorporated into joint employer labour corporations in 1928 under the corporatist system. It is likely, therefore, that Ferrero was a functionary within a local corporatist institution, although there is no evidence of him having joined the Fascist party.[1] By early 1939, he had married and had become a father, but little else changed, and he soon came to the notice of the local police. This arose from his leading role in a hare-brained scheme.

Ferrero, along with two accomplices, decided to uncover a communist subversive conspiracy in their district. This disclosure, they hoped, would win them fame, rewards and promotion. There was, however, an obstacle to achieving their goal: there was no communist subversive activity in the town or in the province of Savona at that time. Undeterred, they set about inventing one. They decided to themselves organise the printing of communist propaganda leaflets, which they could then produce as evidence that they had uncovered underground communist subversion. Finding a printer who would print the material wasn't easy, but Ferrero managed to gain the confidence of an old communist and, through him, located a printer who was willing to produce the goods, cash on delivery. Unknown to Ferrero, one of his accomplices had reservations and informed the authorities of what was afoot. Ferrero and a second accomplice were trailed by the political police and, just as the leaflets were changing hands, they pounced. The conspirators and the printer were arrested.

The police considered Ferrero to be the main instigator and he was sentenced to a year's imprisonment. After serving his jail sentence, he was sent into internal exile in April 1939, first to the hill town of Introdacqua in the province of Aquila and later to a more remote town in Calabria. He was joined by his wife and daughter for at least part of his exile.[2] Italian law from the nineteenth century provided for internal exile – *confino* – initially to isolate mafia and bandits from their community, and this provision was used by the fascists to exile anti-fascists, homosexual men, national minorities, Jehovah's Witnesses and, following the passing of race laws in 1938, Jews, to camps located in remote villages mainly in the south.[3]

Ferrero's period of exile ended in March 1940 when he returned home. In early 1943, he was implicated in another plot; this time an attempt to extort money from a family whose son was in prison. The scam involved a fraudulent promise to arrange for the release of their son, a political prisoner, in exchange for a large sum of money. The police found out about the scheme and Ferrero found himself back in jail. He was only in prison a few months when the momentous political events of that year led to him walking free. Mussolini was overthrown on 25 July and Marshal Badoglio, with the King's blessing, became head of state. Fascism, it seemed, was vanquished, although to the dismay of most, the military alliance with Nazi Germany remained in place.

On 3 September the new government announced an armistice with the Allies, and the Germans sent in troops to take control of the country, or at least the northern and central parts of the peninsula not yet occupied by the Allies. The Italian civil and military administration instantly collapsed. Badoglio, along with King Emmanuel, fled and most officers also abandoned their posts leaving their demoralised soldiers without leadership or orders. In what became known as 'The Catastrophe', nearly all of the Italian army passively surrendered to the Germans. Thousands of soldiers gave themselves up to small units of the

German army before being marched into captivity. As many as 700,000 Italian military personnel were made prisoners by their erstwhile ally.

Before order could be restored, prisoners walked out of their jails and *confinati* left their places of confinement. Also on the move were Italian soldiers avoiding the German round-up and British, Greek and Slavic POWs who had walked out of their Italian camps, attempting to make their way to the Swiss border or south to Allied lines.[4] Ferrero joined the itinerant hordes during that September. The country was in turmoil; food and other basic necessities were scarce and there was widespread disorder and looting.[5]

Ferrero made his way to Asti in Piedmont where he adopted the title of 'Captain Davide' and began to form a partisan group in the commune of Canelli. His recruits were young men who had taken to the hills to avoid deportation or conscription by Mussolini's Social Republic. Various partisan groups had sprung up spontaneously from among these fugitives, in greater numbers in Piedmont than elsewhere.[6] Most became politically affiliated; the Garibaldi brigades to the Communist Party, the Justice and Liberty (GL) groups to the left-wing Action Party and others linked to the Socialist and more conservative political parties. There were also non-political groups – *Autonomi* – which included Ferrero's 'Patriots' Battalion'. Initially, his group acted like other emerging partisan formations. They raided houses for arms and provisions, harassed and ambushed local fascist outposts in remote areas and occasionally fired on German military transports. That was until 1 February 1944 when 'Captain Davide' turned his 'patriots' into collaborators.

The previous month, 150 of his group had been captured by German troops and members of Mussolini's *Guardia Nazionale Repubblicana* during a combined search of the Asti Hills for partisans and draft evaders. In retaliation, Ferrero took as hostages four fascists hoping to trade them for the lives of his men. One of his hostages, a former Italian army officer, observing that the 'Captain' and his followers seemed to be anti-communist and anti-English, offered to act as a peace broker with the Germans. The offer was accepted and negotiations commenced between Ferrero and Otto Grieser, the local SS Commander. The Germans had little confidence that Mussolini's forces would be able to contain the surge in partisan activity in Asti and they may have considered Ferrero's group, at one time comprising over a thousand men, better equipped for this task. The practice of contracting local militia was standard practice for the SS within German-occupied territories. Ferrero was given responsibility to police an area of territory between the Belbo and Bormida rivers where he was expected to maintain the peace and keep the district free of communist partisans. As part of the 'peace agreement', Griesler conceded to Ferrero the right to recruit within his area and allowed exemptions from military service in Mussolini's Social Republic for those who joined his ranks.

The 'Patriots' Battalion' were now allied with the SS. They were allocated a former police barracks and were armed by the Germans who also paid them wages. Not all were happy with this arrangement. Hundreds left although 'Captain Davide' was able to partially replenish these losses by offering sanctuary to others avoiding conscription by the Social Republic. The Fascists were furious about the activities of the 'patriots' for Ferrero made no secret of his disdain for, and hostility towards, them. He took it upon himself to direct local youths not to respond to call-ups and wrote to the fascist authorities declaring that he had withdrawn all draft papers issued to young men in his district. The Fascists made repeated complaints to the German Commander, but these were ignored. To demonstrate publicly that policing authority had been granted to him by the Germans, Ferrero had posters containing a picture of himself shaking hands with a German officer displayed in his area. The poster warned other 'rebels' to follow his lead 'before it is too late',[7] a warning presumably intended for those who had refused to follow him into alliance with the Germans.

On 15 March 1944, the Germans decided they could make better use of Ferrero and his 'patriots' and he and 100 of his men were forcibly transported to a German occupied barracks outside Turin. They were to be deployed in the Trieste region to combat the advance of Titoist Yugoslav partisans and for this assignment they needed to be trained. The 'patriots' were now subject to German military discipline, although they retained their own command structure and a uniform containing Italian tricolour insignia.[8]

A month later, the now 'Colonel' Davide and his battalion was relocated to Gorizia, a town north of Trieste. There were frequent confrontations between them and the forces of the Social Republic.[9] In early June, this escalated to the point of near open warfare. A truckload of the 'patriots', accompanied by two SS men, was stopped by a unit of Mussolini's *Guardia Nazionale Repubblicana* (GNR) who detained and disarmed Ferrero's men.

A captain in charge of the 'patriots' was assaulted by a GNR officer. The confrontation only ended when German police arrived at the scene. Ferrero, was enraged and he promptly arrested the Fascist officers involved, holding them as prisoners in his barracks. Complaints were made by the Fascists to the German military and Mussolini was also informed. However, the Fascists were powerless because the region was part of the Adriatic Operational Zone which was directly under the authority of the German forces. Ferrero felt confident he had the support of the SS for his actions. He told his captives 'I can do anything I want, the SS support me, I also enjoy the unconditional trust of General Wolff.'[10]

General Wolff, the SS commander and police chief for Northern Italy, may not have taken much interest in what Ferrero was up to, but General Odilo Globocnik, the Trieste SS commander, did. Globocnik, described as 'perhaps Himmler's most obsequious follower and ferocious executioner',[11] was an enthusiastic mass murderer who, in September 1942, had returned to his native Trieste to take up a position as SS and Police Leader. One of his first projects was to convert a former rice mill in the San Sabba district of the city to a prisoner transit and extermination camp. He had little regard for the fascists and had the GNR militia removed from his district. But neither was he a fan of Ferrero.

Around this time Ferrero had been in contact with Yugoslav partisans with a view to releasing some Germans they had captured. His motivation for this was entirely mercenary: there was a reward to be collected for their safe delivery. However, Globocnik suspected Ferrero was using these contacts to prepare for another U-turn. His fears may have had some substance for Ferrero had earlier confided to his men: '[A]lthough we made an oath, we are still the rebels, but for now we must go along with them. Soon we will leave for Trieste, to fight against Tito, but when we get there, we will join the other side.'[12] Globocnik decided to have all of the 'patriots' arrested. Some of them resisted and were only subdued after a gun fight. Ferrero, together with 'the most unruly and restless' of his followers, was dispatched to Dachau.[13] The remainder were detained in Trieste where many of them ended up as guards in the notorious San Sabba concentration camp.

A former Italian partisan and later distinguished author, Italo Calvino, like Ferrero from the Italian Riviera, had a fictional partisans leader in one of his books say: 'Just a trifle, a false step, a tipping of the soul, and we find ourselves on the other side.'[14] There were many like Ferrero who took that false step and ended up 'on the other side', but few with such abandon. In his favour, it could be said that his first move was to save 150 of his men captured by the Germans and that everything that followed resulted from this decision. And that, in contemplating going over to Tito's side, he was intending to redeem his initial false step. But to give him credit for this, we would have to assume he had a commitment to something more than just self-survival. Evidence for this is lacking. Everything points to him being a mercenary. He was consistently anti-Fascist and anti-Fascism was the sentiment that unified the diverse Italian partisan groups and later was to become the touchstone of the post-war Italian Republic. But for Ferrero, anti-Fascism seems to have had no political connotation. Like many young people who fell foul of the law, he blamed the authorities, in this instance the Fascists, for the perceived wrongs inflicted upon him. For him, one suspects, it was, and remained, simply personal. He remained a conman, with the talent to win the confidence of others and to use them for his ends. He changed sides casually, but convincingly. He declared himself to be a patriot, a claim that cannot be reconciled with his alliance with the German SS.

Shortly after the war Ferrero's past caught up with him. On 13 May 1945, the Socialist newspaper *Avanti* printed an interview with Mario Badoglio, his former *Prominenten* colleague, in which he praised the role played by Ferrero within the partisan group in Niederdorf. Ferrero must have had mixed feelings about this. The praise would boost his prestige within the partisan movement, but it might also attract unwanted attention to him and his past. By June, seemingly ignoring the risk of being recognised for what he was, he returned to Piedmont. By then he had promoted himself to the rank of general and, with a small retinue, he took up residence in a hotel in the town of Acqui. There he generously distributed much sought-after travel permits and issued promotions to local partisans. The partisan leader for the district, Pietro Minetti, was elsewhere when Ferrero first arrived and decided to meet with him after his return. He was immediately suspicious and began to make enquiries about the 'General'. Ferrero's past as a collaborator was exposed and he was arrested. What was he doing back in his old stomping ground where he was always likely to be recognised? It may be that he was intending to recoup monies or loot stashed away during his time as leader of the 'patriots'.

What exactly happened to Ferrero after his detention has never been revealed. He was taken to Alexandria, the provincial capital, where some believe he was executed, or possibly murdered by rivals. There was also a rumour, taken seriously by some, that he didn't die, but somehow managed to get to Argentina.[15] Should he have done so, it would have been entirely in keeping with his extraordinary ability to talk his way out of trouble.

LIST OF *PROMINENTEN* IN HOTEL PRAGSER WILDSEE

Austria

Konrad Praxmarer
Richard Schmitz
Kurt von Schuschnigg
Maria Dolores von Schuschnigg
Vera von Schuschnigg

Britain and Ireland

Sigismund Payne Best
Jack Churchill
Peter Churchill
Thomas Cushing
Harry Day
Sydney Dowse
Hugh Falconer
Wadim Greenewich
Bertram James
John McGrath
Patrick O'Brien
John Spence
Richard Stevens
Andrew Walsh

Czechoslovakia

Josef Burda
Imrich Karvaś
Jan Rys-Rozsévač
Ján Stanek

Denmark

Hans Hansen
Adolf Larsen
Jörgen Mogensen
Hans Lunding
Max Mikkelsen
Knud Pedersen

France

Jeanne Blum
Léon Blum
Prince Xavier of Bourbon-Parma
Armand Mottet
Gabriel Piguet
Ramond Van Wymeersch

Germany

Bogislaw von Bonin
Fritz Cerrini
Friedrich Engelke
Alexander von Falkenhausen
Wilhelm von Flügge
Prince Friedrich Leopold of Prussia
Franz Halder
Gertrud Halder
Anton Hamm

Erich Heberlein
Margot Heberlein
Horse Hoepner
Joseph Joos
Karl Kunkel
Franz Maria Liedig
Josef Müller
Johann Neuhäusler
Martin Niemöller
Heidel Nowakowski
Horst von Petersdorff
Prince Phillip of Hesse
Hermann Pünder
Hjalmar Schacht
Fabian von Schlabrendorff
Georg Thomas
Amélie Thyssen
Fritz Thyssen
Wilhelm Visintainer
Paul Wauer

Greece

Konstantinos Bakopoulos
Panagiotis Dedes
Vassilis Dimitrion
Nikolaos Grivas
Georgios Kosmas
Alenxandros Papagos
Ioannis Pitsikas

Hungary

Aleksander Ginzery
Josef Hatz

Samuel Hatz
Andreas Hlatky
Miklós Horthy, Jr
Géza Igmándy-Hegyessy
Miklós Kállay
Julius Király
Desiderius Ónody
Péter Schell

Italy

Amechi
Eugenio Apollonio
Mario Badoglio
Burtoli
Davide Ferrero
Sante Garibaldi
Tullio Tamburini

Latvia

Gustavs Celmins

Netherlands

Johannes van Dijk

Norway

Arne Dæhli

Poland

Jan Izycki
Stanislaw Jensen
Count Aleksander Zamoyski

Russia

Ivan Bessonov
Victor Brodnikov
Fyodor Ceredilin
Vassily Kokorin
Pyotr Privalov
Nikolay Rutschenko

Sweden

Carl Edquist

Yugoslavia

Hinko Dragić-Hauer
Novak D. Popovic
Dimitrije Tomalevsky

Prisoners of Kin

Fey von Hassell
Annelise Gisevius
Anneliese Goerdeler
Benigna Goerdeler
Gustav Goerdeler
Marianne Goerdeler
Irma Goerdeler
Jutta Goerdeler
Reinhard Goerdeler
Ulrich Goerdeler
Käte Gudzent
Franz von Hammerstein
Hidur von Hammerstein
Maria von Hammerstein-Equord
Anna-Luise von Hofacker

Eberhard von Hofacker
Ilse Lotte von Hofacker
Elisabeth Kaiser
Therese Kaiser
Arthur Kuhn
Anni von Lerchenfeld
Lini Lindemann
Josef Mohr
Käthe Mohr
Gisela Gräfin von Plettenberg-Lenhausen
Walther Graf von Plettenberg-Lenhausen
Dietrich Schatz
Alexander Schenk Graf von Stauffenberg
Alexandra Schenk Gräfin von Stauffenberg
Inéz Schenk Gräfin von Stauffenberg
Maria Schenk Gräfin von Stauffenberg
Markwart Schenk Graf von Stauffenberg, Sr
Markwart Schenk Graf von Stauffenberg, Jr
Otto Schenk Graf von Stauffenberg
Hans-Dietrich Schröder
Harring Schröder
Ingeborg Schröder
Sybille-Maria Schröder
Isa Vermehren

ENDNOTES

Chapter 1

1 Macintyre, B., *A Spy Among Friends: Philby and the Great Betrayal* (London: Bloomsbury, 2015), p. 12.
2 Payne Best, S., *The Venlo Incident* (London: Hutchinson & Co., 1950), p. 15.
3 Jeffery, K., *MI6: The History of the Secret Intelligence Service, 1909–1949* (London: Bloomsbury, 2011), p. 382.
4 Schellenberg, W., *The Labyrinth: Memoirs of Walter Schellenberg* (Boston: Da Capo Press, 2000), p. 70.
5 Jones, N., 'Introduction', in S. Payne Best, *The Venlo Incident: How the Nazis Fooled Britain* (Yorkshire: Frontline Books, 2010 E-book). For further reference, see Jeffery, *MI6*, p. 383.
6 Payne Best, *The Venlo Incident*, p. 17.
7 Schellenberg, *The Labyrinth*, p. 80.
8 Jeffery, *MI6*, p. 385. Payne Best describes both himself and Stevens compiling a list of people who would have to be evacuated from the Netherlands in the event of a German invasion. He claims, unconvincingly, to have discarded his list before being captured; the implication being that Stevens did not do the same. Payne Best, *The Venlo Incident*, p. 16.
9 Hastings, M., *The Secret War: Spies, Codes and Guerrillas* (London: William Collins, 2015), p. 44.
10 Instutit für Zeitgeschichte Munich: https://www.ifz-muenchen.de/archiv/zs/zs-1939.pdf (accessed 18 October 2018).
11 Haasis, H. and W. Odom (trans.), *Bombing Hitler: The Story of the Man Who Almost Assassinated Hitler* (New York: Skyhorse Publishing, 2011), p. 181. The author states that the Gestapo were so impressed with Elser's work that they put it into their field manual for training purposes.
12 Payne Best, *The Venlo Incident*, p. 53.
13 Ibid., p. 79.
14 Ibid., p. 108.
15 Ibid., p. 68.
16 Jones, N., 'Introduction', in S. Payne Best, *The Venlo Incident* (2010 E-book).

Chapter 2

1 Ferriter, D., *The Transformation of Ireland, 1900–2000* (London: Profile Books, 2005), p. 30.

2 UKNA KV 3/345. Interrogation report of Lt-Col. John McGrath, 14 May 1945.

3 Ibid. Statement made by Jump Hoven in 1945. Hoven claimed McGrath told him 'that he regarded himself an Irishman first of all and that he was prepared to fight for Ireland if an opportunity should arise'. Hoven goes on to state that he then realised that McGrath made these statements to him 'with his own mental reservations'.

4 Carter, C.J., *The Shamrock and the Swastika* (Palo Alto: Pacific Books, 1977), p. 127.

5 'Attempt to Enlist Irishman as Agents', *Irish Independent*, 7 June 1945.

6 UKNA KV 3/345. Memorandum prepared by McGrath for attention of Director M9 War Office and smuggled out of Friesack in 1941.

7 Ibid. Statement of Michael Delaney, who was senior NCO in Friesack for a time in late 1940.

8 Roger Casement formed an 'Irish Brigade' from First World War prisoners with a view to them fighting for Irish independence. The venture attracted new recruits.

9 McDonagh, J., 'Let Ireland Weep', in *Poetry of Loss in the First World War* (Journal of Franco–Irish Studies, Vol. 4, Issue 1, 2015), p. 10.

10 Longden, S., *Dunkirk: The Men They Left Behind* (London: Constable and Robinson, 2008).

11 UKNA KV 3/245. McGrath.

12 Carter, *The Shamrock and the Swastika*, p. 127.

13 Vincent 'Paddy' Byrne, a Belfast-born RAF man, received a coded message from MI9: 'Byrne – double-cross the Germans – any length – great possibilities, but very dangerous,' (see G. Walters, *The Real Great Escape* (London: Bantam Books, 2014), p. 53). Another serviceman, James Brown, acted as a double agent at the instigation of MI9 (see A. Gilbert, *POW: Allied Prisoners in Europe, 1939–1945* (London: John Murray, 2007), p. 247).

14 Carter, *The Shamrock and the Swastika*, p. 127.

15 UKNA KV 3/345. Report of interrogation of John McGrath.

16 Knox, D.B., *Suddenly, While Abroad: Hitler's Irish Slaves* (Dublin: New Island, 2012), p. 108.

17 Hoar, A., *Red and Green* (Dublin: Brandon Books, 2004), p. 255.

18 Carter, *The Shamrock and the Swastika*, p. 125.

19 UKNA KV 2/769. Haller.

20 INA DFA/205/108. In one broadcast, he stated: 'I admired Hitler from the first days in power in Germany.'

21 O'Reilly, T., *Hitler's Irishmen* (Cork: Mercier Press, 2008), p. 66.

22 Ibid., p. 70.

23 UKNA KV 3/345. McGrath.

24 Ibid. Report of interview with Fr Thomas O'Shaughnessy, penned by I.G. Philips of MI9, 30 April 1943.

25 UKNA KV 2/769. Haller.

26 Cushing, T., *Soldier for Hire* (London: Calder, 1962), p. 14.

27 Ibid. Although he claims to have been twelve years old, there is no record of Thomas Cushing in the Irish census returns for 1911, so he must have been at least two years younger.

28 Ibid., p. 186.

29 Author's conversation with Finbar McLaughlin, author of *Left for the Wolves* (Dublin: Irish Academic Press, 2007).

30 O'Reilly, *Hitler's Irishmen*, p. 72.

31 Ibid., pp. 90–1.

32 UKNA KV 2/19. Strogen.

33 UKNA KV2 769. Haller.

34 UKNA KV 2/19.

35 Churchill, P., *The Spirit in the Cage* (London: Hodder and Stoughton, 1954), p. 128.

36 UKNA FO 950/1725. Correspondence from the archives shows that letters were written for him by his wife, adding his signature in a childish scribble.

37 UKNA KV 2/769. Haller.

38 Hull, H., *Irish Secrets: German Espionage in Wartime Ireland, 1939–1945* (Dublin: Irish Academic Press, 2003), p. 219.

39 UKNA 950/1725. This was written on Walsh's behalf by his wife in support of his claim for compensation. He may have exaggerated somewhat, although such treatment by the Gestapo would have been routine.

40 UKNA KV 3/345. Report of interview with Fr Thomas O'Shaughnessy.

41 A number of statements refer to the crime. See UKNA KV 2/1951 (T. Strogen and G.O. Johnson) and UKNA KV 2/769 (Haller).

42 O'Shaughnessy, T., *Rest Your Head in Your Hand* (Dublin: Ward River Press, 1983), p. 86.

43 UKNA KV 3/345. Notes of interview with O'Shaughnessy.

44 O'Shaughnessy, *Rest Your Head in Your Hand*, p. 88.

45 O'Reilly, *Hitler's Irishmen*, p. 74.

46 'Irish Colonel's Life in German Camps', *Irish Times*, 23 October 1945.

47 Interview with Tim Rohen, *Evening Echo*, 30 May 1979.

48 O'Shaughnessy, *Rest Your Head in Your Hand*, pp. 98–9.

49 UKNA KV 2/769. Haller.

50 Ibid. Lahousen was a friend of the head of the *Abwehr*, Admiral Canaris. Both were anti-Nazi conspirators. While Canaris was executed following the 1944 attempt on Hitler's life, Lahousen – then serving on the Russian front – survived.

51 UKNA KV 3/345. McGrath.

52 O'Reilly, *Hitler's Irishmen*, p. 111.

53 Interview with John McGrath, *Irish Times*, 14 June 1945. There may have been substance to the charge, for one former inmate at Friesack recalls McGrath having contact with the Dutch Resistance.

54 Rohan, T., 'Torpedoed, Picked up by a German Ship Flying a US Flag', *Evening Echo*, 30 May 1979.

55 IWM 9/51/1, S. Payne Best Archive. Letter smuggled by McGrath to Payne Best in Dachau in April 1945.

56 Report of address by John McGrath to Rotary Club meeting in Dublin, *Irish Times*, 23 October 1945.

57 Mommsen, H. and A. McGeoch (trans.), *Germans Against Hitler: The Stauffenberg Plot and Resistance Under the Third Reich* (London: I.B. Taurus, 2009), p. 521.

Chapter 3

1   Beevor, A., *Berlin: The Downfall, 1945* (London: Penguin, 2003), p. 136.

2   Sullivan, S., *Stalin's Daughter: The Extraordinary and Tumultuous Life of Svetlana Alliluyeva* (London: Fourth Estate, 2015), p. 27.

3   Kolesnik, A.N., 'Prisoner of War, Sr. Lt Yalov Fzhugashvikli', in *Soviet Military History Journal*, No. 12, December 1988, p. 50.

4   Sullivan, *Stalin's Daughter*, p. 96.

5   Ibid., p. 466.

6   Ibid., p. 27.

7   Richardson, R., *The Long Shadow: Inside Stalin's Factory* (London: BCA, 1993), p. 93.

8   Khlevniuk, O.V. and N. Seligman (trans.), *Stalin: A New Biography of a Dictator* (Connecticut: Yale University Press, 2003), p. 253.

9   Kotkin, S., *Stalin, Vol. I: Paradoxes of Power, 1878–1928* (London: Allen Lane, 2014), p. 595.

10 Ibid., p. 81. Maria and Alexander Svanidze and Mario Svanidze were successively executed in 1941 and 1942. Yakov's wife spent three years in detention but survived.

11 Kolesnik, 'Prisoner of War', *Soviet Military History Journal*, p. 49.

12 Ibid., p. 48.

13 Article written by C. Neef, *Der Spiegel*, 9 February 2013.

14 Sullivan, *Stalin's Daughter*, p. 99.

15 Kolesnik, 'Prisoner of War', *Soviet Military History Journal*, p. 50.

16 Wojciechowska, B., *Waiting to be Heard: The Polish Christian Experience Under Nazi and Stalinist Oppression, 1939–1955* (Indiana: Author House, 2009), p. 103.

17 Kolesnik, 'Prisoner of War', *Soviet Military History Journal*, p. 50.

18 Lacouture, J., *Léon Blum* (New York: Holmes & Meier, 1982), p. 442.

19 Kotkin, *Stalin, Vol. I*, p. 454.

20 Payne Best, S., *The Venlo Incident*, 2010), p. 156.

21 O'Shaughnessy, T., *Rest Your Head in Your Hand* (Dublin: Ward River Press, 1983), p. 101.

22 Cushing, T., *Soldier for Hire* (London: Calder, 1962), p. 257.

23 Simpson, C. and J. Shirley, *The Sunday Times*, 24 February 1980. The journalists based their piece on an interview with Cushing, which is likely to be partisan at best. For further reference, see Ciaran Crossey's online article – http://irelandscw.com/ibvol-CushingStalin.htm (accessed 18 October 2018) – and T. O'Reilly, *Hitler's Irishmen* (Cork: Mercier Press, 2008), p. 113.

24 UKNA FO 371/94812. This aspect of the affray was related by John Dodge, who claims to have heard it from Peter Churchill. Churchill was not a witness and could only have heard it from one of the Irishmen or from Kokorin. Churchill does not recount this in his book. However, he was alone among the British officers in Sachsenhausen, who seem to have liked Cushing.

25 Article written by C. Neef, *Der Spiegel*, 9 February 2013.

26 Simpson, C. and J. Shirley, *The Sunday Times*, 24 February 1980.

27 UKNA FO 371/46714.

28 Interview with Thomas Cushing, *The Sunday Times*, 24 January 1960.

29 Ibid.

30 UKNA FO 371/94812.

31 Payne Best, *The Venlo Incident*, p. 157.

32 Hull, M.H., *Irish Secrets: German Espionage in Wartime Ireland, 1939–1945* (Dublin: Irish Academic Press, 2003), p. 219.

33 UKNA FCO 72/6. Spence arrived in *Sonderlager* 'A' in November 1943.

34 Eckert, A.M., *The Struggle for the Files* (Cambridge: Cambridge University Press, 2012), pp. 47–8.

35 UKNA FO 371/ 94812.

36 Ibid. Dodge's letter to the Foreign Office, January 1951.

37 Montefiore, S.S., *Young Stalin* (London: Weidenfeld and Nicolson, 2007), p. 312.

Chapter 4

1 Churchill, P., *The Spirit in the Cage* (London: Hodder and Stoughton, 1954), pp. 126–7.

2 Burleigh, M., *The Third Reich: A New History* (London: Macmillan, 2000), p. 514.

3 Maslov, A., *Captured Soviet Generals* (Oxford: Routledge, 2001), p. 44.

4 Parrish, M., *Sacrifice of the Generals: Senior Soviet Officer Losses, 1939–1953* (Lanham: Scarecrow Press, 2004), p. 44.

5 Ibid., pp. 43–4.

6 James, B.A., *Moonless Night* (Barnsley: Pen and Sword, 2002), pp. 120–1.

7 Ibid., p. 120.

8 Churchill, *The Spirit in the Cage*, p. 127.

9   Parrish, *Sacrifice of the Generals*, p. 44.

10 Padfield, P., *Himmler Reichsführer–SS* (London: Macmillan, 1990), p. 519.

11 Churchill, *The Spirit in the Cage*, p. 139.

12 Maslov, *Captured Soviet Generals*, pp. 157–8.

13 James, *Moonless Night*, p. 121.

14 Smith, S., *Wings Day: The Man Who Led the RAF's Epic Battle in German Captivity* (London: Collins, 1968), p. 182.

15 Churchill, *The Spirit in the Cage*, p. 133.

16 Donoghue, D., *Hitler's Irish Voices* (Dublin: Beyond the Pale Publications, 1998), p. 46.

17 Kiely, K., *Francis Stuart: Artist and Outcast* (Dublin: The Liffey Press, 2007), p. 148.

18 INA DFA 205/108.

19 Churchill, *The Spirit in the Cage*, pp. 157–67.

20 Carroll, T., *The Dodger: The Extraordinary Story of Churchill's Cousin and the Great Escape* (Edinburgh: Mainstream Publishing, 2012), p. 284.

21 Churchill, *The Spirit in the Cage*, p. 159.

22 UKNA 45/25815.

23 Ibid.

24 INA DFA 205/108.

25 UKNA 45/25815.

26 Churchill, *The Spirit in the Cage*, pp. 159–60.

27 Ibid., p. 160.

28 Ibid., p. 161.

29 Ibid., pp. 166–7.

30 Ibid., p. 138.

31 Smith, *Wings Day*, p. 76.

32 Walters, G., *The Real Great Escape* (London: Bantam Books, 2014), p. 50.

33 Vance, J.F., *A Gallant Company: The Men of the Great Escape* (California: Pacifica Military History, 2000), p. 362.

34 IWM Catalogue No. 27731, Reel 8. Recording of Dowse interview, 2004. Oral History series.

35 Carroll, *The Dodger*, p. 378

36 Vance, *A Gallant Company*, p. 113.

37 Smith, *Wings Day*, p. 207.

38 Vance, *A Gallant Company*, p. 15.

39 James Durney, http://www.kildare.ie/ehistory/index.php/from-clongowes-college-to-the-great-escape/ (accessed 18 October 2018).

40 IWM Catalogue No. 27731, Reel 8.

41 Simon Carr interview with Malcom Churchill, son of Jack Churchill, *Daily Mail*, 28 March 2014. For further reference, see L. Royal, *Safe Return Doubtful* (Oslo: Royal Explorers Club, 2015), pp. 6–9.

42 James, *Moonless Night*, p. 130.

43 Cushing, T., *Soldier for Hire* (London: Calder, 1962), p. 257.
44 Carroll, *The Dodger*, pp. 116–20.
45 James, *Moonless Night*, p. 145.
46 Walters, *The Real Great Escape*, p. 169.
47 Smith, *Wings Day*, p. 88.
48 James, *Moonless Night*, p. 123.
49 Churchill, *The Spirit in the Cage*, p. 144.

Chapter 5

1   Carroll, T., *The Dodger*, p. 302.
2   Carroll, T., *The Great Escape from Stalig Luft III* (New York: Pocket Books, 2005), p. 267.
3   Ibid.
4   Smith, S., *Wings Day: The Man Who Led the RAF's Epic Battle in German Captivity* (London: Collins, 1968), p. 174.
5   James, B.A., *Moonless Night* (Barnsley: Pen and Sword, 2002), p. 124.
6   Smith, *Wings Day*, p. 184.
7   Churchill, P., *The Spirit in the Cage* (London: Hodder and Stoughton, 1954), p. 153
8   Ibid., p. 146.
9   Rolf, D., *Prisoners of the Reich* (London: Leo Cooper, 1988), p. 80.
10 James, *Moonless Night*, p. 131.
11 Ibid., p. 264.
12 Smith, *Wings Day*, pp. 187–8.
13 UKNA WO 208/3336/102. Sydney Dowse.
14 James, *Moonless Night*, p. 140. For further reference, see Churchill, *The Spirit in the Cage*, pp. 180–188.
15 UKNA WO 208/3336/33. Bertram James.
16 Carroll, *The Dodger*, p. 309.
17 Churchill, *The Spirit in the Cage*, pp. 191-7.
18 Carroll, *The Dodger*, p. 321.
19 Smith, *Wings Day*, p. 196.
20 Ibid., p. 205.
21 James, *Moonless Night*, p. 158.

Chapter 6

1   Payne Best, *The Venlo Incident*, p. 113.
2   Ibid., p. 165.
3   Ibid., p. 166.
4   Ibid.

5   Richards, B., *Secret Flotillas, Volume II* (London: Frank Cass, 2004), p. 234.
6   UKNA HS 9/496/6. Falconer.
7   Ibid.
8   Churchill, P., *The Spirit in the Cage* (London: Hodder and Stoughton, 1954), p. 209.
9   Rosa Sala Rose, http://rosasalarose.es/2011/04/el-secuestro-de-los-heberlein/ (accessed 18 October 2018).
10 UKNA WO 328/12. Margot Heberlein. For further reference, see 'Heberlein ist abgereist', *Der Spiegel*, 13 July 1950.
11 UKNA WO 382/12. For further reference, see WO 346/11, deposition of Erich Heberlein.
12 Payne Best, *The Venlo Incident*, p. 118.
13 Berben, P., *Dachau, 1933–1945* (London: Norfolk Press, 1975), pp. 126–34.
14 Shirer, W.L., *The Rise and Fall of the Third Reich* (London: Pan Books, 1964), p. 1177.
15 Payne Best, *The Venlo Incident*, p. 187.
16 James, B.A., *Moonless Night* (Barnsley: Pen and Sword, 2002), p. 127.
17 Smith, S., *Wings Day: The Man Who Led the RAF's Epic Battle in German Captivity* (London: Collins, 1968), p. 208. For further reference, see James, *Moonless Night*, pp. 160–1.
18 Shirer, *The Rise and Fall of the Third Reich*, p. 1307.
19 Hastings, M., *Armageddon: The Battle for Germany, 1944–1945* (London: Macmillan, 2004), p. 446.
20 Kershaw, I., *The End: Hitler's Germany, 1944–1945* (London: Allen Lane, 2011), p. 301.
21 Cushing, T., *Soldier for Hire* (London: Calder, 1962), p. 260.
22 Beevor, A., *Berlin: The Downfall, 1945* (London: Penguin, 2003), p. 72.
23 The other executed men were: Sergeant Jumbo Steele; Wireless Operator Tommy Handley and Jon Kotrba of the Czech Army in Exile. All were captured alongside Cumberlege in occupied Crete. For further reference, see http://www.royalnavyresearcharchive.org.uk/Mike_Cumberlege.htm#.W8i7wy-ZMWp (accessed 18 October 2018).
24 Smith, *Wings Day*, p. 209.
25 Müller J.W., *Contesting Democracy: Political Ideas in Twentieth-Century Europe* (Connecticut: Yale University Press, 2013), p. 119.
26 Smith, *Wings Day*, pp. 191–2.
27 James, *Moonless Night*, p. 169.
28 Persson, S., *Escape from the Third Reich* (Yorkshire: Frontline Books, 2009), p. 179.
29 Churchill, *The Spirit in the Cage*, p. 200.
30 Ibid., p. 202.
31 Smith, *Wings Day*, p. 214.
32 UKNA WO 328/3. Hinko Dragic.

33 Sigler, S., *Corpsstudenten im Widerstand gegen Hitler* (Berlin: Duncker & Humblot, 2014).
34 Smith, *Wings Day*, p. 216.
35 James, *Moonless Night*, p. 175.
36 Churchill, *The Spirit in the Cage*, p. 204.
37 Ibid.

Chapter 7

1   Berben, P., *Dachau, 1933–1945* (London: Norfolk Press, 1975), p. 81.
2   Payne Best, *The Venlo Incident*, p. 204.
3   IWM Image Catalogue, Document 1414.
4   Haasis, H. and W. Odom (trans.), *Bombing Hitler: The Story of the Man Who Almost Assassinated Hitler* (New York: Skyhorse Publishing, 2011), p. 195.
5   Ibid., p. 203.
6   Smith, S., *Wings Day: The Man Who Led the RAF's Epic Battle in German Captivity* (London: Collins, 1968), p. 216.
7   Ibid.
8   Berben, *Dachau*, p. 15.
9   James, B.A., *Moonless Night* (Barnsley: Pen and Sword, 2002), pp. 180–1.
10 Payne Best, *The Venlo Incident*, p. 209.
11 UKNA WO 328/43. Paul Wauer.
12 Wachsmann, N., *KL: A History of the Nazi Concentration Camps* (London: Little, Brown, 2016), p. 127.
13 Payne Best, *The Venlo Incident*, p. 184.
14 Evans, R.J., *The Third Reich at War: How the Nazis Led Germany from Conquest to Disaster* (London: Penguin, 2009), p. 388.
15 Roper, R.T., *The Last Days of Hitler: The Classic Account of Hitler's Fall From Power* (London: Pan Books, 2012), p. 9.
16 Burleigh, M., *The Third Reich: A New History* (London: Macmillan, 2000), p. 686.
17 Von Hassell, U. and G. Brooks (trans.), *The Ulrich von Hassell Diaries* (London: Frontline Books, 2011), p. 86.
18 Shirer, W.L., *The Rise and Fall of the Third Reich* (London: Pan Books, 1964), p. 1092.
19 Evans, *The Third Reich at War*, p. 407.
20 Von Hassell, *The Ulrich von Hassell Diaries*, p. 142.
21 IWM 9/51/1, S. Payne Best Archive, SPB 9. A typed copy of the letter was kept by Payne Best and is among his papers.
22 Jeffery, K., *MI6: The History of the Secret Intelligence Service* (London: Bloomsbury Publishing, 2011), p. 386.
23 Kinrade Dethick, J. and A.M. Corke, *Twixt the Devil and the Deep Blue Sea: The Story of the Crew of HMS Saracen* (2015), p. 104.

24 Payne Best, *The Venlo Incident*, p. 213.

25 IWM 9/51/1, SPB 9.

26 Payne Best, *The Venlo Incident*, p. 216.

Chapter 8

1 Wachsmann, N., *KL: A History of the Nazi Concentration Camps* (London: Little, Brown, 2016), p. 412.

2 Ibid., p. 414.

3 Hedgepeth, S.M. and R.G. Saiden (eds), *Sexual Violence Against Jewish Women During the Holocaust* (New Hampshire: University Press of New England, 2010), p. 48.

4 Berben, P., *Dachau, 1933–1945* (London: Norfolk Press, 1975), pp. 131–2.

5 Neuhäusler, J., *What Was It Like in the Concentration Camp at Dachau?: An Attempt to Come Closer to the Truth* (Munich: A.G. Manz, 1960), p. 33.

6 Moulin, P., *Dachau, Holocaust, and the US Samurai* (Bloomington: Author House, 2007), p. 48.

7 'Leben auf Widerruf Joos,' quoted in Neuhäusler, *What Was It Like in the Concentration Camp at Dachau?: An Attempt to Come Closer to the Truth*, p. 33.

8 'The Righteous Among The Nations', Yad Vashem: http://db.yadvashem.org/righteous/family.html?language=en&itemId=4016907 (accessed 18 October 2018).

9 Smith, S., *Wings Day: The Man Who Led the RAF's Epic Battle in German Captivity* (London: Collins, 1968), p. 217.

10 UKNA WO 328/5. Deposition of Frederick Leopold, Prince of Prussia.

11 Petropoulos, J., *Royals and the Reich: The Princes von Hessen in Nazi Germany* (Oxford: Oxford University Press, 2008), p. 3.

12 Ibid., p. 293.

13 Thomas, H., *The Spanish Civil War* (London: Penguin, 2012), p. 730.

14 Pool, J., and S. Pool, *Who Financed Hitler?: The Secret Funding of Hitler's Rise to Power, 1919–1933* (London: Macdonald and Jane's, 1979), p. 167.

15 Kershaw, I., *Hitler: 1889–1936* (London: Penguin, 2001), p. 357.

16 UKNA WO 328/39. Deposition of Fritz Thyssen.

Chapter 9

1 Blum, L., *Le Dernier Mois* (Paris: Arléa, 2004), pp. 61–2.

2 Birnbaum, P., *Léon Blum: Prime Minister, Socialist, Zionist* (New Haven: Yale University Press, 2015), pp. 134–5.

3 Lacouture, J., *Léon Blum* (New York: Holmes & Meier, 1982), p. 423.

4 Judt, T., *The Burden of Responsibility* (Chicago: University of Chicago Press, 1998), p. 34.

5 Lacouture, *Léon Blum*, p. 441.

6 Blum, *Le Dernier Mois*, p. 63.

7 Ferguson, A., *When Money Dies* (New York: Public Affairs, 2010), p. 211.

8 Kershaw, I., *Hitler: 1889–1936* (London: Penguin, 2001), p. 392.

9 Kershaw, I., *Hitler: The Germans and the Final Solution* (New Haven: Yale University Press, 2008), p. 31.

10 Von Hassell, U. and G. Brooks (trans.), *The Ulrich von Hassell Diaries* (London: Frontline Books, 2011), p. 293, note 110.

11 Ibid., p. 222.

12 Shirer, W.L., *The Rise and Fall of the Third Reich* (London: Pan Books, 1964), p. 184.

13 Colton, J., *Léon Blum: Humanist in Politics* (New York: Alfred A. Knoff, 1966), E-book.

14 Ibid.

15 Kedward, R., *La Vie en bleu: France and the French since 1900* (London: Penguin, 2006), p. 185.

16 Birnbaum, P., *Léon Blum: Prime Minister, Socialist, Zionist* (New Haven: Yale University Press, 2015), p. 103

17 Lacouture, *Léon Blum*, p. 225.

18 Kedward, *La Vie en bleu*, pp. 178–9.

19 Lacouture, *Léon Blum*, p. 297.

20 Colton, *Léon Blum: Humanist in Politics*, E-book.

21 Blum, *Le Dernier Mois*, pp. 63–4.

22 Birnbaum, *Léon Blum*, p. 62.

23 Von Schuschnigg, K. and P. Eckstein (trans.), *Farewell Austria* (London: Cassell & Co., 1938), p. 188.

24 Höbelt, L., 'Fascism and Catholicism in Austria', in J. Nelis, A. Morelli and D. Praet (eds), *Catholicism and Fascism in Europe, 1918–1945* (Hieldesheim: Georg Olms Verlag, 2015), p. 314.

25 Kirk, T., 'Fascism and Austrofascism', in G. Bischof, A. Pelinka and A. Lassner (eds), *The Dollfuss/Schuschnigg Era in Austria* (New Brunswick: Transaction Publishers, 2003), p. 26.

26 Von Schuschnigg, K., *Austrian Requiem* (London: V. Gollancz, 1905), pp. 3–9.

27 Ibid., pp. 76–7.

28 Blum, *Le Dernier Mois*, p. 64.

29 Kirk, 'Fascism and Austrofascism', in *The Dollfuss/Schuschnigg Era in Austria*, p. 22.

30 Blum, *Le Dernier Mois*, p. 64.

31 Ibid.

Chapter 10

1 UKNA FO 371/46888.

2 'Will they attempt to barter with the lives of two kings?', *Sunday Express*, 18 February 1945.

3 UKNA FO 371/46888.

4   Ibid.

5   Blum, L., *Le Dernier Mois* (Paris: Arléa, 2004), pp. 14–15.

6   UKNA FO 371/46888.

7   Schellenberg, W., *Walter Schellenberg: The Memoirs of Hitler's Spymaster* (London: Andre Deutsch, 2006), p. 429.

8   Schellenberg, W., *The Labyrinth: Memoirs of Walter Schellenberg* (Boston: Da Capo Press, 2000), p. 379.

9   Padfield, P., *Himmler Reichsführer – SS* (London: Macmillan, 1990), p. 565.

10   Weale, A., *The SS: A New History* (London: Abacus, 2010), p. 405.

11   Aronson, S., *Hitler, the Allies and the Jews* (Cambridge: Cambridge University Press, 2006), p. 307. The primary source is Schellenberg.

12   UKNA FO 371/46888.

13   Persson, S., *Escape from the Reich* (New York: Skyhorse Publishing, 2009), p. 21.

14   Hastings, M., 'How the Germans Closed Ranks Around Hitler', *The New York Review of Books*, Vol. LXII, No. 16, 22 October 2015.

15   Hastings, M., *Armageddon: The Battle for Germany, 1944–1945* (London: Macmillan, 2004), p. 515.

16   Zeitz, J.M., 'The Nazis and Coco', *The New York Times*, 8 May 2005.

17   Muhlsten, A., 'The Cut of Coco', *The New York Review of Books*, 9 October 2014.

18   Kershaw, I., *The End: The Defiance and Destruction of Hitler's Germany, 1944–1945* (New York: Penguin, 2011), p. 284.

19   For further reference, see Persson, *The Third Reich*.

20   Richardi, H., *SS Hostages on the Pragser Wildsee* (South Tyrol: Zeitgeschichtsarchiv Prags, 2006), p. 26.

21   Ibid., p. 9.

22   Smith, S., *Wings Day: The Man Who Led the RAF's Epic Battle in German Captivity* (London: Collins, 1968), p. 215.

23   Kershaw, I., *The Nazi Dictatorship: Problems and Perspectives of Interpretation* (London: Bloomsbury Academic, 2015), p. 93.

24   Hastings, M., *The Secret War: Spies, Codes and Guerrillas* (London: William Collins, 2015), p. 311.

25   CIA release, 22 September 1993. Memorandum to President Roosevelt, 10 March 1945: https://www.cia.gov/library/center-for-the-study-of-intelligence/kent-csi/vol7no2/html/v07i2a07p. 0001.htm (accessed 18 October 2018).

26   Telegram from Allen Dulles, 9 March 1945, quoted in N.H. Petersen, *Hitler's Doorstep: The Wartime Intelligence Reports of Allen Dulles, 1942–1945* (Philadelphia: Pennsylvania State University Press, 1996), p. 468.

27   CIA release, 22 September 1993. Memorandum to President Roosevelt, 4 April 1945: https://www.cia.gov/library/center-for-the-study-of-intelligence/kent-csi/vol7no2/html/v07i2a07p. 0001.htm (accessed 18 October 2018).

28   Ibid., Memorandum to President Roosevelt, 13 March 1945 (accessed 18 October 2018).

Chapter 11

1   Hitchcock, W.I., *Liberation: The Bitter Road to Freedom, 1944–1945* (London: Faber and Faber, 2009), p. 295.

2   Hastings, M., *Armageddon: The Battle for Germany, 1944–1945* (London: Macmillan, 2004), pp. 502–3.

3   Berben, P., *Dachau, 1933–1945* (London: Norfolk Press, 1975), p. 180.

4   Churchill, P., *The Spirit in the Cage* (London: Hodder and Stoughton, 1954), p. 206.

5   Ibid., p. 207.

6   James, B.A., *Moonless Night* (Barnsley: Pen and Sword, 2002), p. 177.

7   Read, A., *The Devil's Principles* (London: Pimlico, 2004), p. 840.

8   Von Schlabrendorff, F. and H. Simon (trans.), *The Secret War Against Hitler* (London: Hodder and Stoughton, 1966), p. 325.

9   Ibid., pp. 232–8.

10 Kershaw, I., *Luck of the Devil* (London: Penguin, 2009), p. 65.

11 Von Schlabrendorff, *The Secret War Against Hitler*, pp. 331–2.

12 Roper, R.T., *The Last Days of Hitler: The Classic Account of Hitler's Fall From Power* (London: Pan Books, 2012), p. 112.

13 Ibid., p. 113.

14 There were a number of *Prominenten* groups, but as Berger was about to travel to Munich he almost certainly was thinking of those assembled in Dachau.

15 Roper, *The Last Days of Hitler*, p. 113. Prince Rupprecht of Bavaria – an anti-Nazi who spent the war in Italy – had envisaged a South German Kingdom uniting Bavaria, Austria and the South Tyrol. For further reference, see Petropoulos, J., *Royals and the Reich: The Princes von Hessen in Nazi Germany* (Oxford: Oxford University Press, 2008), p. 173.

16 Burleigh, M., *The Third Reich: A New History* (London: Macmillan, 2000), p. 430.

17 Nuremberg Trial Proceedings, Vol. 4, 3 January 1946, pp. 308–9: http://avalon.law.yale.edu/imt/01-03-46.asp (accessed 18 October 2018).

18 Berben, *Dachau*, p. 182.

19 Nuremberg Trials, p. 307. The Munich Gauleiter, Giesler, accused Kaltenbrunner of ordering him to arrange the killings.

20 Berben, *Dachau*, p. 186.

21 Von Schuschnigg, K. and F. von Hildebrand (trans.), *Austrian Requiem* (New York: G.P. Putnam's Sons, 1946), p. 283.

22 Payne Best, *The Venlo Incident*, p. 220.

23 UKNA KV 3/345. Interrogation Report of Lt-Col. John McGrath, 14 May 1945.

24 Von Hassell, F., *A Mother's War* (London: John Murray, 1990), p. 172.

25 Blum, L., *Le Dernier Mois* (Paris: Arléa, 2004), p. 74.

26 Payne Best, *The Venlo Incident*, p. 219.

27 Blum, *Le Dernier Mois*, p. 75.

28 Ibid., p. 76.

29 Berben, *Dachau*, p. 101.
30 Payne Best, *The Venlo Incident*, p. 221.
31 Von Hassell, *A Mother's War*, p. 173.
32 Berben, *Dachau*, p. 134.
33 Hastings, *Armageddon*, p. 503.

Chapter 12

1   Vermehren, I., *Reise durch den letzen Akt* (Hamburg: Rowohlt Taschenbuch Verlag, 2014), pp. 223–4.
2   Churchill, P., *The Spirit in the Cage* (London: Hodder and Stoughton, 1954), p. 210.
3   Payne Best, *The Venlo Incident*, p. 196.
4   James, B.A., *Moonless Night* (Barnsley: Pen and Sword, 2002), p. 179.
5   Smith, S., *Wings Day: The Man Who Led the RAF's Epic Battle in German Captivity* (London: Collins, 1968), p. 221.
6   Ibid., p. 222.
7   Payne Best, *The Venlo Incident*, p. 197.
8   Ibid., p. 196.
9   Vermehren, *Reise durch den letzen Akt*, p. 242.
10 Ibid., p. 223.
11 Ibid., p. 225.
12 Blum, L., *Le Dernier Mois* (Paris: Arléa, 2004), p. 81.
13 James, *Moonless Night*, p. 180.
14 Ibid., p. 227.
15 Vermehren, *Reise durch den letzen Akt*, p. 227.
16 Ibid., p. 226. For further reference, see Smith, *Wings Day*, p. 224.
17 Smith, *Wings Day*, p. 225. For further reference, see James, *Moonless Night*, p. 181.
18 Zangrandi, R. and R. Wolcott-Behnke (eds), *A Train to the Brenner* (London: Galley Press, 1963), p. 198.
19 Smith, *Wings Day*, p. 226.
20 Ibid., p. 225.
21 Vermehren, *Reise durch den letzen Akt*, p. 226.
22 Smith, *Wings Day*, p. 216.
23 Vermehren, *Reise durch den letzen Akt*, p. 227.
24 Churchill, *The Spirit in the Cage*, p. 212.
25 Von Hassell, F., *A Mother's War* (London: John Murray, 1990), pp. 180–1.

Chapter 13

1   Richardi, H., *SS Hostages on the Pragser Wildsee* (South Tyrol: Zeitgeschichtsarchiv Prags, 2006), p. 68.

2 Ibid., p. 10.

3 Lucas, J., *Last Days of the Reich* (London: Book Club Associates, 1986), p. 146.

4 Kaufmann, J.E. and H.W. Kaufmann, *The Forts and Fortifications of Europe: The Neutral States, 1815–1945* (Barnsley: Pen and Sword, 2014), pp. 117–18.

5 Hastings, M., *Armageddon: The Battle for Germany, 1944–1945* (London: Macmillan, 2004), p. 490.

6 Von Schuschnigg, K., *Austrian Requiem* (London: V. Gollancz, 1905), pp. 287–8.

7 Churchill, P., *The Spirit in the Cage* (London: Hodder and Stoughton, 1954), pp. 213–14.

8 Smith, S., *Wings Day: The Man Who Led the RAF's Epic Battle in German Captivity* (London: Collins, 1968), p. 230.

9 Payne Best, *The Venlo Incident*, p. 229.

10 Stieninger, R., *South Tyrol: A Minority Conflict in the Twentieth Century* (New Brunswick: Transaction Publishers, 2003), p. 46.

11 Motta, G., *The Italian Military Governorship in South Tyrol and the Rise of Fascism* (Rome: Edizioni Nuova Cultura, 2012), p. 81.

12 While other political parties in Germany opposed Mussolini's policies concerning the South Tyrol in the 1928 Reichstag elections, Hitler stood aside because he wished for an alliance with Fascist Italy as stated in his unpublished *zweites buch* ('second book').

13 Grote, G., *The South Tyrol Question, 1866–2010* (Bern: Peter Lang, 2012), p. 68.

14 I am indebted to Georg Grote for explaining the process and enlightening me generally on the history of South Tyrol.

15 Bank, J., L. Gevers and B. Doyle (trans.), *Churches and Religion in the Second World War* (London: Bloomsbury Academic, 2016), p. 501.

16 Grote, *The South Tyrol Question*, p. 69.

17 Ibid., p. 70.

18 Wolff, S., *Disputed Territories: The Transnational Dynamics of Ethnic Conflict Settlement* (New York: Berghahn, 2003), p. 121.

19 Steuer, L., M. Verdorfer and W. Pichler, 'Verflogt, Verfemt, Vergessen', in R. Loeffel, *The Family Punishment in Nazi Germany: Sippenhaft, Terror and Myth* (London: Palgrave Macmillan, 2012), p. 73.

20 Pavone, C. and P. Levy (trans.), *A Civil War: A History of the Italian Resistance* (London: Verso, 2014), p. 610.

21 Fowler, W., *The Secret War in Italy: Operation Herring and No. 1 Italian SAS* (Shepperton: Ian Allan Publishing, 2010), p. 87.

22 For further reference, see T. Snyder, *Black Earth: The Holocaust as History and Warning* (London: Vintage, 2016).

Chapter 14

1 Display Exhibition, Neiderdorf Town Hall, May 2015.

2 James, B.A., *Moonless Night* (Barnsley: Pen and Sword, 2002), p. 185.

3 Richardi, H., *SS Hostages on the Pragser Wildsee* (South Tyrol: Zeitgeschichtsarchiv Prags, 2006), p. 69.

4 Smith, S., *Wings Day: The Man Who Led the RAF's Epic Battle in German Captivity* (London: Collins, 1968), p. 229.

5 Payne Best, *The Venlo Incident*, p. 228.

6 Ibid., p. 229. Payne Best wrote that von Bonin knew Vietinghoff, but most accounts point to von Bonin knowing General Hans Röttiger, Vietinghoff's chief of staff. For further reference, see J. von Lang, *Top Nazi: The Man Between Hitler and Himmler* (Oxford: Enigma Books, 2013), p. 302; and Richardi, *SS Hostages on the Pragser Wildsee*, p. 72.

7 Von Lang, *Top Nazi*, pp. 292–5.

8 Ibid., pp. 287–90.

9 James, *Moonless Night*, p. 185.

10 Payne Best, *The Venlo Incident*, pp. 231–2.

11 Vermehren, I., *Reise durch den letzen Akt* (Hamburg: Rowohlt Taschenbuch Verlag, 2014), p. 238.

12 Smith, *Wings Day*, pp. 233–4.

13 James, *Moonless Night*, pp. 186–7.

14 Payne Best, *The Venlo Incident*, p. 232.

15 Smith, *Wings Day*, p. 235.

16 Payne Best, *The Venlo Incident*, p. 233.

17 Smith, *Wings Day*, pp. 236–7.

18 James, *Moonless Night*, p. 189.

19 Richardi, H., *SS-Geiseln in der Alpenfestung* (Bozen: Edition Raetia, 2015), p. 134.

Chapter 15

1 Richardi, H., *SS-Geiseln in der Alpenfestung* (Bozen: Edition Raetia, 2015), p. 132. The profile of individuals within the *Prominenten* were largely self-generated and occupations were what they themselves declared.

2 Ibid., p. 284.

3 Nolte, E., *Three Faces of Fascism* (London: Weidenfeld and Nicolson, 1965), p. 499, note 246.

4 Righi, A., *Italian Reactionary Thought and Critical Theory* (New York: Palgrave Macmillan, 2015), p. 84.

5 Smith, S., *Wings Day: The Man Who Led the RAF's Epic Battle in German Captivity* (London: Collins, 1968), p. 217.

6 Churchill, P., *The Spirit in the Cage* (London: Hodder and Stoughton, 1954), p. 205.

7 James, B.A., *Moonless Night* (Barnsley: Pen and Sword, 2002), p. 175.

8 Von Hassell, F., *A Mother's War* (London: John Murray, 1990), p. 177.

9   What follows is largely based on accounts found in R. Gremmo, *I Partigiani Alleati dei Nazisti* (Piedmont: Storia Ribelle, 2015).

10 Pavone, C. and P. Levy (trans.), *A Civil War: A History of the Italian Resistance* (London: Verso, 2014), p. 23.

11 Gremmo, *I Partigiani Alleati dei Nazisti*, p. 35.

12 Wachsmann, N., *KL: A History of the Nazi Concentration Camps* (London: Little, Brown, 2016), p. 530.

13 Cardosi, G. and G. Marisa, *La giustizia negate* (Varese: Arterigere, 2005), p. 31.

Chapter 16

1   Churchill, P., *The Spirit in the Cage* (London: Hodder and Stoughton, 1954), p. 220.

2   Evans, R.J., *The Third Reich at War: How the Nazis Led Germany from Conquest to Disaster* (London: Penguin, 2009), p. 14.

3   Von Hassell, F., *A Mother's War* (London: John Murray, 1990), p. 182.

4   Payne Best, *The Venlo Incident*, p. 233.

5   Ibid., p. 233.

6   Ibid., p. 235.

7   Ibid., p. 234. The comparison made by Payne Best was not with the Italian partisans, but with the 'Great Escapers'.

8   Ibid., p. 235.

9   Richardi, H., *SS-Geiseln in der Alpenfestung* (Bozen: Edition Raetia, 2015), p. 245.

10 Vermehren, I., *Reise durch den letzten Akt* (Hamburg: Rowohlt Taschenbuch Verlag, 2014), pp. 239–40.

11 IWM 9/51/1, S. Payne Best Archive, SPB 13.

12 There are differing accounts of this incident and some memoirs omit any mention of it, referring only to the departure of most of the SS. This description is mainly based on information extracted from Smith, *Wings Day*, p. 238; B.A. James, *Moonless Night* (Barnsley: Pen and Sword, 2002), p. 190; Payne Best, *The Venlo Incident*, p. 235. (Not surprisingly, Payne Best places himself alongside von Bonin during the final confrontation with Bader; other accounts do not support this.)

13 Von Schuschnigg, K., *Austrian Requiem* (London: V. Gollancz, 1905), p. 289.

14 Blum, L., *Le Dernier Mois* (Paris: Arléa, 2004), p. 87. For further reference, see James, *Moonless Night*, p. 191.

15 Von Hassell, *A Mother's War*, p. 183.

16 Waller, D., *Disciples: The World War II Missions of the CIA Directors who Fought for Wild Bill Donovan* (New York: Simon and Schuster, 2015), p. 371.

17 James, *Moonless Night*, p. 190.

18 Vermehren, *Reise durch den letzten Akt*, p. 244.

19 Cushing, T., *Soldier for Hire* (London: Calder, 1962), p. 262.

Chapter 17

1   Heiss, C.M., H. Richardi and T. Crawford (trans.), *Lake Braies*, booklet, p. 29.
2   Smith, S., *Wings Day: The Man Who Led the RAF's Epic Battle in German Captivity* (London: Collins, 1968), p. 240.
3   Ibid. For further reference, see B.A. James, *Moonless Night* (Barnsley: Pen and Sword, 2002), p. 191.
4   Ibid.
5   Churchill, P., *The Spirit in the Cage* (London: Hodder and Stoughton, 1954), p. 224.
6   Müller, J., *Bis zur letzen Konsequenz: Ein Leben für Frieden und Freiheit* (Munich: Süddeutscher Vertag, 1975), p. 274.
7   Vermehren, I., *Reise durch den letzen Akt* (Hamburg: Rowohlt Taschenbuch Verlag, 2014), p. 247.
8   Payne Best, *The Venlo Incident*, p. 241.
9   Ibid.
10 Ibid., p. 238.
11 Von Hassell, F., *A Mother's War* (London: John Murray, 1990), p. 185.
12 Smith, *Wings Day*, p. 242.
13 Letter from Sydney Dowse to Payne Best, 29 July 1945. Wymeersch is referred to as 'the horrible Frenchman' and Heidi is referred to as 'his terrible girlfriend'. IWM 9/51/1, S. Payne Best Archive, SPB 1.
14 Churchill, *The Spirit in the Cage*, p. 223.
15 Richardi, H., *SS-Geiseln in der Alpenfestung* (Bozen: Edition Raetia, 2015), p. 244.
16 Smith, *Wings Day*, p. 243.
17 Von Schlabrendorff, F. and H. Simon (trans.), *The Secret War Against Hitler* (London: Hodder and Stoughton, 1966), p. 335.
18 Churchill, *The Spirit in the Cage*, pp. 223–4.
19 Payne Best, *The Venlo Incident*, p. 243.
20 James, *Moonless Night*, p. 192.
21 Ibid.
22 Blum, L., *Le Dernier Mois* (Paris: Arléa, 2004), p. 92.
23 Payne Best, *The Venlo Incident*, p. 243.
24 'La cattura degli ostaggi ed il miraggio dell'Alpenfestung' ('The Capture of Hostages and the Mirage of the Alpenfestung'): http://www.isa-fabiani.it/drupal/sites/default/files/Mostra%20Stauffenberg%20parte%20II.pdf (accessed 18 October 2018).
25 Statement of Payne Best, 1945, p. 13. IWM 9/51/1, SPB 1.
26 Payne Best, *The Venlo Incident*, p. 245.
27 James, *Moonless Night*, p. 192.

Chapter 18

1   Smith, *Wings Day*, pp. 247–9.
2   Blum, L., *Le Dernier Mois* (Paris: Arléa, 2004), p. 92.

3   Payne Best, *The Venlo Incident*, pp. 245–6.
4   Churchill, P., *The Spirit in the Cage* (London: Hodder and Stoughton, 1954), p. 224.
5   Vermehren, I., *Reise durch den letzen Akt* (Hamburg: Rowohlt Taschenbuch Verlag, 2014), p. 254.
6   Von Schuschnigg, K., *Austrian Requiem* (London: V. Gollancz, 1905), p. 290.
7   Vermehren, *Reise durch den letzen Akt*, pp. 266–7. Adapted from a translation by S. Whiteside, in W. Kempowski, *Swansong, 1945: A Collective Diary from Hitler's Last Birthday to VE Day* (London: Granta Books, 2014), p. 384.

Chapter 19

1   Smith, *Wings Day*, p. 252.
2   Carroll, T., *The Dodger*, p. 377.
3   Ibid., p. 302.
4   Ibid., p. 380.
5   Ibid., p. 382.
6   Jones, N., 'Introduction', in *The Venlo Incident* (2010 E-book)
7   IWM 9/51/1, SPB.
8   Ibid.
9   UKNA WO 344/87/1.
10 UKNA KV 2/769. Haller.
11 UKNA KV 3/345. Interview with Fr. Thomas O'Shaughnessy.
12 Ibid. Interrogation report of Lt-Col. John McGrath.
13 Ibid. Note on file.
14 Churchill, P., *The Spirit in the Cage* (London: Hodder and Stoughton, 1954), p. 246.
15 IWM 9/51/1, SPB Box 1.
16 UKNA FO 371/94812.
17 UKNA FO 950/1725. A. Walsh.
18 Ibid.
19 Churchill, *The Spirit in the Cage*, p. 233.
20 Tickell, J., *Odette: Secret Agent, Prisoner, Survivor* (London: Chapman and Hall, 1949).
21 Royal, L., *Safe Return Doubtful* (Oslo: Royal Explorers Club Press, 2015), p. 9.
22 Churchill, *The Spirit in the Cage*, p. 126.
23 Payne Best, *The Venlo Incident*, p. 76.
24 O'Hara, G., 'The Parliamentary Commission for Administration, the Foreign Office and the Sachsenhausen Case', *The Historical Journal*, Vol. 53, Issue 3, September 2010, p. 777.
25 House of Commons Debate, 5 February 1968, *Hansard*, Vol. 758, cc.147–8.
26 UKNA FO 950/1725.
27 Lacouture, J., *Léon Blum* (New York: Holmes & Meier, 1982), p. 471.
28 Ibid., pp. 472–3.

29   Von Hassell, F., *A Mother's War* (London: John Murray, 1990), p. 185.
30   Von Lang, J., *Top Nazi: The Man Between Hitler and Himmler* (Oxford: Enigma Books, 2013), p. 302.
31   Churchill, *The Spirit in the Cage*, p. 244.
32   Ibid., p. 245.
33   Maslov, A., *Captured Soviet Generals* (Oxford: Routledge, 2001), p. 44.
34   Ibid., p. 159.
35   *Der Spiegel*, 41, 8 October 1958.
36   From [owner's] private collection.

Addendum I

1   Adapted from T. Wall, 'The Truth and Colonel McGrath', in *Dublin Review of Books*, 1 February 2017: http://www.drb.ie/essays/the-truth-and-colonel-mcgrath (accessed 18 October 2018).
2   My thanks to John Kelly for researching McGrath in Elphin, Co. Roscommon.
3   Information on John McGrath's military career was kindly provided by the Historical Disclosures section of the Army Personnel Centre in Glasgow.
4   *Irish Independent*, 24 September 1945.
5   I am grateful to Tom Callan for discovering this note in the parish register in Elphin, Co. Roscommon, and for providing other details about John McGrath's life.
6   O' Callaghan, M., *For Ireland and Freedom: Roscommon's Contribution to the Fight for Independence* (Cork: Mercier Press, 2012), p. 137.
7   'German Scheme Disclosed: Attempt to enlist Irishmen as Agents', *Irish Independent*, 7 June 1945.
8   O'Shaughnessy, T., *Rest Your Head in Your Hand* (Dublin: Ward River Press, 1983), p. 109.
9   O'Reilly, T., *Hitler's Irishmen* (Cork: Mercier Press, 2008), p. 265.

Addendum II

1   UKNA WO 204/12807. Josef Müller.
2   Riebling, M., *Church of Spies* (New York: Basic Books, 2015), p. 45.
3   UKNA WO 204/12807.
4   Cornwell, J., *Hitler's Pope* (London: Penguin, 2000), p. 240.
5   Ibid., p. 112.
6   Burleigh, M., *Sacred Causes* (London: Harper Perennial, 2006), pp. 225–6. For further reference, see Cornwell, *Hitler's Pope*, p. 237.
7   Schellenberg, W., *Walter Schellenberg: The Memoirs of Hitler's Spymaster* (London: Andre Deutsch, 2006), p. 401.
8   Mueller, M. and G. Brooks (trans.), *Canaris: The Life and Death of Hitler's Spymaster* (London: Chapman Publishing, 2007), pp. 184–5.

9   UKNA WO 204/12807.

10 Cornwell, *Hitler's Pope*, pp. 148–9.

11 Riebling, *Church of Spies*, pp. 95–6.

12 Metaxas, E., *Bonhoeffer: Pastor, Martyr, Prophet, Spy* (Nashville: Thomas Nelson, 2010), p. 109.

13 Ibid., p. 359.

14 Ibid., p. 372.

15 Riebling, *Church of Spies*, p. 166.

16 Mueller, *Canaris*, p. 233.

17 Bonhoeffer, D., *Works, Volume 16: Conspiracy and Imprisonment, 1940–1945* (Minneapolis: Fortress Press, 2006), pp. 434–5.

18 Metaxas, *Bonhoeffer*, p. 441.

19 Riebling, *Church of Spies*, pp. 181–2.

20 Metaxas, *Bonhoeffer*, pp. 475–6.

21 Payne Best, *The Venlo Incident*, p. 181.

22 Bently, J., *Martin Niemöller* (Oxford: Oxford University Press, 1984), p. 148.

23 UKNA WO 204/12807.

Addendum III

1   Kershaw, I., *Hitler: 1889–1936* (London: Penguin, 2001), p. 564.

2   Loeffel, R., *The Family Punishment in Nazi Germany: Sippenhaft, Terror and Myth* (London: Palgrave Macmillan, 2012), pp. 20–1.

3   Evans, R.J., *The Third Reich at War: How the Nazis Led Germany from Conquest to Disaster* (London: Penguin, 2009), p. 642.

4   Kershaw, I., *Luck of the Devil* (London: Penguin, 2009), p. 69.

5   Ibid., p. 67.

6   Mulley, C., *The Women Who Flew for Hitler* (London: Macmillan, 2017), p. 218.

7   Ibid., p. 135.

8   Hoffmann, P., *Stauffenberg: A Family History, 1905–1944* (Montreal: McGill-Queen's University Press, 2003), p. 276.

9   Von Hassell, F., *A Mother's War* (London: John Murray, 1990), pp. 103–4.

10 Ibid., pp. 105–14.

11 Ibid., p. 123.

12 Ibid., p. 131.

13 Wachsmann, N., *KL: A History of the Nazi Concentration Camps* (London: Little, Brown, 2016), p. 280.

14 Merten, U., *Forgotten Voices* (New Brunswick: Transaction Publishers, 2012), p. 27.

15 Von Hassell, *A Mother's War*, pp. 132–3.

16 Ibid., pp. 137–8.

17 Ibid., p. 138.

18 United States Holocaust Memorial Museum: https://encyclopedia.ushmm.org/ content/en/article/stutthof (accessed 18 October 2018).
19 Von Hassell, *A Mother's War*, p. 143.
20 Ibid., p. 151.
21 Ibid., p. 157.
22 Loeffel, *The Family Punishment in Nazi Germany*, p. 176.
23 Hoffmann, *Stauffenberg: A Family History*, pp. 279–80.
24 Von Hassell, *A Mother's War*, pp. 158–9.
25 Hoffmann, *Stauffenberg: A Family History*, pp. 279–80.
26 Hassell, *A Mother's War*, pp. 167–8.
27 Ibid., pp. 169–70.
28 Ibid., p. 185.
29 Ibid., pp. 187–8.
30 Ibid., p. 191.
31 Ibid., p. 225.

Addendum IV

1 Richardi, H., *SS-Geiseln in der Alpenfestung* (Bozen: Edition Raetia, 2015), p. 284. The profile of individuals within the *Prominenten* were largely self-generated and occupations were what they themselves declared.
2 Ibid., p. 132.
3 UKNA FO 371.
4 Sanders, P.W., 'Economic Draining: German Black Market Operations in France, 1940–1943': http://www.academia.edu/9466921/German_black_market_ operations_in_France_and_in_Belgium_1940-1944_PhD_dissertation_Cambridge_ History_Faculty_2000 (accessed 18 October 2018).
5 Curtis, M., *Verdict on Vichy* (London: Phoenix Press, 2004), p. 258.
6 Sanders, 'Economic Draining'.
7 Abramovici, P., *Szkolnikoff: Hitler's Jewish Smuggler* (Barnsley: Pen and Sword, 2016), pp. 18–20.
8 Ibid., p. 34.
9 Ibid., p. 36.
10 Ibid., pp. 102–6.
11 Ibid., p. 32.
12 Ibid., p. 146.
13 Curtis, *Verdict on Vichy*, pp. 178–80.
14 Abramovici, *Szkolnikoff*, p. 190.
15 Hazera, J. and R. de Rochebrune, *Les Patron Sous L'Occupation* (Paris: Éditions Odile Jacob, 1995), p. 229.
16 Sanders, 'Economic Draining'.

17   Abramovici, *Szkolnikoff*, p. 109.
18   Ibid., pp. 105–6.
19   'Zielbewußte Unmoral', *Der Spiegel*, 10 July 1948: http://www.spiegel.de/spiegel/print/d-44417576.html (accessed 18 October 2018).
20   Ibid.
21   Von Schlabrendorff, F. and H. Simon (trans.), *The Secret War Against Hitler* (London: Hodder and Stoughton, 1966), p. 188.
22   'Zielbewußte Unmoral', *Der Spiegel*.
23   Richardi, H., *SS-Geiseln in der Alpenfestung* (Bozen: Edition Raetia, 2015), p. 134.
24   Neuhäusler, J., *What Was It Like in the Concentration Camp at Dachau?: An Attempt to Come Closer to the Truth* (Munich: A.G. Manz, 1960), p. 33.
25   UKNA FO 371.
26   Abramovici, *Szkolnikoff*, pp. 147–55.

Addendum V

1   R. Gremmo, *I Partigiani Alleati dei Nazisti* (Piedmont: Storia Ribelle, 2015), p. 24.
2   Ibid., p. 26.
3   Foot, J., *Modern Italy* (New York: Palgrave Macmillan, 2014), p. 95.
4   Clerk, M., *Modern Italy: 1871 to the Present* (London: Pearson, 2008), p. 373.
5   Pavone, C. and P. Levy (trans.), *A Civil War: A History of the Italian Resistance* (London: Verso, 2014), p. 23.
6   Kelly, M., 'The Italian Resistance in Piedmont: The Myth of Unity', CERC Working Paper No. 2/2006, Contemporary European Research Centre, University of Melbourne, p. 1.
7   Gremmo, *I Partigiani Alleati dei Nazisti*, pp. 65–6.
8   Ibid., pp. 66–7.
9   Ibid., p. 75.
10   Ibid., p. 83.
11   Wachsmann, N., *KL: A History of the Nazi Concentration Camps* (London: Little, Brown, 2016), p. 294.
12   Gremmo, *I Partigiani Alleati dei Nazisti*, p. 67.
13   Ibid., p. 84.
14   Calvino, I., 'Il sentiero dei nidi ragno', quoted in Pavone, *A Civil War*, p. 42.
15   Gremmo, *I Partigiani Alleati dei Nazisti*, p. 130.

INDEX